W9-BHR-715

Netscape Guide To

Internet Research

FOR WINDOWS & MACINTOSH

2ND EDITION

TARA CALISHAIN AND
JILL ALANE NYSTROM

The Coriolis Group, Inc.
An International Thomson Publishing Company
14455 N. Hayden Road, Suite 220
Scottsdale, Arizona 85260

602.483.0192
FAX 602.483.0193
http://www.coriolis.com

Library of Congress Cataloging-In-Publication Data
Calishain, Tara.
   Official Netscape guide to Internet research / by Tara Calishain
and Jill Alane Nystrom. -- 2nd ed.
     p. cm.
  Includes index.
  ISBN 1-56604-845-1
  1. Netscape 2. Internet (Computer Network) 3. World Wide Web
(Information retrieval system) I. Title
TK5105.883.N48C35 1998
001.4'0285'53—dc21   98-11199
                                               CIP

Printed in the United States of America
10 9 8 7 6 5 4 3 2

Publisher
   Keith Weiskamp

Acquisitions
   Jeff Duntemann
   Stephanie Wall

Project Editor
   Mariann Hansen
   Barsolo

Production Coordinator
   Wendy Littley

Cover Design
   Anthony Stock

Layout Design
   April Nielsen

CD-ROM Development
   Robert Clarfield

 an International Thomson Publishing company I(T)P®

Albany, NY • Belmont, CA • Bonn • Boston • Cincinnati • Detroit • Johannesburg • London
Madrid • Melbourne • Mexico City • New York • Paris • Singapore • Tokyo • Toronto • Washington

For my husband and my family.

—Tara Calishain

To Elizabeth, my best girl. You are why I smile.
And to Christopher...C.S. Lewis was right. TMD.

—Jill Alane Nystrom

Acknowledgments

The biggest acknowledgments go to the people who read the first edition of this book, with extra thanks to those who sent ideas, suggestions, and feedback. Thank you. If it wasn't for you, there wouldn't be a second edition. Ventana and Coriolis were helpful as always—thanks to Stephanie, Mariann, Wendy, Tony, Kim, and April.

Jill, thanks. Great job with the book.

—Tara Calishain

Ellen and John Hoffman, who are always there for me on any adventure I choose. Thanks guys! Tara Calishain: What can I say? Once again you've let me share in the fun. Here's to a dozen more! Christopher Butzgy: You get acknowledged, you pay extra! As always, thanks to my family and friends for their encouragement in everything I do.

—Jill Alane Nystrom

About The Authors

Tara Calishain has written a few books and occasionally writes for computer magazines.

Jill Alane Nystrom is a Ph.D. candidate at Northwestern University and co-author of the *Official Netscape Messenger and Collabra* book. She writes regularly about technical expertise and international politics.

Table Of Contents

Introduction

A long time ago—well, not that long, just a few years—all your research efforts focused on the library. Whether you needed books, magazine articles, or pointers to government information, you had to use the library. The information was there for you, but whether or not you were able to get to it depended on how your schedule meshed with the library's, and how many other people needed the information that you were interested in.

Now there's the Internet, with millions of times the space of your neighborhood library and reference information that can be accessed by many people at the same time. Unfortunately, if you've tried to approach the resources of the Internet as you would the resources in your neighborhood library, you probably found yourself quickly overwhelmed.

Imagine an almost infinitely large room, filled with crowds of people. Books, tapes, and movie reels are stacked haphazardly everywhere. There are hundreds of card catalogs, no two of which contain the same information. And books are coming in faster than they can be shelved. "Pandemonium!" you say? Maybe, but this scenario is also analogous to the workings of the Internet.

Take heart; it's crazy, but comprehensible. The sheer size of the Internet makes it incredibly intimidating at first but also makes it an incredible research resource. The World Wide Web (WWW) in particular has come a long way in the few years it has been in existence. In early 1994, for example, Tara's husband grumbled constantly about researching his pet hobby—microbiology—on the Internet. Almost every reference he found online pointed to a book or magazine article that he had to get at a university library. Almost four years later, he gleefully surfs through entire biology textbooks that have been transferred to Web pages and put online.

Libraries will never go out of style. They will always be good places for studying, research, and community interaction. However, they should be your second choice the next time you're trying to get governmental information, finish that thesis, or look into current events in Guatemala. The Internet can help you do a number of research tasks; you can:

■ Browse worldwide news from hundreds of different sources.

■ Get expert feedback and perspectives on all kinds of topics.

■ Find state, national, and international government information.

■ Get business and financial information.

■ Browse historical documents and listen to historical speeches.

■ Check millions of phone numbers in a matter of seconds.

And that's not all, but it's a good sample with which to start.

As you can see, the Internet contains a vast variety of materials. In addition, you can access these materials in a number of ways: newsgroups, mailing lists, and the Internet superpower—the World Wide Web. To make things even more complicated, there are literally thousands of search tools, "link" lists, subject indices, and other collections of information. "Wow!" you say. "Where do I begin?"

That is what this book will strive to teach you: where to begin, how to approach a research problem from different angles when you're ready to tear all your hair out, how to organize the information when you get it, and how to put your report or other research materials back on the Internet.

Who Can Use This Book?

This book is written for anyone who wants to use the Internet as a research tool, be they student, information professional, or hobbyist. Readers should also know their way around Netscape Communicator, the Web software suite that acts as your "toolbox" for online research. Here's what you'll need:

■ An IBM PC-compatible computer with at least 8MB of RAM; 6MB available hard disk space; a 486 or faster processor; and Windows 3.x, Windows 95, or Windows NT. Or...

■ A Mac or Mac clone with at least 8MB of RAM, 5MB available hard disk space, a 68030 or faster processor, and System 7 or higher.

■ Netscape Communicator as your Internet browser (you can use a lot of the information in this book even if you're using a different browser, but some of the chapters won't apply to you).

■ A SLIP or PPP connection to the Internet, with a modem that runs at 14.4 Kbps (28.8 Kbps is strongly recommended), or a direct connection.

You do not have to be a Navigator whiz with knowledge of the hot-key combination to every last little feature in the program. If you're able to move from site to site and you understand how to click on active links, you're at a good starting point.

An Overview Of This Book

Around the Internet world in 25 chapters? With over 50 million pages online, some would say that it can't be done, but we're sure going to give it the old college try. Here's how the book shakes out:

Chapter 1, "The Internet Research Overview," explains what sets the Internet apart from traditional sources of information (like libraries) and where its strengths and weaknesses lie.

Chapter 2, "Configuring Netscape Communicator," shows you how to configure Communicator. Your research efforts can really get off on the right foot when you take the time to get Navigator situated the way you want it.

Chapter 3, "Prepare To Research: Plug-ins And Telnet," takes a look at add-ons and additions to Navigator that can jazz up your Web surfing experience with audio, video, and other multimedia.

Chapter 4, "Helper Applications," takes a look at some software you can use in addition to Communicator to organize your information and make its handling easier.

Chapter 5, "Ten Friendly Tips For Internet Research," gives you some ideas for the best way to approach a research problem and some handy steps you can take to tackle your Internet research effort as painlessly as possible.

Chapter 6, "Making The Most Of Mailing Lists," talks about Messenger, Communicator's e-mail application. Then, we'll talk about using this application to access mailing lists, how to search list archives, and how to communicate with folks on a mailing list without breaking any of the rules of Internet etiquette.

Chapter 7, "The Wild, Wild World Of Newsgroups," first takes a look at the Navigator news reader application. After that, we'll examine the over 5,000 Usenet newsgroups on the Internet and find out how to approach them for information—sometimes without even posting a message. You'll also learn where to find Usenet newsgroups online if your Internet provider doesn't offer them and where you can search Usenet archives. Finally, you'll learn about some of the special hazards of Internet newsgroups and what you can do to avoid them.

Chapter 8, "Other Research Tools Accessible From The Web," introduces you to some lesser-known Internet research tools—Telnet, Finger, Gopher. They're not retro British bands, they're other ways that you can access information online.

Chapter 9, "Push Technology: When Push Comes To Shove," takes a look at a new kind of information distribution technology called *push*, and discusses how you can use it to get information updates on a regular basis without surfing to the same pages over and over.

Chapter 10, "The World Wide Web," gives you the basics of the WWW and shows you a few ways you can use the Web to get information for your everyday life. If you know people who insist that the Internet has no practical use, have them read this chapter.

Chapter 11, "General Searching On The World Wide Web," introduces you to the Web's general searching resources. How many full-scale search engines do you think there are? One? Two? Three, possibly? We'll look at over half a dozen, along with subject indices and clearinghouses. This chapter is also peppered with tips to show you how best to use general search indices.

Chapter 12, "Domestic Government Information Online," covers specific research needs and problems with an overview of what government information is available on the Net on the state, national, or international levels. Do you know how to get to Wyoming's home page? How about how to access the Internal Revenue Service online? Learn here.

Chapter 13, "International Resources Online," covers international information and news online. Here's where you find out how to get to the United Nations, online embassies, and even Yahoo! Canada.

Chapter 14, "Finding Folks Online," shows you how to use the variety of phone books and e-mail listings available on the Internet. Even if you're trying to reach someone who isn't online, there are a number of "white pages" that may be able to give you the information you need. (We'll also take a quick look at genealogy resources online.)

Chapter 15, "Finding Business And Professional Resources Online," gives you the lowdown on finding stock information, financial news, press releases straight from the companies, and even contact information for the Securities and Exchange Commission (SEC). Once you find out where a business is located, you'll learn how to use mapping resources online to get an exact location.

Chapter 16, "Resources For Student Research," covers the essential tools of student researchers—reference works. You'll learn where to find dictionaries (for both English and other languages), thesauri, atlases, historical documents, literature, card catalogs, and other information to which every student should have access.

Chapter 17, "Up-To-The-Minute News And Information," shows you the best places and ways to get up-to-the minute information on current news and events. From online newspapers to customized news services, the Internet can keep you up-to-date on what's new and what's not. Want the scoop on live online events? Here's where you find out about it.

Chapter 18, "Getting The Truth: Legends, Facts And Frauds," gives you a rundown on some of the more pervasive legends on the Internet (like Craig

Shergold's brain tumor and the prevalence of a Good Times virus) and how to double-check your facts before putting them into your research. You'll also learn how to avoid online fraud and where to go if you get ripped off.

Chapter 19, "Fee-Based Databases: When Should You Pay?" tells you about the pay information services available through the Internet (generally through the World Wide Web). We'll also take a look at several different kinds that might make your research a little easier.

Feeling washed away by the tide of information yet?

In Chapter 20, "Help! How Do I Keep Up?" you'll learn how best to stay on top of what's happening on the Internet through "What's New" services, mailing lists, and online newsletters.

In Chapter 21, "Protecting Yourself: Privacy On The Internet," we'll take a look at common sense and other ways to protect your personal information online.

Chapter 22, "Archiving: Keeping Track Of Research Projects," gives you a quick course on saving all your information without driving yourself nuts with piles of paper and enormous files. Learn how to start with a one-page case study and build on it from there.

Chapter 23, "Moving Information Around," gives you ideas on how to handle the information you find on the Internet—whether you want to strip the HTML code or edit an image that you find online. You'll also find suggestions for software you can use to get the job done.

Chapter 24, "Citing Electronic Information," shows you how to use MLA standards to cite what you find online. This chapter also gets into proposals for enhanced MLA standards and shows where you can find those proposals online.

In Chapter 25, "Giving Your Research Back To The Internet," you'll learn what you should consider when putting your research masterpiece back online—everything from how you can learn HTML to where you can get free Web space to showcase your masterwork.

Sound good? Are you ready? Then let's do it!

Part I

Overview Of The Internet And Internet Tools

CHAPTER 1

The Internet Research Overview

Tara has been using bulletin board services—computers strung together with modems, essentially tiny versions of the Internet—for over a dozen years. One thing she noticed early in using the systems is how she could "see" where she was. When she would dial into and connect to a system, she would visualize it as a real place, and all of the subsequent activities—reading mail, transferring files, or playing games—would feel like they were happening in the place she was visualizing. Sometimes it would feel as if she w ere in a large, airy, wooden house, or in a dank cave by the sea, or even in a domed city high above the clouds. Even though it was over the teleph one, Tara was still communicating with people, and she had to imagine a place for that communication to take place.

That was how her brain dealt with the idea of cyberspace. Cyberspace is a daunting concept for most of us. Zillions and zillions of electrons, spanning the planet, linking thousands of computers and millions of people together? It gets a bit mind-blowing. So our brains help us by visualizing a place within the realm of imagination, helping us feel that we have control over where we are and what we're doing.

We would surmise that you're someone who's interested in using the Internet for research; otherwise you wouldn't have picked up this book. Or you're a student and your professor assigned you this book. (Thank them for us.) You have probably heard about the Internet from news programs or magazines, or perhaps you've had an Internet account yourself for some time. Good for you.

In any case, you're probably aware of the vast size of the Internet: more than 150 countries strong and growing. You might even be aware of the history of the Internet—a decades-old project begun by the U.S. Department of Defense.

How do you visualize the Internet? Does it look like a disorganized room full of books? Is it a stomping ground, a wailing wall, or a battlefield? Is it an ocean of information over which hurricanes sometimes rise? Perhaps, because you're interested in using the Internet for research, you think of it as a library.

However you see it, we'd like to give you a new visualization for using the Internet for research. Instead of thinking of it as a library, make the Internet your toolbox.

Anything can be in a toolbox, because almost anything can be a tool. Tara has a little can of Play-Doh in her computer toolbox for picking up tiny computer screws. She has a pair of tweezers for bending pins. Thinking of the Internet as a toolbox allows you to realize all the possibilities.

There's video on the Internet, and audio, in addition to text. There are first-person interviews and historical documents. There are movable, interactive diagrams. There is news that happened just a few minutes ago and pictures of Egyptian hieroglyphics. The Internet is much more fluid than a library, because information is constantly being added, and it is much more long-lasting, because online information can stay for years, getting moldy and outdated, without anyone removing it. This is not pretty.

Trying to imagine the Internet as a library is hard on your head. It's too much information, too much flow, too many resources, and too many types of resources. Think of it instead as a toolbox from which you select one tool at a time. You wouldn't open your toolbox and grab all the screwdrivers at once, would you? Of course not. You'd look at all the screwdrivers that you had, pick the one that was the right size, and go do the job. If you had a nail that you needed to remove, you'd get a hammer. What this book will teach you is where to find the tools, which ones are the right ones for the job, and how to use them.

A World Wide Web Overview

The World Wide Web is to the Internet what Michael Jordan is to professional basketball. In a league of talented people and astonishing athletes, he stands head and shoulders above the rest. He's the excitement-generator, the attention-getter. Michael Jordan is the "killer application" of pro basketball. Likewise, the Web is arguably the "killer application" of the Internet.

The idea of the Web is built around the idea of *hypertext*. Hypertext is a nonlinear way of presenting ideas.

What The Web Is Not

Let's get into what the Web is *not:*

- **A Wall-To-Wall Porn Shop.** Yes, there is pornography on the Web. There is also porn at your local bookstore. Porn is not the majority of the Web's content and it never will be. Should you accidentally stumble across some, we promise it will not jump off the screen and eat your brain.

- **A Den Of Computer Criminals And Con Men.** There are dishonest people and frauds in every situation, and the Internet is no exception. However, the bad apples are more than counterbalanced by legions of helpful, honest people. There are also plenty of online resources to help you protect yourself against online scams. You'll read more about these in Chapter 18 and Chapter 21.

- **A Collection Of Commercial Sites And Pointless Personal Pages.** The best commercial sites educate about both a product and the technology or topics behind a product. Many commercial sites fall within this category. As for the useless home page idea—well, many of the most beloved research sites (WebCrawler and Yahoo!, to name two) started out as personal pages. Even if the myth were true, and there were no commercial sites and personal sites worthwhile, there are still vast numbers of university-related sites that are well worth a look.

Conversely, this book is presented in a traditional paper manner. Chapter by chapter, ideas are presented in a linear fashion. It all flows in a straight line:

Chapter 1 *leads to*

Chapter 2 *leads to*

Chapter 3 *leads to*

Chapter 4, and so forth.

You could skip around if you wanted to, but it's not how the book is written, and it would be difficult for you to maintain your train of thought.

A hypertext document employs *hyperlinks* so that you can get your information without going in a straight line, and without flipping around looking for what you want. Hyperlinks can be put in a Web page anywhere, so you can "jump around" to different parts of a document, or to another document entirely.

Let's take the example of the WRAL-TV News site as shown in Figure 1.1.

Figure 1.1   The WRAL News site.

This is a listing of news stories. If it were a paper object, like a newspaper, you'd have to read, or at least scan, the objects one by one in their proper linear order. With hypertext, all you need is a hypertext headline and a short summary of the story. Find the story in which you're interested and—boom!—you're there, directly at the story that's captured your interest.

Let's take this a little further by looking at a story that has additional information.

As you can see down the left side of the Web page shown in Figure 1.2, the idea of hyperlinks goes beyond the idea of a simple news story. For example, from a news story you could click on a link to hear the radio conversations between NASA and the space shuttle. (The capability for graphics and audio on the Web leads some people to use the term hypermedia as opposed to hypertext, but it all refers to a nonlinear form of information organization.)

TIP

Hyperhuh? We're talking somewhat vaguely about the kinds of different media available online. You're probably wondering exactly what kind of media besides text you'll find online. Well, you can find audio (both regular and MIDI music), pictures, movable and interactive diagrams, slide shows, movies, dancing text—all kinds of things. Probably more different kinds of multimedia than you've seen in your local library!

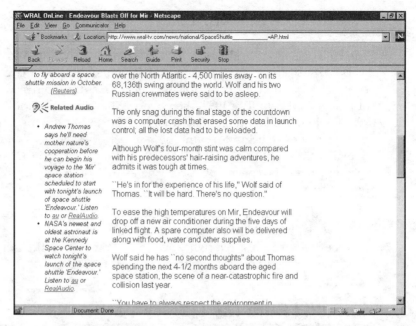

Figure 1.2   A news story.

The danger of a nonlinear progression of information is your susceptibility to get "turned around," or lost in the information. You're reading a news story about Mir, for example, and you see a link to NASA. So you go from WRAL to NASA. At NASA, you may find a link to MIT to learn more about scientific achievements in space technology. From MIT, you might link to a student's home page and learn about his or her interest in the rock group Nirvana.

The next thing you know, you're on a Nirvana fan's Web site in Norway, listening to a sound clip of *Heart-Shaped Box* and you've totally forgotten about NASA!

Of course, that's along the lines of a worst-case scenario for a researcher gathering information about Mir and NASA. In most cases, the advantage of Internet sites hooking up with each other through connections as simple as text notifications is a critical one, allowing us to string together information in ways we never thought possible.

It's important to remember, however, that while the heart of the Web is hypertext linking, not all the tools and elements used within it can use this capacity. (In Chapter 8, we'll be talking about older tools that can't handle multimedia without a little extra trouble.)

A Whale Of A Technology

The Web gets larger and larger with each passing second. According to Network Wizard's (**www.nw.com**) July 1997 Domain Survey, there were 828,000 registered *domains* (a domain is a Web site such as mtv.com or wral-tv.com) as of January 1997. In July 1997, there were 1.3 million—an addition of almost 500,000 domains and more than double the count of the previous year! And that doesn't even begin to count the number of Web pages on each of those domains, the number of people that use the Web, and so on. (Numbers of that sort may never be concretely established—the sprawling, anarchic nature of the Internet prohibits a head count.)

The World Wide Web's rapid rate of growth has swallowed some other Internet tools whole. Information tools like Gopher, Finger, and Usenet newsgroups have been more or less overwhelmed by the rapid growth of the Web. Many may even be accessible from within the Web itself.

Should I Burn My Library Card?

With all this lead-in, you might have come to the conclusion that the Internet is the greatest thing since sliced bread. It is. However, sometimes it's better to use it as a supplement rather than as a stand-alone research solution.

Why? Because the very things that are the Internet's greatest strengths are sometimes its greatest weaknesses. There is no governing body that rules the Internet, and no set of laws that say what information will get placed on the Internet and in what time frame. This makes civil libertarians very happy. However, it does leave a few gaps in what the Internet covers well.

The Local Lack

It's not surprising that the Internet's globe-spanning design leaves a dearth in local news and community information, but it can be disappointing. You're much more likely to find thorough coverage of a national issue than a local one. This can get very frustrating. Some companies are trying to make more local information available online but it remains difficult to find information on community activism, nonprofit organizations, or simply local news.

As the Internet gets even larger and becomes a commonly accepted source for news and information, local news and community resources will become more available. Until then, try the real-world or online versions of your local library, newspapers, and nonprofit organizations.

Going Local

In the interval between the first edition and this second edition, the issue of local content online has become a hot topic (mostly as people have figured out that selling local advertising online could be a very lucrative business.) There's still a lack of comprehensive local information, especially if you live in a non-metropolitan area, but it's getting better. For more information on local content, check out CitySearch at **www.citysearch.com**, Sidewalk at **www.sidewalk.com**, or City.Net at **www.city.net**.

Vital Statistics

Vital records—birth, death, and marriage—are not generally available online, though Kentucky is making great strides in this area. This is one type of information that will not be integrated into the Internet for a long time, simply because of the huge volume of material that would have to be transferred to the Internet. History buffs and genealogists have made significant progress in putting vital records on CD-ROM, but it's still only a dent in a huge task of archiving. There are some great vital records collections online, like the Social Security Death Index, but the best place to find vital records is still your county courthouse or archives.

TIP

It should be noted that even though there are very few vital records online, the Internet is a great place to find out where to go—offline—for vital records, especially historical records.

Archived Materials

Just as it would be close to impossible to gather up all the vital records ever created and put them online quickly, so it is with archived magazines and newspapers. Some newspapers, such as the *Charlotte Observer*, have terrific archives online. (There's also an incredible new online resource called NewsWorks, which we'll talk about later.) Other papers have nothing online, meaning you'll have to go to the local library to get the information you need, if it's available at all.

Many papers and magazines have been building archives from the day they began their presence online, which means that five years from now there will be several places to go to find good archives. Until then, just count this as the penalty of being an Internet pioneer, and go check your local library.

Okay, now that we've bummed you out, let's talk about what *is* available online.

What You Can Find On The Internet

There is no on-high Internet governing body that says what information must be put online and in what time frame. While there are lots of people who want to regulate what may *not* be put online, there are very few people working to regulate what must be made available.

Despite the lack of a governing body, materials on the Internet have two common characteristics:

- **Someone Loves Them.** A friend of ours once said, "The world is so big and so weird that you can probably find 50 people who are interested in anything you can imagine." (We were discussing something like gelatin shotput throwing at the time.) The Internet is an excellent example of this variety—the passions and interests of millions of people, available for you to share.

- **Someone Hates Them.** Of course, the flip side of loving something so much that you put up a Web site dedicated to it is hating something so much that you do the same thing. Such sites and lists are aimed mostly at TV shows and musical groups.

These categories sound a little silly, don't they? Everyone hates something or loves something, right?

The point we're trying to get across here is that putting up a Web page, or starting a mailing list, or submitting materials to be archived on a Gopher takes some work, and very few people are actually paid for doing that work. Therefore, most of the materials on the Internet are things about which the creator feels strongly. Even when the subject matter might seem trivial to you, bear in mind that someone put some time into making those materials available to you (see Figure 1.3).

That said, here's a partial list of what you can expect to find on the Internet:

- Newspapers
- Magazines
- Maps
- Telephone directories
- TV stations
- Shopping malls
- Thousands of books
- Art museums

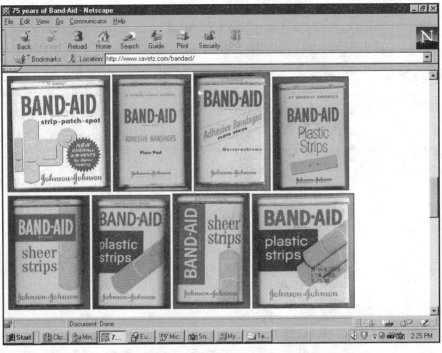

Figure 1.3   The Band-Aid collection. Sometimes what seems trivial to you is important to someone else.

- Dancing lessons
- The Library of Congress
- Job listings for various companies
- Travel information from around the world
- The Professor's (from "Gilligan's Island") real name
- Government information from census records to Small Business Association brochures

You're getting it, right? From the sublime to the ridiculous, the Internet has just about all of it.

The Big So What

"So Tara and Jill," you might be saying to yourself, "there's lots of stuff on the Internet. I can learn The Professor's real name and get the phone number of that ice cream parlor I used to go to when I lived in Fairbanks. But I can get all that without getting on the Internet, without having to learn how to use all this complicated stuff, and without having to merge onto the Information Superhighway…in other words, so what?"

We figured you were going to say that! Cue up the music!

Live, from Raleigh, North Carolina, a city proudly named after a guy that got his head chopped off, it's "Late Night With Tara Letterman!"

Not quite. But we do have a top ten list. Well, let's make a top five list so we don't have to worry about litigation.

The Top Five Reasons The Internet Is A Great Place To Do Research

1. **There are thousands of different perspectives.** The Internet isn't just about your neighborhood, your city, your state, or even your country. It's about the whole world. There are people who can tell you first-hand what it's like to live in South Africa, or what it looks like from the top of a double-decker bus in London. These people have different cultural, economic, and political perspectives to share. This diversity is one of the foremost things that makes the Internet such an interesting place.

2. **Information can be put online instantly.** The instant something happens, someone can report it online. When Hurricane Fran blew over the eastern United States in 1996, folks along the coast posted updates and commentaries. The Associated Press (AP) newswire carried information on traffic flow and the evacuation process. The National Weather Service carried satellite maps and radar images. It wasn't necessary to wait for the "Top of the Hour" on Headline News or for the Weather Channel to return to hurricane coverage. Everything was online very quickly.

3. **Physical space constraints are lessened.** This book is a certain number of pages long because that's the length that was deemed economical. Longer would have made it cost too much, though an exhaustive study of Internet research could take volumes. On the Internet, space constraints are lessened. There are many places online that make free space available for Web pages, and anyone can post their perspectives and ideas onto Usenet.

4. **Information is available 24 hours a day.** If you're a night owl like Tara, you know those pesky daylight hours of some information archives can get annoying. (You mean the library closes at 9:00 PM? What's that about? What if I need to get a phone number or governmental information at

3:00 AM?) The Internet, barring power outages, is available 24 hours a day. You can look up phone numbers at 4:00 AM and peruse the day's headlines at 5:00 AM. You can get tax information from the government at midnight if you want. The Internet conforms with your schedule, not the other way around.

5. **Information is available in a variety of formats.** Don't want to read the day's headlines? Great! You can listen to them. Perhaps you don't want to read about the sports play of the day, you want to see it. Fine! Download a video. Do you want to hear the closing arguments from Roe vs. Wade? No problem. While your local library has some multimedia resources, its holdings remain primarily text. The Internet, and especially the Web, can integrate text, graphics, audio, and video into a rich information resource.

Hopefully, we've knocked the socks off "The Big So What," and you're ready to get on the Internet and do some research. But before we get into configuring Netscape Communicator, let's look down the road a little at the future of the Internet.

The Future Of The Internet

The Internet is spreading like wildfire. You can do so many things online now: make a phone call, have a video conference, or even play Monopoly. The Internet is growing over and through our traditional ideas of community and communication.

Where will it all go from here? The same place it always has—into the things we love and the things we can't stand; and into the things we want to understand better and the things we want to share with other people.

You can be part of it!

Moving On

In just one chapter we've covered a lot of ground. Hopefully we've given you a new way to look at the megalith we call the Internet and some thoughts on how the Internet enhances, but doesn't always replace, traditional research.

We've also discussed what you can find on the Internet and what makes the Internet better than traditional research. Bear in mind, though, that what we've talked about barely scratches the surface. The Internet is very deep and very wide.

So now you're thinking of the Internet as a toolbox. You're aware of the hugeness and the immediacy of the Internet. You can't wait to get out there and stir up some electrons. So what now?

In the next chapter we'll talk about how to configure the tool you'll use first and foremost in searching the Internet—Netscape Communicator.

CHAPTER 2

Configuring Netscape Communicator

It's time to start getting your toolbox in order. And that means making sure that Netscape Communicator is properly configured.

This chapter—actually, this entire book—assumes that you're at least somewhat familiar with Communicator. You don't have to know all the ins and outs, but if you think a Netscape is the skyline of a town called Net, then put this book down and pick up a copy of the best-selling *Official Netscape Communicator Book* by Phil James. (Netscape Press, 1997).

> **TIP**
>
> *Can you use this book if you're not using Netscape Communicator? Yes; there's a lot in here to learn that's not browser-specific. You may, however, want to skip ahead to the next chapter.*

To make sure you're using the most up-to-date version of Netscape Communicator, bop on over to Netscape's site at **home.netscape.com/download/index.html** and grab yourself the latest version. It's pretty huge, so make sure you've got a lot of time to be online, and warn all the family members not to pick up the phone.

TIP

If you want to be a Netscape Navigator guru, then your favorite mantra should be RAM, RAM, RAM! Navigator does so many things that it takes up a lot of system resources. RAM prices are very good right now, and installing memory is a snap.

For Windows 3.1, Windows 95, and Windows NT users, we recommend at least 8MB of RAM, but 16MB would be even better.

For Mac users, 16MB is preferable, although a Mac (or a Mac clone) with only 8MB should have enough RAM to spare in order to run Navigator. However, you may not be able to launch any other applications while Navigator is running.

The Many Faces Of Communicator

You may have noticed when you went to download Communicator that there were several different types of Communicator available. If you bought it at your local software store, you probably had even more choices. What's going on here?

The standard version of Netscape Communicator is what we'll be assuming you use as we go through this book. The standard version has Netscape Navigator (a Web browser), Messenger (e-mail), Collabra (newsgroups), Composer (for creating Web pages), Netcaster (a "push" technology application—we'll talk about that in Chapter 9), and Conference (a real-time conferencing solution with audio chat and a whiteboard).

If you're using the Internet in a corporate setting, you might be using Netscape Communicator Professional. Professional has everything that the standard version of Communicator has, plus Netscape Calendar and a couple of other additions that are useful in a corporate setting. If you're using Communicator Professional, you can use this book just as if you were using the standard version of Communicator.

If you use a different program to read your e-mail and newsgroups, you might be using the Communicator stand-alone edition. The stand-alone edition doesn't include Conference, Messenger, or Collabra. It's basically just Navigator and Netcaster. Though you can still use this book if you use the stand-alone edition of Communicator, you won't be able to use the Messenger and Collabra software.

Finally, if you bought your copy of Netscape Communicator in a software store, you might have bought one of the Netscape Communicator enhanced editions. These have little extras like plug-ins or additional software, and might save you some money and downloading time down the road. Otherwise they're just like the standard edition.

We don't tell you what kind of ice cream to eat and you don't tell Tara not to wear her pink socks with her yellow shirt (although you would probably like to). Configuring Navigator is very much the same way: You've got your own tastes and preferences and you have your own idea of how Navigator should look. Still, some of the configuration options can make a big difference with how well your research efforts go, so let's take a look at them and we'll offer friendly advice when we can. (Bear in mind we're only going to comment on the ones that can have an effect on your research efficiency—tweaking the rest is up to you.)

Head to Edit|Preferences on the Navigator menu bar and we'll get started.

TIP

Looking for the mail and newsgroup preferences? You'll find them in the chapters dealing with e-mail (Chapter 6) and newsgroups (Chapter 7).

General Preferences

General Preferences gives you a chance to change the "look and feel" of Navigator's browser. By making just a few changes to the preferences under the Appearance, Fonts, Navigator, Languages, and Apps subsections, you can make the most of your browser while doing research.

TIP

If you're used to using Netscape Navigator 3.0, you might get a little confused by the new look of the options menu. The "outline" of the options is on the left, while the options themselves are on the right. Click on the part of the outline you want to explore on the left (if it has a plus sign next to it, click on the plus sign to expand the outline) and then adjust the options that appear on the right.

Appearance

The Appearance tab lets you choose how Navigator will look on your screen. You can check out the appearance settings in Figure 2.1.

- **On Startup Launch.** Navigator's default is to launch the Web portion of its package at startup (as opposed to Navigator's e-mail or newsreader clients), which is what you want. If you really wanted to, you could click on these check boxes and open several or even all of Communicator's

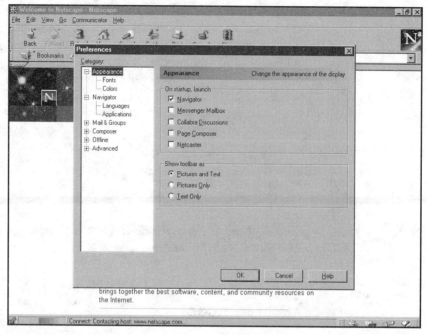

Figure 2.1   The options on the Appearance tab.

different components. Unfortunately, however, this takes up a lot of memory. It's better to open just the Web browser and use the other components as you need them. Leave that setting the way it is.

■ **Show Main Toolbar As.** You have the option of showing the main toolbar as pictures, text, or pictures with text. Unless you can't live without those cute little pictures, choose text only. It gives you a little extra browser window space.

Fonts

You can define the general size and style of fonts (letters) in Navigator when you're browsing the Web. You can choose both the proportional font and the fixed font, but bear in mind that Navigator determines *what kind* of font—proportional or fixed—will be used to display a Web page. After that, it uses your preferences to determine which particular proportional or fixed font it should use to display the page (see Figure 2.2).

A *proportional font* is called that because each letter in the font takes up an amount of space determined by the letter's shape. For example, an *m* will take up more space than an *l*. (This book is printed in a proportional font.) We like to keep our proportional font around 12 points, using a newspaper-type font

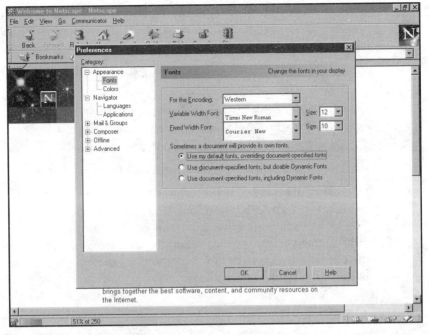

Figure 2.2   The Font options.

like Times New Roman. If you make your letters smaller than 12 points, it can get tough on the eyes. Make them larger, and it can mess up the way a Web page looks on your screen.

A *fixed font* is a font in which each letter takes up the same amount of space. An *l* will take up as much space as an *m*, which will take up as much space as a *v*, and so forth. It looks like this:

```
This is a fixed font.
```

Sometimes, the creator of a Web page wants to show you information that's preformatted in a series of lists or in a table. By having that information show up on your screen in a fixed font, the creator guarantees that it will arrange itself neatly on your screen. Since fixed fonts tend to run a little larger than proportional fonts, we like to have our fixed font a little smaller—around 10 points—using a traditional fixed font like Courier. (You don't have to worry about knowing the difference between fixed and proportional fonts—Navigator lists only the proportional fonts when you're choosing a proportional font and only the fixed fonts when you're choosing a fixed font. However, if you use a Mac, all fonts appear in both the proportional and fixed sections.)

Sometimes a document will provide its own fonts. In this section you have the chance to specify what Communicator should do if it runs across a Web page that has its own fonts. You can:

- Use the default fonts you've already specified and not use the Web page's fonts.

- Use the document-specified fonts (if they're installed in your system) but not use Dynamic Fonts. Dynamic Fonts are downloaded to your computer in order to display the Web page.

- Use the document-specified fonts and Dynamic Fonts.

Dynamic Fonts can make everything look prettier, but the problem is that downloading fonts can take a long time; mainly they're used to make something look prettier, not impart more or better information. Therefore we recommend that you choose the first option and use your default font. You might miss out on some good design, but you'll get the information you need without spending time downloading fonts.

Colors

As you can see in Figure 2.3, you have the options to set the colors that Communicator uses to display Web pages.

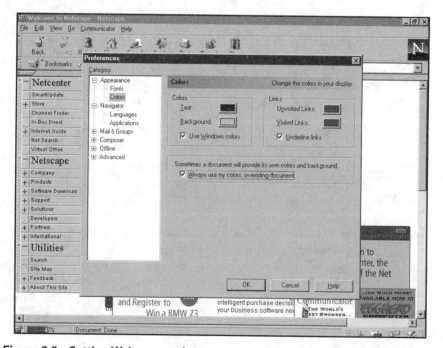

Figure 2.3   Setting Web page colors.

The first colors you can set are the text and background of the Web pages. (Click on the colored box to the right of the words "Text" or "Background" to get a palette of colors from which to choose.) To reset the colors to their defaults, click on the "Use Windows color" check box.

You also need to set the colors for hyperlinks. There are settings for *visited links* (links you've clicked on) or *unvisited links* (links you haven't clicked on).

It doesn't really matter which colors you use; just make sure they're different. If you don't have a way to distinguish your visited sites from your unvisited sites, you run the risk of crossing over your own tracks too often and wasting a lot of time.

There's a check box under this option to specify that hyperlinks should be underlined. Make sure that box is checked; underlines make it easier to distinguish the hyperlinks from other text.

Sometimes a Web page has its own colors and background. There's a check box here to specify that your colors should always be used, overriding the design in the document.

Again, it's a matter of easy access to information. If you click the check box, you're missing out on design. On the other hand, you're assuring that Web pages will always be displayed in a uniform way, with text and colors that'll make any page easy to read.

Navigator

In the Navigator section you get to make a few decisions about how you want your Web browser to work, as you can see in Figure 2.4.

First you need to decide how Navigator starts. You've got a set of three radio buttons here to specify if Navigator starts with a blank page, a home page (more about that in a moment) or the last page visited.

If you work with a lot of different pages, you may want to use a blank page. That way, when you first start Navigator you don't have to wait for a page to download. On the other hand, if you often use the same pages, you may want to start Navigator on the last page you visited or on a home page.

A home page is simply the first Web page you get when you start Navigator. You'll see that there's a text box here to specify a page. The default home page is the Netscape page. You can also click the Use Current Page button if you're already online and connected to a Web page you really like.

Maybe you have an HTML file on your hard drive that you want to use as a home page. Can you do that? Sure thing. Click on the browse button underneath

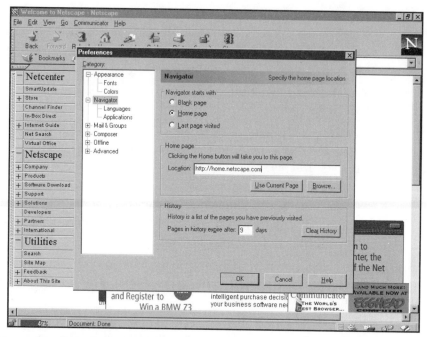

Figure 2.4 The Navigator options.

the Home page location text box, and you'll get a file locator box to choose an HTML file on your hard drive.

The last item in this section is a box for you to specify when the pages in your history list should expire. These pages are ones you have previously visited, and therefore will be a different color. (You set the colors for visited links a few minutes ago, remember?) Here you have the option of setting how many days they'll appear as visited links. If you put 7 in the box, for example, then for seven days after you click on a link, that link will appear in the visited link color. On the eighth day, however, the link's color will change and it will appear as an unvisited link until you click on it again.

Some people don't like to have their visited links last a long time. They get too many visited links, or they get confused about when they last went to visit a resource.

We like having a pretty high number in this box, however. If there's a low number we might forget when we visited a site and cross our own tracks while looking for a resource. We recommend you put 30 days in here. That gives a resource enough time to change before you go back to it.

Skip down to the advanced preferences and click on cache.

Advanced Preferences

Advanced Preferences is where you can set up Cache, Proxies, and Disk Space.

Cache

A cache is an area that Navigator sets aside to store recently viewed Web pages. That way, if you keep flipping back and forth between two Web pages, Navigator doesn't have to make you wait for them to reload every time—it simply pulls the already-loaded copies from the cache and puts them on the screen. As you see in Figure 2.5, setting the cache is just a matter of filling in a few blanks.

While there's no reason, theoretically, that you couldn't make your cache as large as possible so that Navigator has to do as little reloading as possible, there are a couple of practical difficulties involved. First, Navigator has to do cache maintenance every time it shuts down. A large disk cache can make maintenance take a long time. Second, there's the issue of hard drive space to consider—you have to have room to download the latest version of Marathon, right?

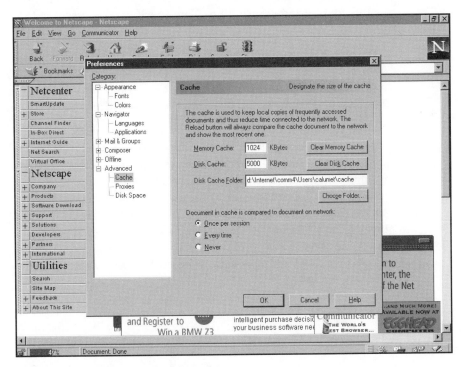

Figure 2.5   Navigator's Cache option.

There are two kinds of cache—Memory cache, which uses your RAM, and Disk cache, which uses your hard drive. For most users, the default disk cache size (5000K) should work fine, though your memory cache should be substantially smaller (you need that RAM!). Cache can be useful even when you're not online—there are software programs designed especially to let you look at your Communicator cache. They're called "Cache Browsers," and we'll talk about a couple of them in Chapter 4.

TIP

Did you know you can look at your cache without using a cache browser? You can! Check it out. Click in the Navigator text box that usually contains the address of the Web page you're visiting and type about:cache. Pretty neat, huh? You can also type about: by itself to learn about Communicator.

Moving On

Your Internet research adventure will get off on the right foot now that you've begun configuring your toolbox. The specifications discussed in this chapter will make your Internet surfing more hassle-free.

As time goes by, you may find yourself returning to the preferences with your own options and ideas on how things should look. That's okay. As you get more comfortable, feel free to do anything you want with the configuration. The important thing is that Navigator looks and works the way you want it to.

So, the Internet is the greatest thing since sliced bread, and Navigator is the greatest thing since sliced Internet. Unfortunately, as great as it is, Navigator cannot do everything—Internet standards and applications change too quickly for that. That's why Navigator has a place for *helper applications*, so Navigator can quickly apply an outside application to something on a Web page. (There are also *plug-ins*, which work within Navigator to display different document types.) The difference between a plug-in and a helper application is that plug-ins do not start a new program in order to display a document. In the next chapter we'll be looking at various kinds of plug-ins you can use to make your research job easier.

CHAPTER 3

Prepare To Research: Plug-ins And Telnet

Netscape Navigator is one heck of a program, but it simply cannot provide you with a way to view and listen to every kind of document on the Internet. New document types are created every day—who could keep up? So instead, Navigator allows you to use *plug-ins*.

A *plug-in* is a browser extension added directly to Navigator; it plays or shows you the document from within Navigator. This is very different from a *helper application*, which is an external program that runs when Navigator finds a document that requires it. (The only helper application we'll be covering in this chapter is Telnet.)

Here's what happens: Navigator is merrily surfing through the Internet when it finds a document it doesn't understand and can't display. It pops up a dialog box that lets you know you don't have the proper plug-in and gives you the option of downloading and installing it. (You can see an example of this alert in Figure 3.1.)

If you answer in the affirmative, Navigator walks you through the process of installing the plug-in. After that, Navigator remembers the application, and from then on can use the plug-in automatically. Pretty neat, huh?

There are over 100 different plug-ins for Navigator at the moment. Listing them all would take far more pages than we have here and would also leave us glumly aware that our list would be outdated almost the instant it was typed. Instead, we're going to concentrate on great plug-ins and helper applications

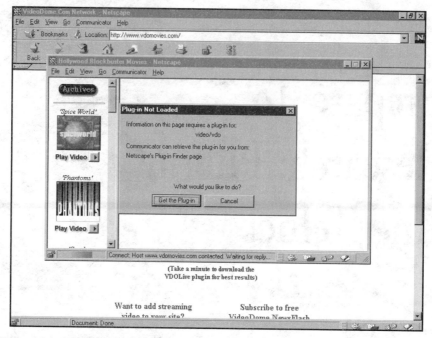

Figure 3.1 Navigator needs a plug-in.

for researchers. In the next chapter, we'll talk about utility software that can make your research application easier. But before we get into the next chapter and before we get into plug-ins, let's talk Telnet.

TIP

*Until they invent books that can be updated by radio waves, information will become outdated. Eventually, you'll have to find new plug-ins by yourself. Netscape will automatically take you to its plug-in page, but if you want to explore finding your own, we suggest you try TUCOWS (**www.tucows.com**), ZDNet (**www.zdnet.com**), and Stroud's Consummate Winsock Applications (**www.stroud.com**).*

Talkin' Telnet

Let's talk Telnet. As was said earlier, Telnet is a helper application that launches from Navigator to handle direct connections with library card catalogs and things like that. Instead of having a Web interface, a Telnet session gives you a very fast non-graphical interface (see Figure 3.2). It's just like standing in a terminal at the library!

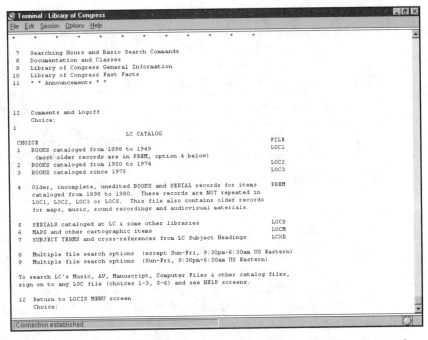

```
Terminal - Library of Congress                                            _ ∂ ✕
File  Edit  Session  Options  Help
*   *    *    *    *    *    *    *    *    *    *    *

   7   Searching Hours and Basic Search Commands
   8   Documentation and Classes
   9   Library of Congress General Information
  10   Library of Congress Fast Facts
  11   * * Announcements * *



  12   Comments and Logoff
       Choice:
1
                              LC CATALOG

  CHOICE                                                        FILE
  1   BOOKS cataloged from 1898 to 1949                         LOC1
         (most older records are in PREM, option 4 below)
  2   BOOKS cataloged from 1950 to 1974                         LOC2
  3   BOOKS cataloged since 1975                                LOC3

  4   Older, incomplete, unedited BOOKS and SERIAL records for items    PREM
      cataloged from 1898 to 1980.  These records are NOT repeated in
      LOC1, LOC2, LOC3 or LOCS.  This file also contains older records
      for maps, music, sound recordings and audiovisual materials.

  5   SERIALS cataloged at LC & some other libraries            LOCS
  6   MAPS and other cartographic items                         LOCM
  7   SUBJECT TERMS and cross-references from LC Subject Headings    LCXR

  8   Multiple file search options   (except Sun-Fri, 9:30pm-6:30am US Eastern)
  9   Multiple file search options   (Sun-Fri, 9:30pm-6:30am US Eastern)

  To search LC's Music, AV, Manuscript, Computer Files & other catalog files,
  sign on to any LOC file (choices 1-3, 5-6) and see HELP screens.

  12   Return to LOCIS MENU screen
       Choice:

Connection established
```

Figure 3.2   Nothin' but Telnet. Take a non-graphical look at the Library of Congress.

Windows 95 has its own Telnet application built-in, and if you want to use it that's fine. However, you might find other software more to your liking. Our personal recommendation is a program called EWAN. It's easy to use and very reliable. You can find the latest version at **www.lysator.liu.se/~zander/ewan.html**.

Many times you can begin a Telnet session just by clicking on a Web link. But sometimes you're going to want to connect to a Telnet site without going through the Web. Here's a quick tutorial in using EWAN:

1. Launch EWAN.

2. Select File|Open. A pop-up menu of pre-selected sites appears.

3. Pick the New option on the right-hand side of the screen. A dialog box opens, asking for:

   ■ **The name of the site**. Use any name you want; this helps you select it from the dialog box later.

   ■ **The network address or host name**. The host name is the series of words separated by periods; for example, news.mindspring.com is a host name. When it's given as words, it's a host name. When it's given as a string of numbers separated by periods, it's a network address.

For example, if you wanted to Telnet to **law.fictionalexample.edu 3000**, then the host name would be law.fictionalexample.edu. However, the network address of the same place might be 111.23.84.31. (The 3000 is the port number; we'll talk about that in the next bullet.)

■ **The port number**. If there isn't a number after the host name, make sure the button next to Telnet is clicked on. If there is a number, like 3000 in the previous example, then make sure the Custom button is selected and the number (in this case, 3000) is in the box next to it. (The Port number just tells the computer what connection to use.)

Next, click on OK and watch the red light at the bottom right part of the screen. When the light turns green, you're connected. Sometimes you have to wait a couple of minutes to get anything on the screen. If you wait a few minutes and don't get anything, press the Enter key a couple of times.

Once you've connected to a site, you can usually begin using its resources immediately. Sometimes, however, you'll have to use a login name and password. These are usually noted somewhere when you first connect. (For example, "Enter username LAW and password GUEST to access the Fictionalexample Law Library.")

For the research nut, Telnet is one of the most vital programs to have. But to really get the most out of your Web browsing, you need to have plug-ins. There are so many of them that we can't cover them all in this book, but we can go over the most vital ones.

Plug-ins For Research

Tara and her husband both love music, and consequently they've developed quite a collection of audio CDs. If you were ever to come to their house and say something like, "I've never listened to music before, and I'm kind of interested. What's good?" Tara's brain would probably short-circuit. She'd mutter a few words and then proceed to run all over the house. You would have to dodge Jane Siberry, Professor Longhair, and Bob Marley CDs as they went flying through the air. She'd fill your arms with Frank Zappa and Billie Holliday and Kate Bush. Once in a while, she would laugh maniacally.

Faced with the prospect of choosing the best helper applications and plug-ins from a vast collection, we are tempted to the do the same thing—toss CDs in the air, mutter, and of course, laugh maniacally. Instead, we will do a few deep breathing exercises, compose ourselves as best we can and give it our best try.

TIP

Interested in learning more about plug-ins? Check out The Official Netscape Plug-in Book, *by Shannon Turlington, from Netscape Press. It lists dozens of plug-ins, along with tricks for using them as a Web surfer and as a Web designer.*

Please Support The Shareware Concept

While some of the programs mentioned in this chapter are free, many of them are shareware, meaning that you can use them free for a certain period of time, but after that you must pay for them. Everybody benefits from this system—designers can keep their overhead costs low, and you get to sample a product before you commit some of your hard-earned moolah. Please don't abuse this system—register your shareware. Most publishers don't want more than $20 or $30 for products that they worked very hard to bring to you, and you're helping to keep a great software publishing system alive.

Viewing Documents

To view and listen to documents within Navigator, there are three must-have add-ons: RealPlayer, Shockwave, and Acrobat. These add-ons increase Navigator's ability to bring you sound, graphics, and animation.

Navigator's Built-in Multimedia

Don't think that Navigator is a weakling without some assistance; plain vanilla Navigator has a robust array of multimedia support. Before we get into add-ons, let's talk about what Navigator can do without any outside help.

Graphics

Navigator can display several graphics files without any helper applications or plug-ins at all. It supports Graphics Interchange Format (GIF), Joint Photographic Experts Group (JPEG or JPG), and X-Bitmap (XBM) graphics files. You'll find GIF and JPG files all over the Internet, but XBM files are more rare.

Wondering about the format of a particular graphics image? Right-click (for Mac users, click and hold the mouse button) on the image and you'll get a whole bunch of options. One of the options is "View Image," followed by the name of the graphics file. Take note of the file's *extension*—the letters that follow the dot—that says what kind of file it is. Besides GIF, XBM, and JPG, other file types are PICT, BMP, PCX, TIF, PNG, and EPS. However, the most popular by far are GIF and JPG.

Sound

All Macs (and Mac clones) come with built-in multimedia capabilities (16-bit stereo sound and the ability to play movie files at 30 frames per second). For Windows users, we'll assume that you have a sound card and speakers connected to your computer. Navigator can play the following file types: AIFF, MIDI, WAV, and AU. All of these files, except MIDI, are simply sound files produced by different computer types. (WAV, as you probably know, is the Windows sound file type.) MIDI, however, is not a sound file in the traditional sense—it is not a recording of a sound, but rather a digital set of instructions that tells your computer to play a certain sequence of musical notes in a certain way. Since it's just a set of instructions and not a recording, MIDI files are much smaller than other types of sound files. On the other hand, your sound card has to be MIDI-compatible to be able to play MIDI files, and the kind of music quality you'll hear can vary greatly depending on the kind of sound card you have. If your computer is less than two years old, it's a good bet that its sound card is MIDI-compatible, but check your documentation if you're not sure.

Moving Images

Navigator supports two movie file formats: QuickTime (which we'll talk more about in just a moment) and AVI, the Microsoft format for video files. Windows users can view AVI files without the assistance of a plug-in or helper application, but Mac users will need to download a plug-in such as MacZilla to view AVI files. MacZilla is really a mega plug-in because it allows you to view QuickTime, AVI, and MPEG movies as well as listen to AU, WAV, MIDI, AIFF, and MP2 sound files. You can download MacZilla from **www.macszilla.com**, but it will cost you about $10.

If you're a Mac user and have installed MacZilla, you can click on a link to an AVI movie to download and then play it on your screen. (It's usually in a small window.) When the movie is finished downloading, you can play it again, or move forward frame by frame, move backward frame by frame, rewind it to the beginning, or fast forward it to the end. Not all AVI files have sound (because sound makes a large video file even larger) so don't be surprised if you end up watching a silent movie.

If you want to see an AVI file in action but don't want to download a really large file, try going to **www.cwci.com/bdl/bdl2.shtml**, and click on the picture of the dog and the bike (check out the dog and the bike in Figure 3.3). This video is silent and short—just a few seconds—but it's less than 300K and is a quick demonstration of how an AVI file looks in Navigator.

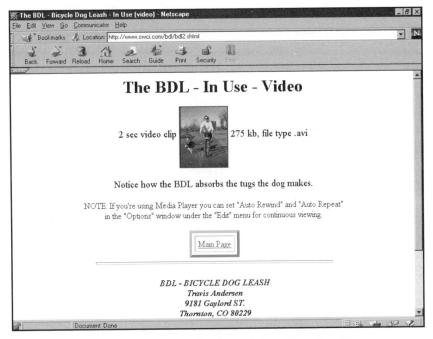

Figure 3.3   ***Check out a few seconds of man's best friend getting some
exercise in this short AVI file.***

Most movie files are much, much larger than 300K—they can run anywhere
from 1MB to over 20MB! Most Web pages will warn you when you're about to
download something large.

A Quick Look At QuickTime

QuickTime, which uses the file extension .MOV or .QT, is a format developed
by Apple that has spread to Windows computers. QuickTime is capable of
playing movies, movies with audio or MIDI tracks, and movie animations.
Navigator plays QuickTime files, but you need to have the latest version of Apple
QuickTime installed to view it properly. You can download the latest version of
QuickTime for the Mac OS or Windows at **www.apple.com/quicktime**. To
view QuickTime VR movies you'll also need to download the QTVR component from **qtvr.quicktime.apple.com/**.

Moving Worlds

Two dimensions. How boring! Sure, you can watch images move on the screen,
but they're flat. Wouldn't you rather have nice 3D images that have depth and
vibrancy? If your answer is yes, read on.

Navigator supports VRML, which is short for Virtual Reality Modeling Language. (Some people pronounce it V-R-M-L, some people say VER-mul. Tara says VER-mul-chelli. Get it?) VRML gives depth to Web pages, turning them into 3D landscapes in which you can move around. In this file type, which has an extension of *.WRL, you can walk, slide, or even fly through a Web page, and yes, it is every bit as cool as it sounds. In the future, instead of having to go through a menu at a library Web site, you'll be able to walk through a virtual lobby and click on the card catalog if you want to search for materials, or click on the help desk if you have a question or want to read a FAQ.

If you'd like to give VRML a try go to **www.marketcentral.com/vrml/gallery.wrl** (shown in Figure 3.4) for an interesting take on a museum. Once the page is loaded, click on the question mark to learn how to move around. For more VRML fun, try the VRML models page at **www.ocnus.com/models/**. You'll find a variety of models here, from a pair of pliers to a skeletal model of the human foot.

If a flat movie takes a lot of time to download, a 3D world would take hours, right? Wrong. VRML landscapes have considerably less detail than reality and generally run from 100K to 400K, which would take less than 10 minutes to download with a 28.8 modem connection. Better yet, once you've downloaded

Figure 3.4 *An online art museum. Admire the pictures or play kamikaze and fly through them.*

the landscape, you don't have to refresh it by downloading new details from the Internet, so it's very fast and easy to move around.

There's also a version of QuickTime called QuickTime VR (for Virtual Reality) that allows you to walk through a movie, turn around, look up or down, zoom in and out, or manipulate objects. For example, we've seen one QTVR movie of a vase that you can inspect by turning it upside down, spinning it end-over-end, and zooming in or out. Visit the QuickTime VR home page at **qtvr.quicktime.apple.com/** for software downloads and samples.

Conference

Communicator installs with Conference, a conferencing tool. (Users of 3.0 might remember something like this, only it was called CoolTalk.) Instead of sending e-mail back and forth or posting messages on a newsgroup, Conference lets you communicate in real-time. You can send text and graphics back and forth, or even, if you have a sound card, communicate by voice. You can even draw pictures and share them on a virtual "white board." Now that's multimedia.

RealPlayer

If you've been around the Internet for a while, you might remember a product called RealAudio. RealAudio played streaming audio—audio that played as it downloaded, instead of downloading completely before playing.

The updated all-new version of RealAudio is called RealPlayer. It plays both streaming audio and streaming video. Streaming video—you guessed it—plays video as it downloads.

That's the good news, that you don't have to wait for an entire video before you view it. Here's the bad news. The quality of the video and the audio depends on the speed of your Internet connection. If you're connected at 14.4 or less, streaming video won't do you any good and you should probably stick to streaming audio. (You have the choice of one or the other. In some cases, only streaming audio is available.) If you're one of the lucky ones who has an ISDN or T1 connection, you'll get a lot of use out of streaming audio and video.

And if you're one of the many with a 28.8 connection or a 56K modem? You'll know that you're not watching television, but you can get decent video quality and excellent audio quality over a 28.8 connection.

You can download the free version of RealPlayer at **www.realplayer.com/ products/player/index.html**. For some interesting RealPlayer content, try C-SPAN's collection of content (see Figure 3.5) at **www.c-span.org/realvid.htm**, historic footage from the MIR space station at **xyber.irisz.hu/mir/**, and the National Public Radio archives at **www.realaudio.com/contentp/npr.index.html**.

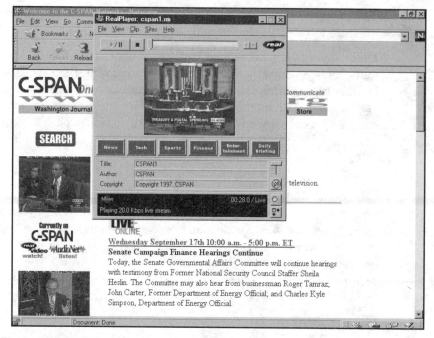

Figure 3.5   It ain't cable, but it ain't bad. It's C-SPAN via RealPlayer.

Shockwave

Shockwave provides diagrams, animation, and other Internet multimedia in relatively small, easily downloadable packages. But more than that, Shockwave modules provide a high level of interactivity. This is where you as a researcher will get the most use out of them. To explore car parts made from Reynolds Metals aluminum parts, see **www.rmc.com/divs/millprod/sae/autopilot.html**. For more shocked sites, check out **www.shocker.com/shocker/**.

Sometimes you might encounter a Shockwave site that doesn't seem to accept your Director plug-in. That's because Shockwave has a younger sibling, Shockwave Flash, which is used mostly for animation and a minimum of interactivity. You can get both the Shockwave Flash and the Shockwave plug-ins at the same place: **www.macromedia.com**.

Acrobat

The Adobe Acrobat reader was developed to read any files created with the Adobe Acrobat application. That tells you a lot, doesn't it? Adobe Acrobat takes electronic documents created using a variety of applications—word processing programs, CAD programs, and publishing programs, to name a few—

and turns them into Adobe Acrobat documents which have an extension of .pdf and are readable by anyone using the Adobe Acrobat Reader.

You can see the advantage to this system. A library or publication might use several different applications to create its research or periodical. With Adobe Acrobat, a library or publication can transform its publications to the same format, which is readable via a freely distributed program.

As a researcher you'll find a variety of interesting items available in the .pdf format. The GATT agreement is available in .pdf format at **trading.wmw.com/ gatt/**. The Florida State University Law Review is available in .pdf format at **www.law.fsu.edu/lawreview/**.

The Adobe Acrobat reader is available at **www.adobe.com/prodindex/acrobat/ readstep.html**.

Moving On

In this chapter, we've taken a look at what you can add to Navigator to view all kinds of Internet documents. We also took a look at Telnet and how you can use it to access online resources like card catalogs.

We're almost there—almost ready to step out into the Internet and get some research done. But there are few more things to discuss. In the next chapter we'll talk about utility software—a set of software you can use to make your researchin' life easier.

CHAPTER 4

Helper Applications

In the first edition of this book, we put the plug-ins and the helper applications in the same chapter, and that wasn't a popular decision. More people wanted guidance on how they could make their Web surfing easier, and how they could best handle the results of their research once they got it to their computers.

Okay, we can see that. So in this chapter, we're going to take an expanded look at the applications that can make your surfing and information handling experiences easier. A helper application can make your life easier in two very different instances—during your use of the Internet, and post-Internet use when you're trying to organize and handle the information that you've got. Let's take a look at using the Internet now.

Using The Internet

Reading e-mail and using newsgroups are pretty immediate activities. You read an e-mail, you answer it, you go on to the next one. Pretty simple. However, with using the Web, you have to wait for Web pages to load. You click on a link, and either the page loads pretty quickly (if you've got image loading turned off, and it's not a very big page) or you wait for a long time, go make yourself a sandwich, do a load of laundry, or whatever.

If you have a lot of Web pages that you want to look at, you can save some time by having your computer download the Web pages automatically. Communicator has a built-in component that will download pages for you automatically on a regular basis called Netcaster. (You'll learn more about it in Chapter 9.) However, if you want to download lots of pages, you might want to use a more specialized program called an *offline browser*.

Now, if you've already downloaded a page using Navigator and you want to go back and look at something, you want to view the disk cache. You can do this from within Navigator, or you can use a cache browser. We'll take a look at an offline browser first, then a couple of cache browsers.

TIP

*Do you want to do your own searching for Internet helper applications? Start at Tucows at **www.tucows.com** and Stroud's Consummate Winsock Apps list at **cws.internet.com**/.*

Offline Browsing

Sometimes after a long round of research, you've got a pile of URLs you want to investigate, but you don't want to sit there and wait for tons of pages to load. Instead, you can have a computer program download all the pages for you, then zip through them very quickly—since all the images and text are on your computer, you can whip through them in a flash.

For offline browsing we like Anawave's WebSnake. (You can download the demo version at **www.anawave.com**.) What you do is enter the URLs you want to have downloaded to your computer, then you add some specifics—what kind of files you want to download, whether you want to leave the domain from which you're downloading files, and so on. Most important is the specification for how many *levels* of a Web site you want to download. The first level is the URL you specify. The second level is the URL you specify and every URL it links to. The third level is the same as level two, plus every URL that *those* URLs link to, and on and on.

As you might imagine, downloading more than a couple of levels of a URL will rapidly get you into using some serious disk space, so be careful when you're using an offline browser.

Sometimes, however, you don't need an offline browser. You just need to find a text file, an image file, or something else that you've previously looked at that's already in Navigator's cache. For that, you need a cache browser.

Viewing The Disk Cache

Has the following ever happened to you? Two minutes after you quit Navigator, you realize that you wanted to save some information you saw on the last page. Too bad it's too late to do anything about it—or is it?

In Chapter 2, we told you about the cache, a way that Navigator saves a certain amount of your surfing session to your hard drive, so you don't have to download the same things over and over again as you skip back and forth within a particular set of pages. Now some companies have taken that idea a bit further by making it possible to explore the cache offline. Of course, if you want some really basic cache exploration, type **about:cache** in Navigator's URL window. As you can see in Figure 4.1, you'll get a basic listing of what's in your disk cache.

If you exit Navigator, but want to review the pages that you've just looked at (how many pages you can view depends on how large you've made your cache), you can do it with cache explorer programs. The two we really like are the Netscape Cache Explorer and UnMozify.

Netscape Cache Explorer

Netscape Cache Explorer (see Figure 4.2) is a no-nonsense program. Functional and simple to use, it examines your cache and comes up with a list of

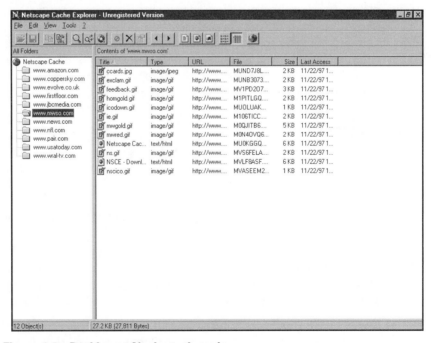

Figure 4.1   Peeking at Navigator's cache.

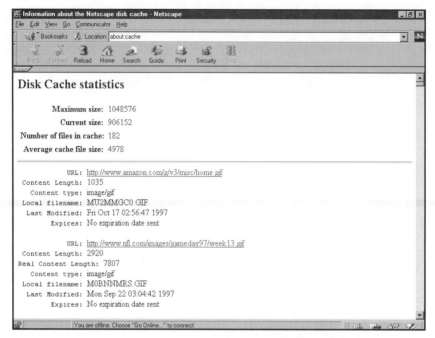

Figure 4.2   Netscape Cache Explorer is simple but powerful.

what documents are in it and what kind of documents they are (text files, pictures, sound clips, etc.); it then presents you with that list. Double-click on the document to view it. Simple. However, if you have your cache set at a very high number, you might find yourself waiting as the Explorer goes through your cache file and puts the list together. If you want only one or two things from the list, this can get tiring. Netscape Cache Explorer still gets our "simple but oh so functional" award. You can pick it up at **www.mwso.com/**.

UnMozify

UnMozify (named after Mozilla, the Netscape mascot) is a little more complicated and a little more savvy than Netscape Cache Explorer. Instead of just going through your cache and giving you a list of files to choose from, UnMozify checks which domains you've visited and gives you that list. As you can see in Figure 4.3, you can choose materials to extract from the cache on a domain-by-domain basis and view them the same way. You can even narrow down the list of extracted files further by choosing text or multimedia files and by choosing files based on age. Once the files have been extracted from Navigator's cache, UnMozify launches Navigator and presents you with a nice menu of the materials available. You can even search the entire cache!

If you have a small cache and you want to browse through it, or if you don't look through your cache very often, this program is overkill. But if you have a

Figure 4.3   UnMozify takes the mystery out of your Navigator cache.

large cache and need to be more selective about which files you extract, this program is a big winner. Pick it up at **www.evolve.co.uk/unmozify/**.

Okay, now you know how to download lots of pages without doing a lot of pointing and clicking, and you also know how to go back and retrieve a file from Navigator's cache.

Hopefully knowing how to go back and look at the list of pages you visited will give you some URLs to add to your bookmark list. How do you keep your bookmark list from growing like kudzu and taking over your hard drive?

Managing Your Bookmarks

Your bookmark list will grow like anything as you get more involved in exploring the Internet—"I have to remember this place, I have to remember that place." Soon your list is 45 miles long, and you're spending so much time scrolling through it trying to find what you're looking for that you don't get much actual surfing done.

While you can do some fundamental things to avoid overly huge bookmark lists (and we'll discuss those in Chapter 11), you can also tame them with the judicious application of bookmark manager programs. These programs help you keep your bookmark lists sorted, and they sometimes give you ways to search your bookmarks by keyword or category, instead of eternal scrolling. We'll tell you about four bookmark programs, two for Windows and two for the Mac OS.

While we haven't seen a bookmark manager program for Windows that completely knocked us out of our chairs, we like these two: URL Manager Jr. and First Floor Smart Bookmarks.

URL Manager Jr.

The *freeware* (absolutely without cost) version of a more extensive commercial product called URL Manager, URL Manager Jr. is a bare-bones URL manager. Some nice features include adding category names, searching keywords, and displaying only one category of your bookmarks at a time. We don't feel that the freeware version will hold up well under a bunch of bookmarks, but it has the advantages of loading quickly and not taking up a lot of your system resources. You can pick it up at **www.dlcwest.com/~sorev**.

First Floor Smart Bookmarks

Calling Smart Bookmarks (see Figure 4.4) a bookmark manager is like calling "The Magnificent Ambersons" just some black-and-white flick.

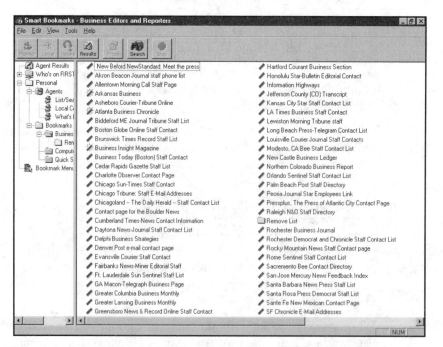

Figure 4.4   Smart Bookmarks is more than a bookmark organizer.

First Floor Smart Bookmarks integrates seamlessly with Netscape Navigator, loading when you load Navigator. It gives Navigator a boost in the Bookmark menu, making it easier to use right off the bat. Instead of going to a separate screen when you need to see more bookmarks, the bookmarks are put in a gray box on the screen. In addition, Smart Bookmarks uses *agents* (we'll also talk about agents in Chapter 11) to check pages for possible changes and then reports those changes to you.

So what are the drawbacks? Absolutely none, if you have a Pentium processor and plenty of memory. But if you don't, Smart Bookmarks is going to cause a hiccup in your program loading time and memory application. If you don't need that kind of power, it might be a little annoying to have to wait for it every time you load Navigator. However, it's a tremendously powerful and useful program. If you have the memory and the processor speed, we recommend it wholeheartedly. You can download a trial version of Smart Bookmarks by visiting the First Floor site at **www.firstfloor.com**.

On the Mac side, you'll find plenty of really cool shareware and commercial bookmark managers, two of which we'll cover here: DragNet and URL Manager.

DragNet

DragNet is a commercial URL manager from OnBase Technology that works well with Navigator and costs about $40. This is a significant sum for an Internet utility, but you'll probably find that it's worth the money. DragNet is capable of storing not only Web URLs, but FTP URLs and e-mail addresses as well. It stores all the URL information in a database whose interface is highly configurable and manageable. You can create categories of URLs to which you may add, edit, and delete entries. OnBase recently created a Windows version as well. You can download a demo of DragNet from **www.onbasetech.com/**.

URL Manager

URL Manager is a shareware bookmark and Internet URL manager that works extremely well with Navigator and comes in two versions, URL Manager ($15) and URL Manager Pro ($25). The main difference between the two versions is that URL Manager Pro adds a new pull-down menu to Navigator that includes the addition of a keyboard shortcut that allows you to easily switch between URL Manager Pro and Navigator. In fact, it works so well that you'll probably never want to go back to using Navigator's bookmarks. In addition to storing Web URLs, URL Manager also sorts bookmarks for FTP, Usenet News, Gopher, e-mail addresses, and any other URL that can be used by Navigator. You can label and sort bookmarks by name, URL, or label. Its Find feature is fairly basic, however, and doesn't provide the powerful searching capabilities of DragNet's database-driven approach to bookmark management.

URL Manager does add an important feature to the concept of the bookmark manager in the form of a helper application *dock*. The Internet Helpers dock allows you to launch or switch to your commonly used Internet applications by double-clicking the application's icon from the dock. This feature is optional and may be cut on or off as you see fit, bit we think it's a great addition to a bookmark manager. You can download URL Manager and URL Manager Pro from **www.url-manager.com/**.

Sometimes, in your quest to do Internet research, you'll find yourself stumbling—not because of the Internet, but because you're having trouble handling the information you're using.

Handling Information Post-Internet

The two biggest stumbling blocks we've found to making the most of our Internet research through Windows are: (1) using the Clipboard feature effectively and (2) organizing the information without using a program so large that we have to exit in and out of Navigator to use it. We've found satisfactory answers to both problems.

The Clipboard Problem

The Windows Clipboard presents a challenge because it allows you to save only one bit of information at a time. Whenever you save a new bit of information, the previous one is overwritten. This becomes a hassle when you come to a mail message with several bits of information that you'd like to save separately, or when you want to combine several bits of information into one document. Clip the information you want, paste it in the document. Clip another bit, paste. Clip, paste. Clip, paste. Ugh! Luckily, enough users have voiced their dislike, and this has led to several elegant solutions for the problem, mostly in the form of clipboard replacements for Windows and the Mac. Our favorites are ClipMate (for Windows) and Sanctus (for the Mac).

ClipMate

ClipMate is the Windows Clipboard you always wanted. It, like the Windows Clipboard, captures every piece of text or graphics that you choose to clip. But unlike the Windows Clipboard, it can hold hundreds of these items at a time. Once it has the item, you can do all kinds of things with it—edit it, print it, give it a different title, glue it together with a bunch of other clipped items, and more (see Figure 4.5).

When you get the hang of using ClipMate (it doesn't take long), you save a lot of time by copying or pasting several things at once. ClipMate presents you

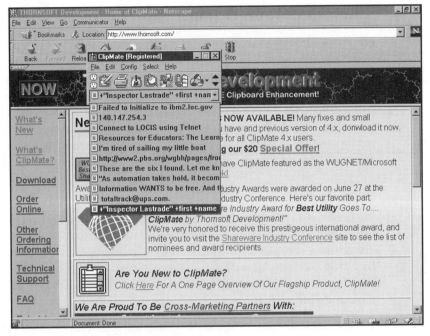

Figure 4.5 *ClipMate lets you choose, erase, and edit clipped text, all from one window.*

with a list of items that you've clipped recently. (That's the one drawback to this program; if you're a clip-fiend like Tara, you'll end up with 400 items on your list in no time.) You can select one item to move to the front, which becomes the item that will be pasted when you use the Ctrl+V command. Or, you can use the glue utility to put some of the items together and paste them all at once. It's one of Tara's favorite programs ever. Put it in your startup file so you can reap its benefits all of the time, not just when you're doing Internet research. You can get a copy at **www.thornsoft.com**.

Sanctus

On the Mac side, a postcardware utility by D.L. Kraakman called Sanctus does the trick. You can download Sanctus (it's a control panel, in case you're wondering) from the MIT HyperArchive at **hyperarchive.lcs.mit.edu/HyperArchive/ HyperArchive.html**. Like ClipMate, Sanctus offers you several options when you have copied an item to the Mac Clipboard. Select the hotkeys to press once the item has been copied to the Clipboard. Sanctus presents a dialog box of options, including Leave in Clipboard, Save in Scrapbook, Save as a Disk File, or Send to a Printer—each option having a keyboard shortcut itself.

Once we know how to get all those little bits and pieces of information, how do we put them together?

The Information Organization Problem

For a long time, we had a real problem figuring out how to organize the information we found online. Usually we just needed a "holding pen" for information until we could turn it into a report or a proposal. We tried using personal information managers, but that wasn't quite what we needed; we then tried using databases, but that wasn't the answer, either. These kinds of programs were either too bulky, weren't easy to use, or didn't have places to store information and get to it quickly. And they almost always took up too much memory. We finally found two programs that did the job for us: InfoSelect and askSam.

InfoSelect

InfoSelect is a friendly information manager. Instead of giving you a bunch of forms that you have to fill out to keep your information straight, InfoSelect gives you a completely form-free, but searchable, way to store information. Included is a calendar with reminder capacity, and the ability to use databases based on forms, if you really want to do that. You'll learn it in about five minutes, and you'll use it forever.

Tara has used it with CopperSky Writing and Research like this: If she's searching the Internet for a particular topic and finds things of interest, she'll clip them and dump them into InfoSelect for later review or for comparison. If she's preparing a report on Internet resources over a week-long period, she adds everything she finds to InfoSelect, then uses its tools and ClipMate to rearrange the information into a presentable format. She doesn't have to cut the information up to please a forms-based database, and she doesn't have to pull down several database records to get what she wants. As you can see in Figure 4.6, InfoSelect keeps a list of records and folders at the side of the screen, so everything's at your virtual fingertips. You don't have to hunt across two or three menus to get a specific phone number or date that you saved.

Its interface won't win any beauty contests, and it's some of the most expensive shareware mentioned in this chapter, but it's worth every nickel. You can get a trial copy at **www.miclog.com**.

> **TIP**
>
> *Mac users might find a great solution to personal infoglut management with a $25 shareware utility from Chronos. This is actually a superb personal information manager, and for the price, we just couldn't live without it. It manages calendars, has multiple alarm capabilities, and has a great search capability. You can download it from* ***www.chronosnet.com/*** *on a trial basis.*

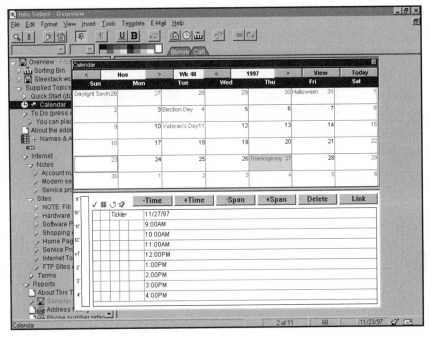

Figure 4.6   InfoSelect keeps information at your fingertips.

askSam

While InfoSelect is good for adding bits and pieces of information and then putting them together into organized documents, askSam (**www.asksam.com**) is excellent for dumping large chunks of information into one place and then referring to them later, over and over, through a fast search-and-retrieve system (see Figure 4.7).

Like InfoSelect, askSam is a free-form database. You can add forms to it if you wish, but you can also just dump information into it and sort it out in different ways without using forms. You can import various types of data into askSam, including HTML, comma-delimited, and tab-delimited. Once you have it there, you can search askSam with case-sensitive searching, fuzzy searching, or full-text searching. And askSam holds up very well under large databases. We've dumped lots of text in it and haven't slowed it down yet.

It's more of a long-range tool and is more "just" a database than InfoSelect. InfoSelect, for example, has a calendar with an alarm built in, an "outline" type view on its left-hand side, and other features that make it easy to view several lists at once, schedule items, and create to-do lists. In askSam, you'll find time- and date-stamp features, but no calendar, and while you can open more than one database at a time, you won't find an easy way to look at them

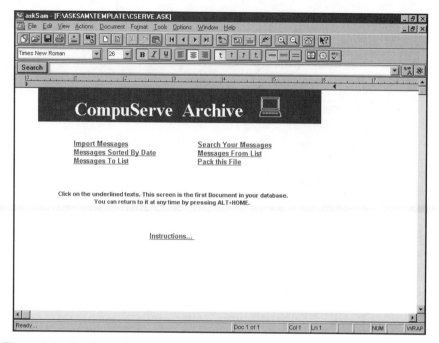

Figure 4.7   Got lots of text? Toss it in askSam.

both at once. On the other hand, if you've got a lot of information that you want to put in one place, askSam really does the trick.

Who Needs A Paper Trail?

The computer is a lovely invention, but unfortunately it's at the mercy of too many elements like electricity surges and fickle electronics. Relying on your computer to keep your information forever—and problem-free—is taking a big risk.

Don't do it. While it's very nice to have backups, an even better idea is to sometimes print out your most essential data. If you do a lot of projects, eventually you'll have too much information to print everything out. However, you can print out your Navigator bookmarks file, your list of favorite e-mail addresses, or other small-but-vital collections of information on occasion.

Paper has the advantage of not relying on electricity to produce readable data. A paper version of your most vital data will act as an insurance policy against computer accidents or emergencies.

Moving On

In this chapter, we looked at external software that you can add to Windows and the Mac to improve your research efficiency.

Don't haul out your wallet, though, if you don't feel like you can afford these programs; they're optional. They will make your life a lot easier, but they are not absolutely necessary. (If you can afford only one of these programs, we recommend ClipMate. It's excellent.)

We're almost there—almost ready to step out into the Internet and get some research done. But first, let's consider a few more things; actually, there are 10 considerations. The next chapter contains our 10 friendly suggestions for Internet research—ideas that you can keep in mind throughout your online research endeavors.

CHAPTER 5

Ten Friendly Tips For Internet Research

To complete the preparation phase for getting out there and researching, we tried to figure out what was missing from your toolbox. We realized that while we've given you a good start on the kinds of hardware and software you'll need and how to configure them, we have not given you a set of guidelines that will serve you over and above specific instructions on this or that technique.

Thus, this chapter was created. These rules are ones that apply to all of the Internet research you'll want to do, and you should keep them in mind at all times. Originally we were going to call this chapter "The 10 Commandments of Internet Research," but it seemed arrogant on our part. So instead, here are 10 Friendly Tips for Internet Research.

I. Search Wisely

You've heard the adage, "a little knowledge is a dangerous thing." Well, too much knowledge may flatten you. There is so much information on the Web these days that it's hard to compile (no two Web search sites contain the same information) and hard to track (no large-scale search engine is without a few outdated or "problem" links).

Don't Get Too General

A sure path to madness is to search for the word "tree" using an Internet search engine. If you want to do a report on trees, make your search phrase as specific as you can and then work your way outward, getting more and more general. For example, say you needed to do a paper on objectivism for your American Philosophy class. You decide to focus on Gwen Ives, a minor character in objectivist Ayn Rand's novel *Atlas Shrugged*. Gwen Ives is a very specific character, and searching for her name might be difficult. Developing a very specific to very general list for Gwen Ives might look like this:

Gwen Ives
Atlas Shrugged
Ayn Rand
Objectivism
American Philosophy

Gwen Ives is probably too narrow a search topic and American Philosophy is too broad. Your best research bets will be in the middle of the spectrum: Ayn Rand and *Atlas Shrugged*. In Chapter 11, we'll get into how you can use Boolean modifiers to phrase very specific research requests.

Use The Appropriate Index

If you're researching a reasonably common topic with a reasonably common theme, use a general index (a site that divides pages up into categories, like Yahoo!) before you use a general search engine (a site that indexes every word of every page it catalogs, like AltaVista). If there's one available, use a topic-specific index before you use a general one. For example, if you're researching vitamins, you'd want to use a health index like Achoo (**www.achoo.com**), shown in Figure 5.1, before you used the general index Yahoo! (**www.yahoo.com**). If Achoo doesn't have what you need, then you'd want to use Yahoo! before you used a general search engine like AltaVista (**altavista.digital.com**).

II. Keep Time On Your Side

Because of its reluctance to be governed extensively by a central body, the Web has no way of automatically adding a site to the many general subject catalogs and indexes available. There is no single "librarian" making sure that all online resources are available from one "card catalog" (a primary reason that trying to approach the Internet as a library can lead to frustration). While Web-crawling spiders (more about them in a bit) make the assimilation and indexing of Web sites easier (and there are a variety of ways to submit a Web site's information to the search engines), it is up to humans to initiate and

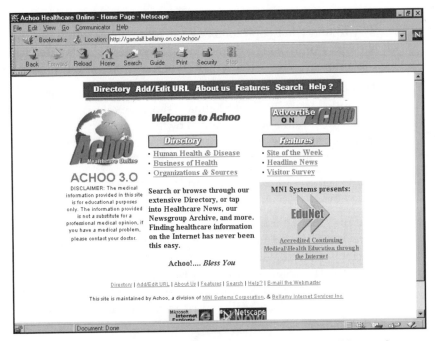

Figure 5.1   A topic-specific index like Achoo can make searching easier.

perform this process and the many other tasks of public relations and publicity that will get their site into the public eye.

Unfortunately, too many site creators love the creation and design process but have a marked distaste for publicizing the fruit of their efforts. This means too many good resources are relegated to dark corners and can result in complicated hunts for the unfortunate seeker of knowledge. (Yes, we said seeker of knowledge. And here you thought you were just trying to finish your comparative economics paper on time.)

When researching a breaking event or an ongoing topic, bear in mind that search engines sometimes take awhile to add things to their databases. Depending on the search engine, the process of adding something may take from a couple of hours to a few weeks. For recent developments, check newsgroup and mailing list archives first.

III. Use Every Scrap Of Information

Did you ever do logic puzzles in math class? They were puzzles in which you were given a group of people and a group of things or activities. By using a limited set of clues, you connect the proper person to the proper thing or activity.

Internet research is much the same way. Every scrap of information is necessary to find what you're looking for. Many times you'll pick up scraps along the way. Don't disregard any scrap of knowledge, no matter how minor. Keep the different scraps of information in mind and be prepared to use them.

Example: Tara has a friend—call her Velma—who has a friend—call him Fred—in South Africa. Fred sent Velma a short e-mail saying that he was having a rough time. Velma was concerned by this short, mysterious note. She was even more concerned when she tried to *Finger* his account (check a user's account for last use and other statistics, more about that in Chapter 8) and wasn't able to.

Velma sent Tara Fred's e-mail address—fakefred@milkyway.co.za. That's all she knew.

The first thing Tara did was try to find the company using milkyway as a *domain name* (main name for a set of computers on the Internet). No luck. Then she looked on a database of South African companies for the name milkyway. No luck. However, she did find her first scrap of information—commercial enterprises in South Africa put a "co" before the za when they make an address, so the address **milkway.co.za** means **companyname.commercialsite. SouthAfrica**.

With that in mind, she went to a World Wide Web search engine and looked for the phrase "milkyway.co.za." She found a lot of things—mostly e-mail addresses. That's where Tara discovered that most of these e-mail addresses were on World Wide Web pages on a World Wide Web machine called **www.pcb.co.za**.

She tried to open the main page of **www.pcb.co.za**, and lo and behold, there on the page (which was the page of PCB Technologies) was an invitation to visit the Milky Way Cafe, an Internet cafe located in Johannesburg. Fred had created a mailbox at the Milky Way Cafe, which apparently didn't let outside machines finger its account.

It was kind of a roundabout search, but by using the scraps of information picked up on the way, Tara was able to figure out where Fred was getting his e-mail from and why his account couldn't be fingered. (He's fine, by the way.) Be sure to use what you find along the way to help you carry out your research.

IV. Attack Your Research Problem From Many Different Angles

Finding a good angle is as important as getting specific. For a more sporting example, let's consider basketball. Say you're doing a newspaper story on the

WNBA vs. the NBA. You decide to focus on California, covering the Los Angeles Sparks and the Los Angeles Lakers. You could do a simple search for Lisa Leslie or Shaquille O'Neal, but you're going to get a lot of game recaps and news stories you're not looking for.

One way to go about finding the information you do need is to think about the different aspects of what you're researching. If you want to compare scoring among the different players in the two leagues, you might want to search for *both* Shaquille O'Neal and Lisa Leslie. Maybe you want to focus on one of the team coaches. Maybe you want to look for files that have both WNBA and NBA in them. Or maybe you want to pull completely back from the L.A. teams and focus on popular players from other areas of the league, like Rebecca Lobo or Michael Jordan.

A lot of your potential success in searching the Internet depends on your flexibility—how you phrase your questions and look for clues. This is not your high school algebra exam; there is no flat right or wrong answer, just the answer you find.

V. Don't Be Afraid To Guess

You can go far on the Net by taking an educated guess or two. You can guess at the addresses where you might logically expect to find information. Conversely, you can guess at the many unexpected ways the topic that you're searching for may have been misspelled, turning up gems that would otherwise escape you.

Play The Name Game

When searching for a particular name, do not assume that everyone knows how to spell it. When Tara has published materials on the Internet, she's been credited as Tara Calishane, Tara Calashain, and Tara Calshain. These spellings are not very wrong, but they are wrong enough that they would not be found under a search for the correctly spelled name. If you are looking for someone named Ridout, search under Rideout and Rideowt as well. If you're looking for references to Louisa May Alcott, try Allcot and Alcot. And of course, first names are even more diverse—someone you know as Andrew might go by Andy or Drew online.

This misspelling rule applies to common English words as well. There is no law that says that people have to run their materials through a spell checker before they put them online, so a lot of lesser-known words are misspelled. Say someone wanted to find references to the word "usufruct." A search for that word would find some references, but not quite what they were looking for. However, a search for "usafruct," a misspelling of the same word, may find a great reference. Many search engines support *wild cards*, which allow you to replace a letter or many letters in a word with a wild card, allowing an Internet search to match on any letter. For example, if the wild card character is a *, then a wild card search for c*t would find cat, cut, cot, and so forth.

Experiment With Addresses

If you're looking for a site on the Web, try typing in **www.<companyname>.com**, for example, **www.microsoft.com**. This usually works if you're trying to find a company name—Philips, Budweiser, Sony, and so on. If you're trying to find a nonprofit organization, try **www.<companyname>.org**, and if you're trying to find a college, try **www.<college>.edu**.

VI. Resist The Temptation To Get Distracted

There's so much stuff out there that you'll often find yourself going, "Hey, that resource looks kind of interesting. I think I'll check that site for a minute." The next thing you know, it's three hours later and you haven't done any of the research you originally intended to do (see Figure 5.2).

Information presented in a hypertext format gives you a raft of possibilities for going off on a fun, exciting, and extensive—but ultimately time-wasting and counterproductive—cyber-escapade. Fortunately for you, we've got solutions. The next time you're traveling across the rocky Internet, try these tips:

- **Write an itinerary.** Sit down with a question or a list of questions and don't sway from it. Every time you want to follow a link, ask yourself, "Is this going to help answer my question?"

- **Set a timer.** When traversing the multidimensional spiral of the Internet, a timer helps eliminate the temptation to take off on an interesting link. We find hunting in blocks of 30 or 45 minutes works well; less time and it's hard to get anything done, more time and it's hard to keep focused. Bear in mind that when you do your hunting can also affect your chances of research success. The Internet has a "rush hour," just like a freeway. If you're doing work around noon, or around 8:00 p.m., you might find that some of your favorite research haunts are so busy that they're unreachable. Don't fret; if you can't get through just go on to the next one, and try again at a less busy time—early in the morning or very late at night.

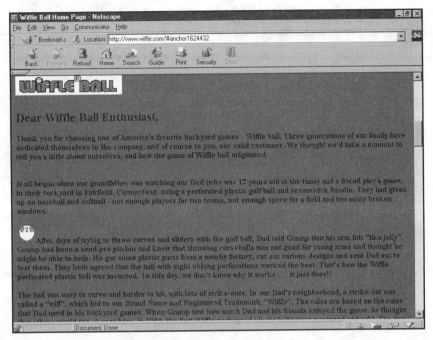

Figure 5.2   It can get pretty tempting, but try to stick with what you're researching.

VII. Mark Your Trail

You don't have to have a sheaf of Alice's Restaurant-style "8x10 glossy photographs with circles and arrows and a paragraph on the back explaining each one," but it's good to mark your trail so you can remember where you went and learn from how you got there.

Bookmarks are a bad way to keep your trail. Since it's easy to add a bookmark every time you're looking for something, a small bookmark file can quickly evolve into a huge unusable mess. If you have only used a resource once to solve a problem and don't plan on using it again, don't put it in your bookmark file. A better thing to do is to write yourself a note, or even a brief e-mail, explaining each unique research problem and how you solved it. Then print it out and keep it. The next time you need to research a problem, you'll have a summary of a problem that you solved before. If the same resource pops up again and again in your problem-solving files, put it in your bookmarks.

For example, we read online newspapers a lot. Invariably we find ourselves going to the terrific online newspaper index Newslink (**www.newslink.org**). Since we use it often—at least five or six times a week—it sits up at the top of our bookmark list.

VIII. Ask For Help

Bad press notwithstanding, most people on the Internet are friendly and help-ful. If you take the time to learn how to ask a question properly, many people will share whatever information they have with you.

The operative part of the above paragraph is the phrase "learn how to ask a question properly." Newsgroups and mailing lists—the primary means of group interaction on the Internet—have standards of culture and communica-tion that vary considerably from place to place. One mailing list may have strict rules about staying on the topic. Another may tolerate straying from the topic, but strictly forbid profanity. A newsgroup may also be moderated, mean-ing that your posts will have to be approved by someone before the rest of the newsgroup sees them.

In chapters 6 and 7, we'll show you how to best familiarize yourself with the rules of a particular group or mailing list. By taking some time to learn the standards of each group with which you wish to communicate, you'll make the most of your posts and e-mails.

IX. Share

Keep the spirit of Internet kindness alive by sharing what you know when you're asked a question.

Sometimes it will be very tempting to *flame* (insult or harass) someone be-cause they've just asked a question that you've heard a million times before, or they've just asked a question that you consider the stupidest thing that you've ever heard. Just count to 10 and forget it.

By taking the time to kindly answer a question that was politely asked, you're doing your bit to keep Internet culture friendly and nice. Heaven knows, all of us can use all of the friendly and nice we can get.

X. Use The Information Responsibly

The power of the Internet and the amount of data it has available make it possible to abuse privacy in ways previously unimaginable. You've probably experienced this already with *spam*—people finding your e-mail address from an online resource and sending you unsolicited advertisements. It's a fairly benign invasion of privacy, but it's still annoying.

Information alone is a powerful tool. By comparison, in terms of sheer power, the Internet is probably one bad nuclear-powered titanium chainsaw. A tool that powerful can do tremendous amounts of good or bad. The responsibility for proper care of it is up to you. Treat the information you get with respect, and don't use it inappropriately.

Moving On

As you see, some of the rules for Internet research are common sense, and some of them are cyberspace-specific. The watchword for all of them, though, is flexibility. The more flexibility with which you can view a problem or answer a question, the better chance you'll have of finding the answer to your question or the information that you're looking for. The best tool in your Internet toolbox is still your brain.

The next chapter brings us to the first of two chapters about communicating with groups over the Internet. The communication medium we'll check out first brings together groups, through e-mail, to discuss everything from quantum physics to the A-Team. Turn the page and let's learn about mailing lists.

Part II

Using The Different Aspects Of The Internet

CHAPTER 6

Making The Most Of Mailing Lists

A few chapters ago we mentioned a friend's theory that no matter what outlandish thought you come up with, there probably will be 50 people interested in it. The number of mailing lists on the Internet seems to bear out that theory; there are close to 72,000 available, on topics ranging from singer/ songwriter Suzanne Vega to people researching ancestors with the last name of Hamilton. There are mailing lists devoted to computer products, cars, sports teams, obscure hobbies, small business, pets, and lots of scientific issues. Needless to say, mailing lists are an incredible research resource!

Before we go any further, let's distinguish between a *mailing list* and a *newsgroup*. A newsgroup is available to pretty much anyone, if their Internet Service Provider offers it (however, there are some newsgroups that are not offered universally). Anyone can read it at any time, and on most newsgroups anyone can post a message. You read newsgroups using either Navigator or a separate software application called a newsreader. We'll cover this and other newsgroup issues in Chapter 7.

Mailing lists, on the other hand, you must request before you can read. They come straight to your mailbox so you get them as part of e-mail. Some mailing lists are *restricted-access,* and you have to have permission to join them. Some mailing lists are *moderated*—anytime anyone puts a post on a moderated list, it goes to the owner of the list, who then decides if anyone else gets to see the message.

Because they are more private, mailing lists usually have a better signal-to-noise ratio than newsgroups. Messages are more relevant, and more users are interested in and informed about the subject. There are fewer irrelevant advertisements, and people who behave badly generally are removed by the mailing list owner before becoming too disruptive.

Of course, there also are problems with mailing lists. Sometimes it's hard to deal with the number of e-mail messages a mailing list generates. Very active ones might generate more than 100 e-mail messages a day. If you don't check your e-mail very often, you're in for a big shock when you decide to get it. Also, there are occasional problems with the mechanics of an e-mail list. You may want to quit reading a list and find that you're still getting it anyway. You may end up getting five copies of the same e-mail. While not earth-shattering problems, these little things can get frustrating.

Still, most of the time the advantages outweigh the disadvantages. Mailing lists can be a good research tool.

Accessing Mailing Lists: Using Messenger

Just in case you're not familiar with Messenger, here's a brief overview. (For a more in-depth look at how it works, pick up a copy of the *Official Netscape Messenger & Collabra Book* from Netscape Press.)

When looking at the main Messenger Mail screen, you'll notice that it is divided into two panes, one for message titles and the other for the message itself, as shown in Figure 6.1. Messenger can also display one undivided pane, with message titles on one screen and the messages on another one, as shown in Figure 6.2.

- **The Message List Pane.** The message list pane shows the title and author of the messages in your message folder. If you've flagged a message as important, a red flag appears next to it. If you've viewed a message already, a green box appears next to it. Choose which message you want to read, click on it, and you'll see the message come up in the mail text pane.

- **The Mail Text Pane.** This is simply the text of the message that you've clicked on in the message list pane. (Not all this stuff is complicated, you know!)

Configuring Messenger

Worried about making the transition from Navigator 3.0's Mail Application to Messenger? Don't be—Messenger has an Account Setup Wizard, which makes the switch a snap.

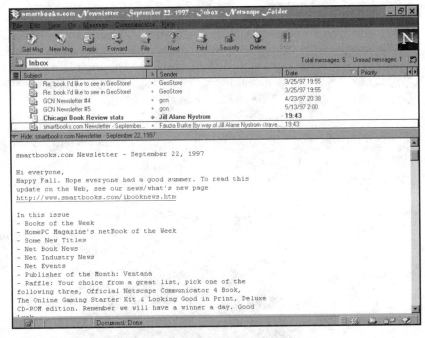

Figure 6.1   Messenger's mail screen divided into panes.

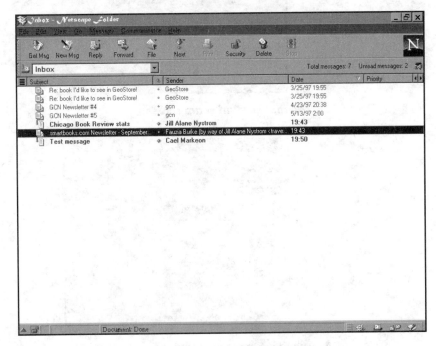

Figure 6.2   Messenger's mail screen not divided into panes.

Using Messenger's Account Setup Wizard

Messenger's Account Setup Wizard helps you set up your account. Once you've installed Navigator, simply choose the Messenger Inbox icon (it's the third icon from the right in the lower right hand corner; it looks like a folder, an in-box, or a yellow question mark beside an envelope). Choose Edit|Account setup. The first screen will look like Figure 6.3.

This screen simply announces that the Wizard will help you set up Preferences for Messenger. Click the Next button to go to the second screen, Figure 6.4.

This is called the identity setup screen because it lets you establish who you are to the cyberworld. Your choices are actually broader than those presented by the Wizard. For example, if you are a hotshot agriculture extension agent with a free Q&A site, you could type "Ask the Grain Guru" in the Name field instead of Jackie Doe. You even have some flexibility for the e-mail address

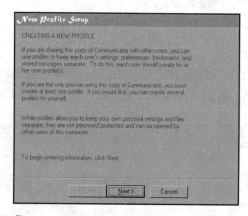

Figure 6.3   The first account setup screen.

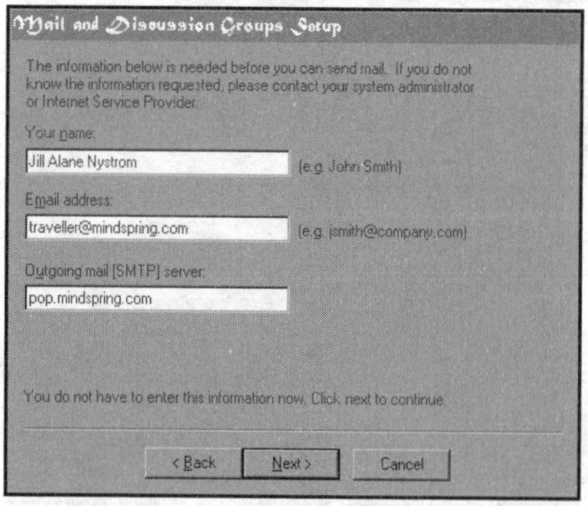

Figure 6.4   The identity setup screen.

space. While many people may have only one e-mail address, you may be one of the growing number of people with a private address and a work address, or several of both. You don't need to put the address you'll be using to download new mail; if you use one address to receive business mail and another to e-mail your garden club, put the latter in this field.

The last field is for the name of your outgoing mail server. The outgoing mail server is often in the form **pop.companyname.com** (our service provider is Mindspring, so our server is **pop.mindspring.com**), but it isn't universally true. Be sure to verify the form of the address with your service provider if you aren't positive. Then click Next to go to the third screen, Figure 6.5.

On this screen you will need to type in the address where you receive mail. Enter only your username, not your whole e-mail address. If your e-mail address is george@sand.com, you would enter **george** in the Mail Server User Name field, *not* george@sand.com. You will also need to enter your incoming mail server, which in many cases is the same as the outgoing mail server. Finally, you will need to choose the type of server, POP3 or IMAP. Most home users will be using an access account with a POP3 server (Mindspring, Earthlink, etc.). However, many business users will be on a local area network (LAN) or other IMAP server. Again, if you aren't sure of your system's configuration, check with your access provider or system administrator. Once you've entered this information click Next and move to the final screen, Figure 6.6.

This last screen asks you to enter the name of your news server, the server your access provider uses to send you Usenet postings. The format is often **news.companyname.com**, but it depends on your provider. Again, check with your user manual or help desk if you are unsure. After you've entered this information, click Finish to establish the settings. Anytime your information changes you can go through the Account Setup Wizard again and make the necessary changes.

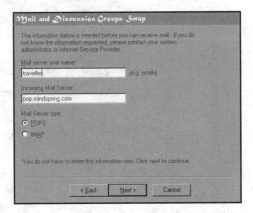

Figure 6.5   Configuring Messenger to receive mail.

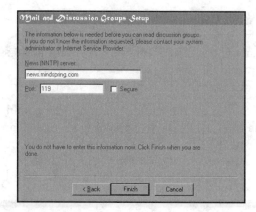

Figure 6.6   The final Messenger Account setup screen.

But wait—that's not all! The Setup Wizard puts basic information into place, but what if you want to control the formatting or even the font of your messages? We'll show you how to configure your preferences in the next section.

Setting Mail & Groups Preferences

Once you go to the Preferences dialog box, you'll see the Mail & Groups tab first, which looks like Figure 6.7.

You'll see several tabs under the Mail & Groups category. Since we went through the contents of the Mail Server and Groups Server tabs when we ran the Account Setup Wizard, we will only briefly cover the Mail & Groups, Identity, Messages, and Directory tabs.

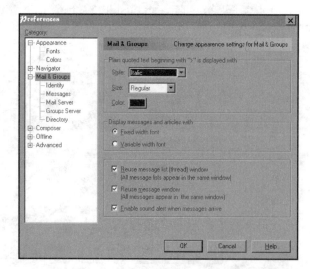

Figure 6.7   The Mail & Groups tab of the Preferences dialog box.

The Mail & Groups Tab

This tab lets you choose the style, size, and color of your message text along with font width and message handling. The first three characteristics are largely a matter of taste (you might like Times New Roman; your colleague may prefer Garamond—although you may not want to go too small on the font size). Font-width is also becoming less of an issue with the emergence of HTML e-mail; what used to require meticulous planning to ensure proper column width can now be guaranteed by using tables, and hence whether you use fixed- or variable-width font becomes less important.

The last section, which deals with message handling, is a little more important. The first option allows you to reuse the message list window or, as it says below, have all message lists appear in the same window. Don't get claustrophobic—all 10 messages in your in-box won't be stuffed into one window. Instead it will simply replace one message with the next in the screen you are reading, rather than opening a new window for each message. This feature is a great advantage if you tend to forget to close your windows after each message, since having multiple windows running can devour memory.

The second option allows you to choose whether to split the screen so that you can display both your message list and message text at the same time. As you can see in Figure 6.8, this allows you to keep an eye on where you are in your list without opening separate windows for each message. This convenience can become annoying, however, if you tend to get long messages and are constantly scrolling through frames to read them.

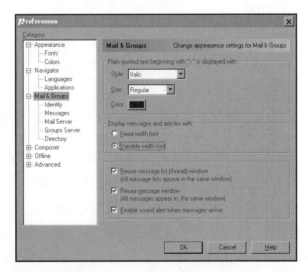

Figure 6.8   The Mail & Groups tab of the Preferences window.

The Identity Tab

This tab gives you the chance to establish who you are to the rest of the world. There are five main fields, as you can see in Figure 6.9.

You'll need to enter your name (real or a suitable alias), e-mail address, reply-to address (only if different from your e-mail address), and organization, if applicable. The last field, signature file, is a small text file which will be automatically attached to the end of any messages you send out. You can create a signature, or .sig, file in Windows Notepad, save it as a text file, and insert the name of the file into this field. You will want to be brief in your .sig—it is considered a breach of Netiquette to tack on a long .sig file, particularly one that is exceedingly "tall" (more than four lines of text). Nonetheless, you will find your .sig a great way to add personality, wit, or a professional edge to your virtual correspondence.

The Messages Tab

Figure 6.10 shows you the Messages tab, the tab which lets you choose how your outgoing messages will appear and be saved.

The first section lets you choose whether to send HTML messages. You may want to leave this one unchecked unless you are certain that most of your correspondents are using a mail reader capable of handling HTML. You can also elect to quote the original message automatically. This option is a good one to leave checked as it will help both the recipient and you (when you look through your out-box) remember what you were referring to days or weeks down the road.

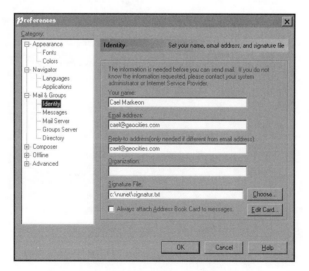

Figure 6.9   The Identity tab of the Preferences window.

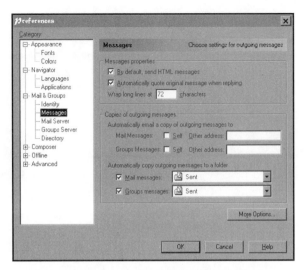

Figure 6.10   The Messages tab of the Preferences window.

The most critical part of this window at this point is to decide whether you want to e-mail copies of your message to someone automatically and if you want to set up a special folder for outbound messages. Unless you are writing something like business correspondence, which requires that you send copies of *every* e-mail to a particular address, we don't recommend that you check this one (you can always cc: people on individual notes). However, it might be a good idea to save your messages to a special folder, although Messenger will store them by default in a "sent" folder if you don't check this one.

The Directory Tab

The Directory tab allows you to choose an online phone book to look up e-mail addresses. As you can see in Figure 6.11, you have several options, including a personal address book. If you want to modify the list, just click "New" to add a reference, "Delete" to remove it, or "Edit" to modify one already posted. You can also choose whether to display individual entries by first or last name.

Now that you've set up all of your preferences, you're ready to get started on your messages. The next section will give you an overview of the Messenger toolbar and how to send mail with Messenger.

The Messenger Toolbar

You'll probably have noticed that the toolbar—the buttons across the top of the screen—change when you're in the mail application. Check Table 6.1 for a quick reference guide to what they mean.

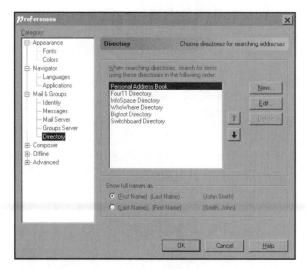

Figure 6.11   The Directory tab of the Preferences window.

Sending Mail With Messenger

Let's walk through sending an e-mail message using Messenger. We'll send this one to your own e-mail address, so you'll know that what you did worked when you get the message.

Table 6.1   Netscape mail commands.

Command	Result
Get Mail	Retrieve unread mail from your service provider's computer to your computer.
Compose	Create a new message.
Re:Mail	Reply to a message.
Forward	Forward a message to another address.
Delete	Delete a message.
Next*	Read the next unread message.
Backtrack*	Read the previous unread e-mail message in your list of messages.
Security*	Displays security information (e.g. encryption, digital signatures).
Stop*	Stop downloading or sending mail to your service provider's mail server; this comes in handy when you're tired of waiting for a hundred messages to download.
*These commands may be "grayed out" and the button is unusable if you don't have any e-mail. Don't panic; they'll work when you do have e-mail.	

The first thing you should do is click on the Compose button on the toolbar. (You also can send a new e-mail message from any Netscape window by choosing New|Message under the File menu or pressing Ctrl+M.)

When you've clicked on that button, you'll get a message composition screen.

Click on the white space beside the To: button, and type your e-mail address. (If you click on the To: button itself, you'll get copy options, including cc: and bcc:. You can also click on the Address Book button on the toolbar to use your address book.)

TIP

The address book is an easy way to keep up with e-mail addresses and insert them into outgoing messages. Select Address Book from Messenger's Toolbar. A window will pop up. Type in a name in the first blank field, and the Address Book will give you the option to find it in one of the directories or to add the name to your personal list.

When you've finished that, press your tab key. Your cursor will automatically go to the next field, the Subject. We recommend you always put a subject in an e-mail message. It saves the recipient time—a glance at the subject line to see what it's about—and it probably will get you a response sooner.

You will notice two other tabs beneath the To: tab. The second one after To:, which has a paper clip on it, is for sending attachments—files that are not part of the e-mail message but are sent along with it. They can include documents like Word files or even entire programs. Generally it's considered rude to send attachments to people without asking their permission first, because program files can contain viruses. Use this feature very carefully. The last tab is for sending options, including encrypting the message or changing its priority.

Press tab again and you're in the message text section. Type whatever you want here, and edit it as you wish. When you're done, your screen should look something like Figure 6.12.

Click the Send button to send the message away. Now, the next time you get your mail (which, as you remember, you can do from the main Messenger screen by clicking the Get Mail button on the toolbar), you should have a nice message from yourself.

Now you know how to send and receive e-mail messages, so let's talk about the mechanics of mailing lists and how to subscribe.

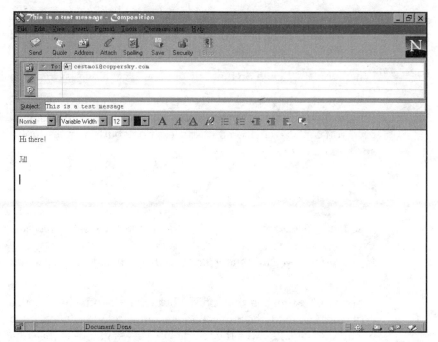

Figure 6.12   The completed Messenger editing screen.

Accessing Mailing Lists: List Servers And How They Work

Although there are some mailing lists that are run manually by humans, most are cared for by programs called *list servers*. A list server is an automated way of adding people to the list, removing people from it, and distributing posts to it. The three main types of list servers are *Listserv, Majordomo,* and *Listproc*. We'll get to each of these in a minute.

When you want to subscribe to a mailing list, you send a message to the list server with your request to join. The list server then adds you to the mailing list or, in the case of some restricted-access lists, forwards your request to the human in charge of the list so he or she can give you permission to join. Then the list server automatically sends you additional information about the list, the two e-mail addresses you'll need to use the list, and more information about the list.

Wait a minute. Two e-mail addresses? Why two e-mail addresses?

Mailing lists run by list servers require that you use two e-mail addresses, one to send commands to the list server and one to send messages to all the humans reading the list. If the list weren't divided this way, you'd have to read a lot of boring subscribe and unsubscribe messages.

For example, let's imagine a list called NERUDA-L, for the discussion of Pablo Neruda and his poetry. In order to subscribe, you have to send a message to **listserv@pablo.neruda.com**. This is the address for talking to the list server and telling it what you want. However, if you want to give the other humans on the list your opinion of page 53 of *The Captain's Verses*, you have to send your message to **NERUDA-L@pablo.neruda.com**. If you send it to the **listserv@pablo.neruda.com** address, no one but the list server program will read it (and the listserver program *doesn't* care about Pablo Neruda). Conversely, if you send the NERUDA-L address a request to subscribe or unsubscribe, the humans on it will be irritated. Be sure you send the right information to the right address.

List Server Language: Talking To The Robots

Because they are computer programs, list servers are very finicky about what you say to them and how you say it. If you don't ask to subscribe or unsubscribe in exactly the right way, they will return your e-mail to you, tell you they didn't understand you, and you have to try again.

To make things even more complicated, each of the three main types of list servers has a slightly different language that you have to learn. Read on for a list of the main commands for the three main types of list servers, with examples of each.

TIP

When sending mail to list servers, there isn't any need to include anything in the subject line; most list servers read only the body of the message. Be sure to turn off your mail signature before you send a message, though—it can confuse the list server. Remember, though, that you'll occasionally find a list server that wants you to put your commands in the subject heading of your e-mail. Keep an eye out.

Listserv

Listserv usually has an address like **listserv@***domain*.

To subscribe, type: **subscribe** *name of list first name last name*:

```
subscribe  SUPERNATURAL-L  Fox Mulder
```

To unsubscribe, type: **unsubscribe** *name of list*:

```
unsubscribe  SUPERNATURAL-L
```

To receive the digest form of the list, which gives you all the day's post in one large e-mail instead of several little e-mails (this option isn't available for all mailing lists), you would type: **set** *name of list* **digest**:

```
set  SUPERNATURAL-L digest
```

You have to subscribe to a mailing list before you can set it for digest mode.

Majordomo

Majordomo usually has an address like **majordomo@***domain*.

To subscribe, type: **subscribe** *name of list e-mail address*:

```
subscribe  KICKBOX jackie@chan.com
```

To unsubscribe, type: **unsubscribe** *name of list*:

```
unsubscribe  KICKBOX
```

To receive the digest, type: **subscribe** *name of list*-**digest:**

```
subscribe - KICKBOX digest
```

Listproc

A Listproc address is usually **listproc@***domain*.

To subscribe, type: **subscribe** *name of list first name last name*:

```
subscribe  WRITE-L George Sand
```

To unsubscribe, type: **unsubscribe** *name of list first name last name*:

```
unsubscribe  WRITE-L George Sand
```

To receive the digest, type: **set** *name of list* **mail digest**:

```
set WRITE-L mail digest
```

Now that you know the language you need to subscribe to mailing lists, where are you going to find them?

Finding Mailing Lists

Because they are more private than newsgroups, mailing lists that discuss the topics in which you're interested may be hard to find.

The best resource we've found for locating mailing lists is LISZT (**www.liszt.com**). It's the most complete we've seen, with more than 71,600 lists, and, because it's even searchable by keyword, is fast to use. Its biggest drawback is that the amount of information in the search summaries varies wildly from mailing list to mailing list; some mailing lists have an excellent description, while some have almost nothing.

CataList (**www.lsoft.com/lists/listref.html**) tracks only mailing lists using the Listserv listserver software. It has far fewer lists than LISZT—about 15,000 total—but is searchable by site, country, and number of subscribers on lists. (Sometimes it's good to know if you're going to be sending an e-mail to a hundred or a thousand people.) Its summary information is consistent for all lists but is nothing special.

Publicly Accessible Mailing Lists (PAML) is available at **www.neosoft.com/ internet/paml**. Obviously a labor of much love, PAML has extensive information on around 2,000 mailing lists—a thorough description, as well as Web home pages and contact addresses when available. It's nicely organized as well—a very friendly resource.

Now you know how to find a mailing list in which you are interested. Now what do you *say?* Furthermore, do you need to say anything at all? Perhaps you can get your answers without asking any questions.

Getting Answers Without Asking Questions

How can you get answers without asking questions?

Many mailing lists keep archives and sometimes Frequently Asked Questions (FAQs). You may discover that you don't need to ask any questions at all to get the answers you need.

To check for an archive or a FAQ, first get an index of the mailing list's files. You do this by sending the command "index *listname*" to the listserver address of the list you want to check. For example, if you want to see what the index of files is for NERUDA-L, the Pablo Neruda mailing list, you would send an e-mail to **listserv@pablo.neruda.com** with the text message:

```
index NERUDA-L
```

That returns you a list of all the files maintained for NERUDA-L. (The index command works for Majordomo and Listproc listservers, as well.)

A Real Example

Okay, enough fictional Neruda examples. Let's take the real example of CARR-L. CARR stands for Computer-Aided Reporting and Research. It's a terrific list for journalists and research nuts like us. CARR-L's listserver address is **listserv@ulkyvm.louisville.edu**.

The first step is to subscribe to CARR-L; some mailing lists do not make their files available to nonsubscribers. The next step—e-mailing the command "index CARR-L" to **listserv@ulkyvm.louisville.edu**—results in your receiving an e-mail message that looks something like this:

```
*   CARR-L FILELIST for LISTSERV@ULKYVM.
*   ::::::::::::::::::::::::::::::::::::::::::::::::::
*
*   The GET/PUT authorization codes shown with each file entry describe
    who is authorized to GET or PUT the file:
*      ALL = Everybody
*      CTL = Local LISTSERV controllers (also known as "postmasters")
*
*
::::::::::::::::::::::::::::::::::::::::::::::::::::::::::::::::::::::::::::
    CARR-L   FAREWELLALL CTL V  74    106 96/08/02 11:12:33 Farewell note
    CAR      IDEAS    ALL CTL V  77    349 94/12/22 16:35:03 Presstime
                                                             sidebar
    COMMTECH JUNE94   ALL CTL V  65    716 94/07/13 16:17:21 CT&P News,
                                                             June 1994
    BREYER   MEDIA    ALL CTL V  69   1198 94/05/26 09:14:16 Summary of
                                                             Judge Breyer's
                                                             Decisions on
                                                             Media Issues
    CARR-L   WELCOME ALL CTL V  77    286 96/08/02
```

You see that there are many files up for grabs in the CARR-L file list. Although there aren't any files called FAQ, there is one called WELCOME. This title generally indicates an introduction for new users.

That file looks interesting. To retrieve it, you send the following command to listserv@ulkyvm.louisville.edu:

```
get carr-l welcome
```

Get tells the computer to retrieve a file. CARR-L is the name of the mailing list that contains the file, and WELCOME is the name of the file itself. The get command also works with Majordomo and Listproc mailing lists. The CARR-L listserver will send you the WELCOME file in a separate e-mail message.

Perhaps even by using the index command you're not finding the information you want. Is it time to ask your question? Not quite. You should search the archives first.

Searching A Mailing List's Archives

Not all mailing lists have archives; the Majordomo list server doesn't even support archive searches. Sometimes a mailing list's introductory message will indicate whether archives are kept. If you're not sure, you can try to search the archives anyway. The worst that will happen is you'll get an error message from the listserver software.

Searching With Listproc

Searching with Listproc is very easy. To do an archive search, simply send the following message to the listproc address of the mailing list you want to search:

```
search [name of list] "keywords"
```

Boolean searches (searches in which the words being searched can be linked together using the qualifiers *and, or,* or *not*) are possible using symbols in the keyword area. See Table 6.2 for the symbol list.

For example, if you type **search toondogs "Astro|Scooby Doo,"** the function searches the Toondogs archives for mentions of Astro or Scooby Doo. On the other hand, if you type **search toondogs "Scooby Doo ~ Scrappy Doo,"** it searches for mentions of Scooby Doo that don't include his nephew Scrappy Doo.

Searching With Listserv

Listserv has far more powerful search features than does Listproc. Listserv's search engine can do everything but make toast. Explaining all it can do would take hundreds of pages. If you want the whole story on archive searching with Listserv, send the following message to **listserv@lsoft.com**:

```
get listdb memo f=mail
```

Table 6.2   Boolean operators.

Boolean Operator	Symbol
And	&
Or	|
Not	~

Warning: This file is extremely long (more than 2,000 lines). We'll give you the short version. Archive searches in Listserv are submitted in a template like this:

```
//
Database Search dd=rules
//rules dd *
Search keywords in name of list since yy/mm/dd
Index
/*
```

The first three lines are always the same. In the line that starts with the word *search,* you start to customize your search.

Let's go back to CARR-L. Say you're wondering what resources on the North American Free Trade Agreement (NAFTA) are available. Your search line might look like this:

```
Search NAFTA in CARR-L since 93/1/1
```

But wait. You're ignoring one of the basics of online research. You always want to start as specific as you can and then get more general. Do you really want to search for every message in which someone mentioned NAFTA? Probably not. You'll get hundreds of "hits," or message listings.

Listserv archive searches also support Boolean searches, which makes narrowing down your NAFTA search an easy task. Say you're wondering about online NAFTA resources. Your search line might look like this:

```
Search NAFTA & WWW & resource|online in CARR-L since 93/1/1
```

What you are telling the Listserv address, in English, is this: Search the CARR-L archives for messages containing the words *NAFTA* and *WWW* and either the words *resource* or *online* since January 1, 1993.

Let's put it all together. Your message to the CARR-L listserver, at **listserv@ ulkyvm.louisville.edu**, would look like this:

```
//
Database search dd=rules
//rules dd *
Search NAFTA and WWW and(resource or online) in CARR-L since 93/1/1
Index
/*
```

The last line, Index, will give you a list of what messages were found.

Sending the above command to the CARR-L archives yields this result:

```
> Search NAFTA and WWW and(resource or online) in CARR-L since 93/1/1
--> Database CARR-L, 7 hits.

> Index
Item #   Date      Time   Recs   Subject
------   ----      ----   ----   ------
002028 95/10/24  10:03    208   Fwd: Government sites; for Bookmarks
003240 95/12/10  11:34    114   Latin American Newsletters-Editors
003981 96/01/20  17:28    156   Fwd: EDUPAGE commo excerpts
005406 96/03/11  10:43     33   Fwd: Free trade and NAFTA issues page
007003 96/05/07  08:33    749   Fwd: Communications technology newsletter,
                                 sample +
007392 96/05/20  17:26    234   Re: Fwd: BONG Bull No. 373!
008729 96/07/18  10:48     85   Government Servers - Business, Commerce
                                 & Economics
```

Hmm...the free trade and NAFTA issues page! That looks like *exactly* what you're looking for. The communications technology newsletter also could be interesting.

You need to send another message to the CARR-L listserver, this time asking to retrieve those messages. The NAFTA issues message number is 005406, and the communications technology newsletter number is 007003.

To retrieve those articles, you send the following message to **listserv@ulkyvm. louisville.edu**:

```
//
Database search dd=rules
//rules dd *
Search NAFTA and WWW and(resource or online) in CARR-L since 93/1/1
Print all of 005406,007003
/*
```

That retrieves the body of those two messages and sends them to you for you to use. Now wasn't that easier than asking a question about NAFTA and then waiting around for a long time?

I Still Haven't Found What I'm Looking For

Still can't find what you're looking for? Okay, now's the time to ask the question. But how do you ask?

Communication Rules Of Thumb

When you subscribe to a mailing list, it's a little like going to someone's house to socialize. So, if you're nice, you wipe your feet, admire the decor, and bring a nice hot dish to share...if that's the proper behavior for that party, of course. Some mailing lists are more for slam dancing and food fights. So how can you tell the difference?

Introductory Messages

Most mailing lists send you an introductory message when you subscribe. It details to varying degrees what the mailing list is about, what topics are discussed, and what behavior is acceptable. Following is an excerpt from an introductory message from the "Haynet" model horse club mailing list:

```
[Last updated on Monday, 03-Jun-96 07:55:59 PDT]
                 The Official Haynet FAQ
Welcome to the Official Haynet FAQ (Frequently Asked Questions)
Document for the Model Horse Mailing List. Below you will find a list
of questions about Haynet that get asked a lot with the all important
answers! This document is long and thorough. It is expected that you
read and/or (at least) keep a copy of this document for your
references. You should refer to this document BEFORE you post a
question about the mailing list to Haynet.
If after reading this document you still do not find an answer to your
question, send email to model-horse-owner@qiclab.scn.rain.com, NOT to
the list.
The Official Haynet FAQ is made available via the following methods:
Web: http://nehalem.rain.com/haynet/faq.txt
Email: send to majordomo@qiclab.scn.rain.com:info model-horse
Haynet is an electronic mailing list which provides a forum for model
horse hobbyists to discuss all aspects of the model horse hobby. Topics
in the past have included: showing (live and photo), collecting,
customizing, racing, real horse breeds and colors (as they pertain to
models) and breeding. In order for other subscribers to know who you
are and how to contact you directly, please remember to sign off with
your real name and your email address at the bottom of your email.
In general, non-model topics are not appropriate; while Haynetters are
a chatty and (mostly) friendly group, it is asked by the list
administrator that posts that are not about model horses be relegated
to personal replies.
```

Use this introductory message to give you basic guidelines on how to behave and what to say on a list. From the guidelines for the mailing list, it seems that it would be acceptable to ask about how to customize your model Arabian horse or where to get professional horse model shots done.

Introductory messages don't cover every aspect of behavior on a mailing list. That's because mailing list managers don't have time to think up every possible action that you might take and then come up with a rule for it. Therefore, there may be things you want to send to a mailing list that you aren't sure are appropriate. In those cases, keep the following rules of thumb in mind, but remember that the rules outlined in the mailing list's introductory message always take precedence!

No Commercial E-mail

Unless it's specifically permitted by a mailing list, don't send messages advertising products or services. If you really think the product or service would be well received and helpful for a list, ask first.

Avoid Grammar And Spelling Flames

Sometimes a grammar or spelling error will be so severe that it will actually affect the meaning of the message posted. In those cases, it is okay to request clarification of meaning, but try to avoid *flaming* (insulting) someone for poor grammar or spelling. English is not the native language of many people on the Net, and it's not fair to belittle their efforts to communicate.

Check Before You Answer

Say you're on a mailing list, and someone sends an e-mail to the list saying that Bill Gates lives in Rhode Island.

The fool! Obviously Bill Gates can't live in Rhode Island; all his money wouldn't fit there. You must correct this person at once!

Check yourself. The problem with obvious errors is that they're, well, obvious; when everyone on the list can correct an error, there's the chance they all might. Then you have to slog through 400 e-mail messages that say, "You dummy—Bill Gates doesn't live in Rhode Island."

When you receive a message that has an obvious error that needs correcting or asks an obvious question, wait until you've received a few more messages before jumping in. You'll save everyone a lot of time.

When In Doubt, Don't Distribute

Unless we're all a lot luckier than we deserve, there comes a day when we get something in our mailbox that looks extremely urgent. It may be a warning about the Good Times virus or a plea to send greeting cards to a young man named Craig Shergold who has a brain tumor. "Gosh," you may think to yourself, "I ought to tell my friends about this!" So merrily you forward it to everyone in your address book.

With the best of intentions, you have just contributed to the insidious half-truth mill of the Internet, the folklore that won't die. There is no such thing as the Good Times virus. Craig Shergold has continued to receive get well cards several years after his tumor was removed. Still, these rumors and others like them have been drifting around the Net for what seems like eons. They're very hard to get rid of, because they take advantage of people's best intentions. People want to help or distribute information, so they spread it around. (We'll be talking more about the legends of the Internet in Chapter 18.)

When you get an e-mail message that warns of a virus or requests cards or letters, do some checking first. If there's an Internet address for more information, get that. If that isn't available, check with the person who sent it to you. If they're not sure when they got it or why, don't forward it.

Communicating Clearly In A Text-Based Medium

Communicating in a text-based medium can be kind of strange at first. It's hard to communicate feelings easily without facial expressions or vocal tone, making it easy for misunderstandings to begin.

To make communication in text a little bit easier, there have evolved substitutes for facial expressions and abbreviations for long phrases. We haven't tried to include a complete list of emoticons and abbreviations; you'll see more as you use the Internet.

Emoticons

:-> Look at that. Looks like a colon, a hyphen, and a greater-than sign, doesn't it? However, if you tilt your head to the left, it magically transforms itself into a smiley face. These sideways faces are called *emoticons*.

Love 'em or hate 'em, emoticons are useful in saying what can't be said quickly in simple words. "I'm kidding," "I'm kidding but I'm kind of serious, too," and "I'm *really* kidding" are the kinds of messages that can be communicated most effectively and quickly through the use of emoticons. How would you like to have to type "I'm kidding" every time you make a joke?

Take these two examples:

Listening to James T. Kirk gives us a headache.

Listening to James T. Kirk gives us a headache :->

In the first example, it's anybody's guess whether we're kidding or not, and James T. Kirk fans can feel free to take offense. However, in the second example, it's obvious that we're kidding and nobody should feel offended.

If you can't bring yourself to make sideways smiley faces, you always can use *g* for grin, or *vbg* for very big grin, and so forth. Table 6.3 shows some common emoticons.

Abbreviations

Online abbreviations evolved as quick replacements for common phrases to eliminate time-consuming typing over and over again. The most common is probably BTW for by the way. Table 6.4 contains a few others.

Table 6.3   Some common emoticons.

Emoticon	Definition
:->	Smile
:-p	Grin
:-D	Big grin
:-/	Half smile
:-0	Shout
;-)	Smile with a wink
:-(	Frown

Table 6.4   Common online abbreviations.

Acronymn	Definition
IMHO	In my humble opinion
AFAIK	As far as I know
LOL	Laughing out loud
ROFL	Rolling on the floor laughing
RTFM	Read the friendly manual (sometimes the F stands for something a little less family oriented)
FWIW	For what it's worth
FYI	For your information

Markups

Markups are fairly new. They began as an offshoot of HyperText Markup Language (HTML), the language used to write World Wide Web pages. In HTML, commands to make text appear as boldface or underlined begin like this: <bold> and end like this: </bold>.

Markups do the same thing for well-known phrases. For example, the following

```
<Homer>
D'oh!
</Homer>
```

means that you should read it in a Homer Simpson–type voice. Or you could use a musical type instead of a person:

```
<Schoolhouse Rock>
Conjunction junction, what's your function?
</Schoolhouse Rock>
```

Abbreviations, emoticons, and markups make communicating through text easier. However, they're no substitute for a well-asked question.

Popping The Question

No, no, not a marriage proposal. The question we're talking about is the research you're trying to do.

When you ask a question on a mailing list, be sure to include the following:

- A good subject line.
- A summary of what you're looking for.
- Where you've already looked.
- Why you're looking, if appropriate.
- How you should be contacted.
- A big thank you.

A Good Subject Line

Be sure to use a clear subject line when writing a message. That way, people who might be able to help you will find your message more quickly. A good subject line is something like "Looking for DUPREEs in Johnston County, NC, ca. 1850." A bad subject line is something like "Dupree."

A Summary Of What You're Looking For

Try to put in one sentence what you're looking for.

Good example: "I'm trying to find birth records and marriage bonds for Johnston County, North Carolina, between 1800 and 1860, especially for the Dupree and Turlington surnames."

Bad example: "I need the birth record for Nathaniel Dupree."

Where You've Already Looked

Mention where you've already looked. If you don't, you may get references to places you've already checked. If you do, someone who has already done that type of research may tell you that you've covered all your bases and you're going to have to go to the (gulp!) library.

Why You're Looking, If Appropriate

It's not required to you say why you're looking for particular information, but sometimes sharing your reasons can prove helpful. If you're a Dupree doing research on the Dupree surname and you say so, someone might invite you to the Dupree reunion. Someone else might invite you to request a copy of the Dupree newsletter. If you're doing research for a social studies project, perhaps another social studies student will offer to team up with you.

How You Should Be Contacted

If e-mail concerning your question should be sent directly to you instead of to the entire mailing list, say so. Or if you'd rather people call you with information, leave your phone number and ask them to call.

A Big Thank You

You're asking people to take time out of their lives and help you with a research problem. Thank them.

Moving On

In this chapter, we've covered everything you needed to know about mailing lists but didn't have the right e-mail address to ask.

As you use the mail application within Navigator, you'll find that some mailing lists cater to your style and communication, and some don't. Don't worry about leaving a mailing list if it hasn't been quite what you wanted. There are thousands of mailing lists out there; you can find the one you're looking for.

Mailing lists are private, have higher signal-to-noise ratios than newsgroups, and can be controlled by the owner of the mailing list. Are you ready to step out into a wilder world? A world populated by sinister things like trolls, flames, and spam? A world called...Usenet?

Then turn the page already!

CHAPTER 7

The Wild, Wild World Of Newsgroups

The Internet is not civilized. The government has not managed to legislate it—not as of this writing, anyway. Aside from some blatant offenses, just about anything goes on the Internet. Nowhere is this more evident than on Usenet.

Usenet is a set of message discussion groups, called *newsgroups*, which are read by millions of people all over the world. Newsgroups are organized around a single topic—from the sublime (**soc.culture.french**) to the ridiculous (**alt.tv. dinosaurs.barney.die.die.die**). There are tens of thousands of newsgroups; new ones are added and old ones deleted every day.

How Are The Newsgroups Organized?

Although newsgroups are organized around a single topic, groups of newsgroups are organized according to their type of topic. These groupings are called *hierarchies*; they call for a prefix to come first, followed with more details about the newsgroup. The words in the newsgroup are separated by dots. For example, *rec* is a hierarchy and always shows up at the beginning of a newsgroup name. **rec.arts** is a subgroup of the hierarchy. **rec.arts.tv** is a real newsgroup, but it can get more detailed than that. **rec.arts.tv** is for discussing all kinds of television, but **rec.arts.tv.mst3k** is only for discussing the TV show "Mystery Science Theater 3000." If you want to get even more detailed, you can check out **rec.arts.tv.mst3k.announce**, which is solely for announcements of important "Mystery Science Theater 3000" events, and so on.

Following is a list of the major hierarchies (there are other ones based on locality, language, Internet Service Provider, etc.):

■ **Comp** Comp refers to computers. Fairly straightforward, isn't it? Newsgroups in this list will have names like **comp.sys.ibm-pc.games. strategic**.

■ **Misc** Misc pertains to those things that don't fit into other categories, or that fit too many categories to easily fit into one. You might have **misc.survivalism**, for example.

■ **News** The news hierarchy is more for news about the Usenet network itself than for discussion. The most important **news.*** group for you to know about is **news.answers**, which carries the FAQs for many Usenet newsgroups (we'll talk about that later).

■ **Rec** Rec stands for recreation: hobbies as well as outdoor activities. Less active pursuits like television watching are also covered. An example is **rec.arts.tv**.

■ **Sci** Newsgroups under the sci hierarchy are for technical scientific discussion and are usually populated by folks who know whereof they speak. These are not the newsgroups where you post something like, "Hey! Do you know if you put vinegar on a seashell it'll fizz?" An example is **sci.geology**.

■ **Soc** These are for social topics. Most countries have **soc.culture.*** **newsgroups**, like **soc.culture.pakistan** or **soc.culture.french**.

■ **Talk** Talk newsgroups are not for the faint of heart. They're for endless (or at least seemingly endless) arguments on the more touchy subjects, like abortion, religion, and politics.

■ **Alt** We saved alt for last, even though it's completely out of alphabetical order, as a special case. If the Internet is anarchy, then the alt newsgroups are anarchy on steroids. All other group hierarchies have to go through a nomination, debate, and voting process before they are added to newsgroups. Alt newsgroups, on the other hand, can be created by pretty much anyone. Almost everything except the mundane appears here, from bizarre sex (**alt.sex.particle-physics**) to personally derogatory newsgroups (**alt.bonehead.joel-furr**) to newsgroups that are not quite as strange as the first two but didn't get enough support to make it on a regular hierarchy (**alt.tv.comedy-central**).

Because of the nature of the hierarchy, the alt group can be prone to spawning huge numbers of newsgroups. For that reason, some service providers will not carry the **alt.*** groups. That's okay, you can get them elsewhere online. (We'll talk about that in a little bit also.)

You Will Be Offended

Unless you've got the patience of a saint and the hide of a battleship, you are going to be offended by things you see on Usenet.

You can avert a lot of ulcers and torn-out hair by realizing that there isn't a lot you can do about these things. Short of actual threats, free speech protects the discourses that go on in cyberspace—even if they bother you personally.

The freedom to argue, discuss, share, and otherwise attempt to understand each other is, in the long run, a big positive. Look at it from that perspective, and avoid the newsgroups that really bother you.

Using Collabra

The program with which one reads newsgroups is called, strangely enough, a *newsreader*. Communicator comes with a newsreader called *Collabra* that you can access by clicking on the Collabra icon in your Message Center or on the lower right corner of any Communicator application screen (the Collabra icon looks like two little dialog bubbles). You can also access Collabra by going to Communicator | Collabra Discussion Groups on the menu bar or by clicking on a newsgroup title when you're Web surfing.

This overview will be brief. For a more detailed look at how to use all aspects of Collabra, check out the *Official Netscape Messenger & Collabra Book* from Netscape Press.

TIP

*Before you start trying to read news, make sure your options are set correctly. Select Edit | Preferences from the menu bar. Make sure that you have selected a Group (NNTP) server. (If you're not connected to an NNTP server, you can't download newsgroup messages to your computer.) NNTP servers are usually called something like this: **news.serviceprovider.com**. For example, we use Mindspring and our NNTP server is **news.ral.mindspring.com**. If you're not sure what your NNTP server is called, check the manual your service provider gave you or call their tech support.*

Selecting Collabra gives you a screen that looks like Figure 7.1.

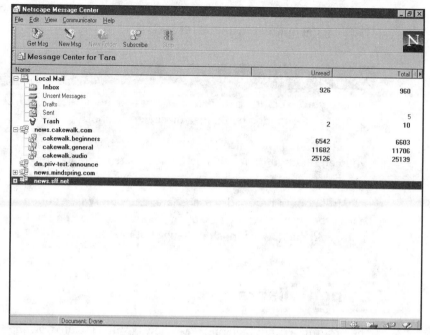

Figure 7.1   Collabra's Message Center.

You'll notice that the Message Center has information about your e-mail (Messenger) account and Collabra's newsgroups. Not only can you access both applications, you can also manage the bulk of your newsgroup needs from this main screen, including downloading new messages and subscribing to newsgroups.

Subscribing To And Selecting Newsgroups

The main screen of the Message Center shows you the status of your e-mail and newsgroups. The first section of the Message Center has information about your e-mail account. To check on your newsgroups, look for the second section, which is indicated by the dialog bubbles icon and the word "news" or the name of your NNTP server (in our example, **news.ral.mindspring.com**).

Immediately below the news header is the list of newsgroups to which you are subscribed. The subscription information is divided into three columns: the name of the newsgroup, how many unread messages are in that group, and the total number of messages.

If you wish to subscribe to a listed newsgroup, go to File|Subscribe to Discussion Groups. A Subscribe dialog box appears, as you can see in Figure 7.2. (You can learn more about what newsgroups are available later in this chapter.)

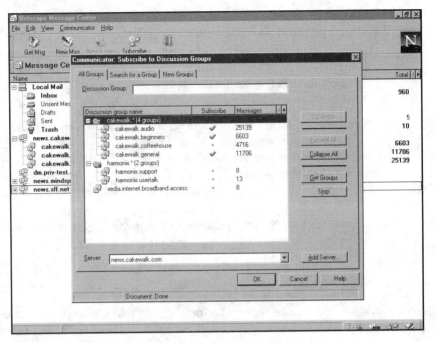

Figure 7.2   Collabra's Subscribe dialog box.

If you haven't downloaded the list of newsgroups available from your news server, Collabra will begin gathering them automatically at this point. Be prepared to do a couple of loads of laundry while this is happening—it will take awhile, especially if your service provider gives you access to most of the groups available. You can always click on stop if you are tired of waiting, but remember that doing this may cheat you out of a fun or helpful group.

After the list has finished, you'll notice that the hierarchies are organized alphabetically, as folders. If you want to expand the hierarchy, just click on the plus sign to the left of the folder, or on Expand All to have every hierarchy expanded at once. To collapse the hierarchies, click on Collapse All or on the minus sign beside an individual folder. The Unread column shows how many unread messages there are in the newsgroup. If you haven't downloaded any messages for that group, it'll display "?". Finally, the Total column shows the total number of read and unread messages in a newsgroup.

If you know the subject you're interested in but don't have the time or inclination to search through every hierarchy to find the perfect newsgroup, Collabra has a couple of handy features to make your quest easier. You'll notice a Search for a Group tab directly behind the All Groups tab we are currently using. Click on the tab and insert a keyword in the Search For box, then click on Search Now. Collabra searches for and lists all of the groups containing that word. Alternatively, if you haven't checked the list of available newsgroups in awhile and want to see what's new, go to the last tab, New Groups, and Collabra posts all of the groups that have been added since the last time you updated your resources. Either way, once you've found the newsgroup you like, just highlight it and click on Subscribe or press the small button beside the name of the newsgroup. Either action changes the button into a checkmark.

When you're at the news reading screen, select Options from the menu. You'll see that you have several new options for viewing messages and newsgroups. You can set your newsreader to show you all available newsgroups (probably not a good idea, because opening Netscape News will take about three days and nights), all newsgroups to which you are subscribed, all newsgroups with new messages, and so forth. In addition, you can set your newsreader to show all messages, only new messages, etc. As you use the newsreader you will determine which settings are comfortable to you.

Managing Your Messages

When you double-click on the newsgroup that you want to read, a split screen pops up. The upper pane contains a list of messages in the newsgroup, and the lower pane contains the text of the message you've highlighted in the upper pane.

If you look at the upper pane, you'll notice that it is organized into seven columns: Flag, Subject, Sender, Status, Date, Priority, and Thread. To flag a message for special attention, click in the box under the Flag column. The Subject column lets you know which issue a person is addressing, and the Sender column shows the name of the person who sent the message. The status of a message—whether it is read or unread—is indicated by a green diamond and bold type if it is unread, or a small, grayer button and normal type if it's read. The Date column shows when a message was posted, and the Priority column indicates the relative position of a message in a larger thread.

What's a thread, you ask? When we say messages in Collabra are *threaded*, that means that they're grouped by subject heading. A spool icon indicates the start of a thread. Say we post a message on **alt.radioactive-grannies** with the subject title of "Where can we find a granny-calibrated Geiger counter?" Ten people answer our question; their messages show up on the Netscape newsreader grouped in order of posting time. Threading makes it easy to follow a conversation—or to ignore one in which you're not interested.

Reading And Responding To Messages

When you find a message heading in which you're interested and click on it, the body text of the message shows up in the message body pane, along with information like who sent it, the date it was sent, what other newsgroups it was sent to, and so on.

The Collabra toolbar contains a number of tools you can use. It runs across the top of the news reading screen and resembles the toolbar you worked with in Messenger:

- **Get Message** Downloads new messages posted to the newsgroup.

- **New Message** Displays a window for composing a new message. (We discussed this in Chapter 6.)

- **Reply** Displays a window for replying either exclusively to the author of the current message via e-mail or to the entire newsgroup.

- **Forward** Brings up a mail composition window and puts an *attachment* to your message, a text file that contains the newsgroup message that you were reading.

- **Next** Shows the next unread message in a thread.

- **Print** Prints the message you're reading.

- **Security** Indicates the security level of a message and newsgroup, such as whether messages were sent encrypted.

- **Mark** Allows you to mark an individual message, entire thread, or all messages in a newsgroup as read or unread.

- **Stop** Stops the news server from uploading or downloading messages.

Writing A Message In Collabra

Ready to send a message in Collabra? Check out Figure 7.3 for how the message composition screen should look. It looks a lot like the Messenger composition screen, doesn't it? Let's go over its elements quickly:

- **CC** Enter an e-mail address here if you want to send a copy of your posting to someone. Don't enter your own address if you've already set your news options to keep a copy of your own postings.

- **Newsgroups** Indicate in which newsgroup you would like your message to appear.

- **Subject** Enter a subject. The same rules apply to news posting subjects as mail subjects—try to make them as meaningful and clear as possible.

- **Attachment** Optionally, add an attachment to your posting. Don't do this unless you're absolutely sure it's okay with the rules of the newsgroup.

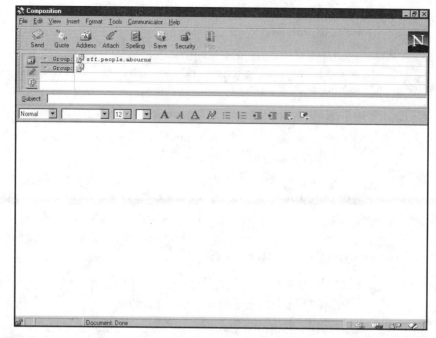

Figure 7.3   Collabra's message composition screen.

Try filling out the message composition window. (Don't click on the Send button, however, unless you're really ready to post.) The finished product should look something like Figure 7.4.

Feeling more comfortable with Collabra? Great. Let's talk about finding the newsgroups in which you're the most interested. (If you just want to play around for a while, try reading **news.newusers.questions**—it's a good place to get your feet wet.)

Looking For Newsgroups In All The Right Places

There are over 18,000 Usenet newsgroups, and they're very specifically named. You can't just type in **television** and read all the newsgroups related to television. You have to enter the exact name of the newsgroup you wish to read. Since new newsgroups are added and old ones deleted every day, it's sometimes hard to find the one you're looking for. Fortunately, there are some nice resources on the Internet for finding the newsgroups you need:

■ *Usenet Info Center Launch Pad*

sunsite.unc.edu/usenet-i/

This newsgroup's search engine is incredibly powerful, helping you find the exact newsgroup you're looking for with a variety of search options.

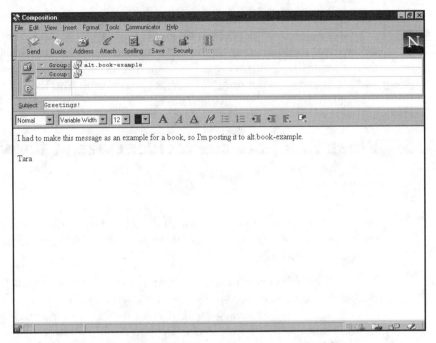

Figure 7.4 Completed Netscape News message composition screen.

When it does find the group you're looking for, it gives you an interesting variety of stats, including the number of messages posted per month on the group, the percentage of Usenet sites that carries the group, and so on.

■ *Infinite Ink Finding News Groups*

www.ii.com/internet/messaging/newsgroups/

Infinite Ink Finding News Groups is updated regularly and recently underwent a major face (and content) lift. It still organizes its Usenet listing hotlinks beautifully and is so user-friendly one might call it cuddly. It doesn't lack in functionality. You can find a variety of resources here, like a breakdown of newsgroups by hierarchy or a list of newsgroup search tools.

■ *Robot Wisdom Newsgroup Finder*

www.mcs.net/~jorn/html/finder/finder.html

This one is your best connection if you have a slower modem or navigating the Internet is going slowly. You can search for newsgroups by historical period, numbers, country, or region or state of the United States. Clickable maps of the world and of the United States are available, but they're made of text so they don't take a long time to load. Exhaustive data on newsgroups returns with the search, including description, charter, and FAQs, when available.

Once you find the newsgroup, go to the File menu and choose Add Newsgroup. Type in the name of the newsgroup and Collabra will add it to your list. If you get an error message, there is one of two possible problems: Either you typed the name of the group wrong—try it again—or the newsgroup you want to add is not carried by your NNTP server. You can still find those groups on the Internet, though, as we'll explain next.

When Your Service Provider Doesn't Carry A Newsgroup

Some Internet Service Providers don't carry all Usenet newsgroups, citing a lack of resources like disk space. We can't say that we blame them. Newsgroup messages take up huge amounts of bandwidth and disk space. Message traffic can get overwhelming.

This might not be comforting if you need to read a newsgroup that isn't included on your provider's news server. If you run across a mention of the newsgroup **alt.spices.texas-pete**, but you can't access it through your NNTP server, what are you going to do? Do you have to switch providers or just give up?

Of course not—this is the Internet. What you'll need to do is access one of the publicly available news servers via the Web.

The most stable news server we've found is Zippo, at **www.zippo.com**. Most newsgroups are available to the general public, and messages display quickly and easily. If you need a newsgroup, try here first.

If you can't find what you need on Zippo, you might want to try a public NNTP news site. These are news servers that allow users other than the ones on their own site to read their newsgroups. Sometimes this is out of altruism, and sometimes it's ignorance; they don't know they're allowing anonymous access. When their traffic picks up from users taking advantage of their site, they end up shutting down anonymous access. Therefore, the list of publicly accessible news sites shifts a lot.

You can get started at FeedME, **www.feedme.org/**, which lists over 30,000 Usenet groups in eleven major categories that parallel many of the hierarchy names (alternative, recreation, science, etc.). The site is fully searchable and includes a "Groups of the Week" feature, which highlights topics popular in the news or gossip world that week.

Remember that when you're using a publicly accessible news site, you're taking advantage of someone else's system resources. Treat this as the favor it is, and don't abuse it.

Okay, you've found the newsgroup you want, and you know how to read it with Collabra. Is it time to ask questions? Not quite. You need to check your FAQs and archives first.

Newsgroup Netiquette

Before we get into FAQs and archives, let's go off on a little tangent.

We know we're spending a lot of time talking about manners and good online citizenship. The reason for this is simple: anarchy. There is little in the way of formal regulation of Internet resources. Even countries that object strongly to the Internet's content—like China—cannot stop the flow of information. It can only restrict its citizens' access.

The only thing that we have to make sure that everyone uses Internet resources responsibly is our own sense of what's right and what's wrong. As long as we maintain freedom of use, access, and discourse, everyone benefits.

However, if the Internet's resources are abused, new users are made to feel unwelcome, or discourse is crushed by tides of rudeness and hostility, it is not going to remain the free and open communication medium it now is.

Of course you wouldn't do that. We know. If you've gotten this far into the book, we wouldn't suspect you of anything but the best of intentions. However, just in case you ever have any questions, we want to give you pointers, hints, and friendly suggestions, so that you can help make the Internet the best it can be. You and billions of other people have a unique perspective and ideas to contribute to the Internet.

Enough ranting. We're finally going to tell you what a FAQ is.

FAQs

FAQs are not newsgroup archives; they are lists of the most *Frequently Asked Questions* on a particular subject. The acronym is pronounced "fack." (One should not use this acronym around an easily offended older relative with poor hearing.) FAQs usually come with a table of contents and can be divided up into several sections, depending on the depth of the subject covered. A newsgroup can have more than one FAQ. A newsgroup doesn't *have* to have a FAQ, but many do.

Big FAQ Attack

The Usenet equivalent of putting a "kick me" sign on your own back is asking a question that has been answered already in a well-publicized FAQ.

We used to read the newsgroup **rec.arts.tv.mst3k**, which dealt with matters concerning the TV show "Mystery Science Theater 3000." A major event rocked the show when Joel Hodgson, one of the show's creators, left and was replaced on-camera by Mike Nelson. Needless to say, the whys and wherefores of this major switch quickly became a part of the newsgoup's FAQ.

That didn't stop folks new to the show from posting the questions over and over, "Why did Joel leave? Where did he go? Who is Mike? How did Mike get shot into space?" Despite the fact that the FAQ was posted periodically on the newsgroup, the questions didn't stop.

Response from veteran newsgroup participants began patiently, but skidded down the scale to annoyed, irritated, disgusted, and finally sarcastic. Readers vied with each other to see who could create the most outrageous version of Joel's demise.

Not reading the FAQ in this case not only disrupted the flow of conversation on the newsgroup, but also gave the questioner, unlucky enough to believe what he read, completely erroneous information. As Mystery Science Theater's resident mad scientist Dr. Forrester might have said: "Bad question, bad answer—bad for you! Deal with it, Joel-prole-mole."

Finding the FAQs

Luckily, finding a FAQ is pretty easy. There are two main places to look: newsgroups themselves and online archives.

Lots of newsgroups post their FAQs periodically—weekly or monthly, usually. If you can just hang around long enough, you'll catch it. There are also ***.answers** newsgroups for every major newsgroup hierarchy—**rec.answers**, **soc.answers**, and so forth. They carry the FAQs of every newsgroup in that hierarchy; **rec.answers**, for example, carries the **rec.arts.tv.mst3k FAQ**.

If you can't get enough FAQs, you can also try **news.answers**, which carries most FAQs from all the newsgroups.

FAQ Archives

To find FAQs by category, newsgroup, or even by search, you can't beat **www.lib.ox.ac.uk/internet/news**. This site is especially handy because if a newsgroup FAQ is available, you can click on it, then click on the newsgroup itself for more discussion.

For more guidance try Infinite Ink's Finding and Writing Periodic Postings at **www.ii.com/internet/faqs/writing/**. Over 2,500 FAQs are at this site, arranged in an easy-to-use manner.

Newsgroup Archives

FAQs are good for answering basic questions and getting an introduction to a particular topic. Sometimes, however, you need more specific information. But don't post to that newsgroup—you haven't checked the online archives yet.

Online archives do not keep track of every post put on the Internet, but they do track enough so that they are a valuable resource. Archives can not only provide you with the answers you're looking for, they can also give you a different angle on your research problem by allowing you to follow conversations on a particular subject. They are also a better resource when you're researching a time-sensitive subject. Newsgroups tend to have information on a particular subject or event faster than Web pages can add it and then get caught up in the Internet search engines.

The two best newsgroup archives we have found are Deja News and Reference.COM.

Deja News

www.dejanews.com

Check out Deja News's opening screen in Figure 7.5. As you can see, it's not too difficult to use Deja News right off the bat. Put a few words in that Quick Search line and then click on Find. When you've stopped fooling around, use the Back button in Navigator to come back to this opening screen and we'll explain a few things.

Searching With Deja News

Deja News uses *Boolean searching*. As you probably remember, Boolean logic allows modifiers for you to specify complex search parameters. Deja News defaults to the Boolean modifier *and*. Each word that you type in the Quick Search list has to show up in an archived post before it is returned to you as a result. If you use the Quick Search line to search for **Cokie Roberts Radio**

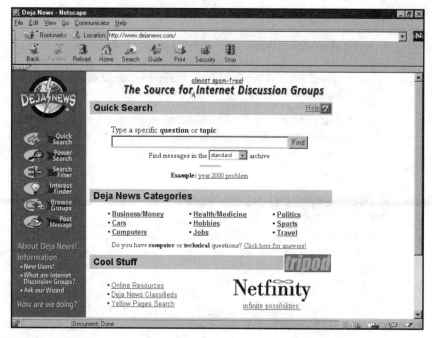

Figure 7.5   Deja News's opening screen.

NPR reporter, the only results you get will have all those words included. Consider your words carefully.

> *Don't worry about capitalizing your words just right, though; Deja News is not case-sensitive. If you used the query **Jo Clayton** or **JO CLAYTON**, you would get the same results.*

A Word About Stopwords

There are some words for which Deja News and other search engines won't search. These are called *stopwords*. They occur in the search engine's database too many times to act as good search words. Examples of stopwords are: *the*, *is*, *that*, *date*, *of*, and *or*. Be sure your search has at least one nonstopword, or it won't work.

Of course, there are other modifiers available as well:

■ *""* This isn't Boolean but it's something you need to know about. When you're searching for a particular phrase, surround the words of the phrase with quotes, for example, **"We the people"**, **"Have you never been mellow?"** and **"See Jane run"**.

■ **&** This is the official Boolean modifier to specify *and*. You don't need to use it in a quick search where you're just putting in several words, but you will need to use it during more complex search phrases, where you're using a number of different Boolean operators.

■ **|** This means *or*. For example, if you did a search for **Rudolph | Santa**, you would get back all messages that contained either Rudolph or Santa.

■ **&!** This means *and not*. Use it when you don't want to find words in your search. If we wanted to get references to Louisa May Alcott but didn't want a list of her books for sale, we could use **Alcott &! FS &! Forsale**.

■ ***** This is a wildcard. Use it when you're not sure of how a word might be spelled, whether or not it's plural, and so forth. Use this modifier extremely carefully, otherwise you're going to get more returns than you can handle. Searching for **Colum*** returns Columbus, Columbia, and so on. If you are uncertain about the spelling of a word, you may want to use the *or* modifier instead (for example, **Calishain | Calishane**).

■ **( )** Parentheses allow you to combine search terms. They group words together but do not allow you to search for a phrase; rather, they make sure the Boolean modifiers are used where you want them used. For example, if we want to know about the towns of Fairbanks and Anchorage in Alaska, we would search this way: **Alaska & (Anchorage | Fairbanks)**.

■ **{ }** Brackets search for the range of difference between two words. For example, if you used the search expression **{quick quicktime}**, Deja News would include all the words between those two values—quick, quickly, quicksand, and so on.

Stupid Search Tricks

Want to amaze and delight your friends? Try this nifty search phrase: **NFL & (ABC Monday | Monday Night Football) &! (Dallas | Cowboys)**.

Looks complicated, but it's actually simple: This phrase searches for the word NFL and either the phrase ABC Monday or Monday Night Football, but not including the words Dallas or Cowboys. Three cheers for Boolean logic!

Using Near Searching

You're probably getting the idea by now that Deja News has 1,001 different ways to help you find what you're looking for, and that Boolean searching is the greatest thing since sliced toothpaste. You're right. But Deja News goes even further, with two concepts called *near searching* and *field searching*.

Near searching works kind of like the *and* modifier, but it's more flexible. It helps you find words that are likely to occur near each other. It works like this: <keyword> ^<distance> <keyword>. The distance is measured in characters. If you want to find a couple of words within 50 characters of one another, the search phrase would look like this: **brass ^50 giraffe**. Bear in mind that this search technique doesn't find the words in any particular order—this search phrase could as easily find *giraffe made of brass* as *big brass giraffe*.

Field Searching

Field searching allows you to narrow your search even more by searching for the field of a newsgroup article—parts of the article like the subject, author, or the date of creation. The Boolean elements work in conjunction with field searching, though parentheses will not—you'll get a syntax error if you try to use them. The two best field search commands for research are:

- **~a** Searches within the author field for a particular word or set of words. **~a Ruth Buzzi | buzzi@laughin.com** would search the author field for either the name Ruth Buzzi or the e-mail address **buzzi@laughin.com**.

- **~s** Searches in the subject field. **~s Sock it to me &! Veddy interestink** would search for the phrase, "Sock it to me," but would exclude all results that contain the phrase, "Veddy interestink."

Deja News Search Results

You now know how to search Deja News eight ways to Sunday. Pick a search phrase. We're going to use **Dorthy Parker**. Click on the Find button. You'll get a page that looks like Figure 7.6.

Let's talk about the columns from left to right:

- **Date** Self-explanatory.

- **Scr** The computer-assigned score for that particular search result. The score seems to weigh heavily by date because mostly the new results show up on top.

- **Subject** The subject line of the original message.

- **Newsgroup** Which newsgroup carried the original message.

- **Author** Who wrote the original message. Clicking on this e-mail address does not allow you to e-mail the author. It will, however, give you an author profile of all the messages that this e-mail address has posted on the Internet, broken down by newsgroup. Pretty cool, huh?

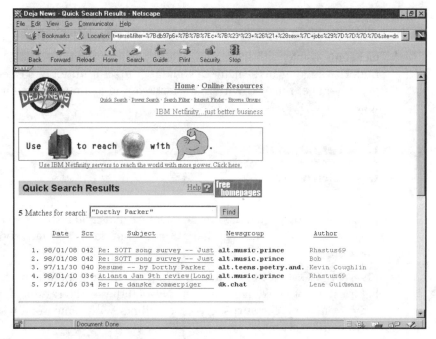

Figure 7.6   Deja News results screen.

The last things on the results page are the individual word hit counts. Pay attention to this—this helps you refine your search. Delete search terms that are limiting you if you're not getting enough results, and add more terms if you're getting too many results. For example, say we search for **solar powered radios crank battery**. (We got very interested in solar-powered radios after the last hurricane.)

We might get back six results, with the individual word hit counts looking like this:

- solar: 10438
- powered: 11807
- radios: 5217
- crank: 2351
- battery: 24208

There are only 2,351 instances of the word "crank." If we remove that word from our search phrase, we would probably get more than the six hits we originally got.

Play around on that Quick Search line for a while. As soon as you get to a search where you think, "Hmm, I wonder if I can—" click on the Power Search logo at the top of the page. In addition to the standard search box, you'll get fill-in-the-blank opportunities to refine your search further.

Get comfortable with Deja News. Put your name in there and see what you find. Try plugging in the name of your favorite sci-fi author or basketball player. When you get finished with that, start reading again and we'll head over to Reference.COM.

Reference.COM

www.reference.com

Reference.COM (see Figure 7.7) isn't quite as far up there on the Cool Meter as Deja News. However, it has one neat feature that can't be beat by Deja News— e-mailable queries. Let's set that aside for a moment and talk about its main functions.

Reference.COM indexes both newsgroups and some mailing lists. As we said before, it is not as extensive as Deja News if the search results we get are any indication. But it can surprise you sometimes with some great results. It's always worth a search.

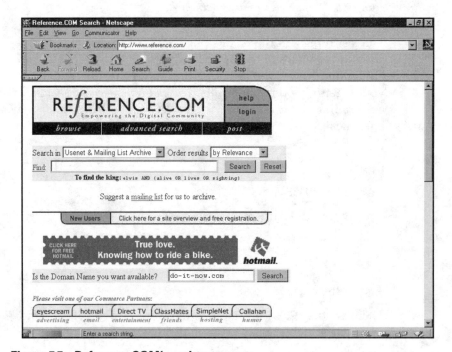

Figure 7.7　Reference.COM's main screen.

As is true with Deja News, Reference.COM uses Boolean logic modifiers as well, though its modifiers are limited to *and*, *or*, and *not*. Handily, it doesn't require arcane symbols to activate its Boolean properties—just use the words themselves. If you want to find the words "boy" and "girl" in a message, use the search phrase **boy and girl**. Reference.COM's wildcard search works just like Deja News's with an asterisk representing parts of words.

TIP

> *Reference.COM isn't case-sensitive, either; searching for **Elvis**, **elvis**, or **ELVIS** gives the same results.*

Words can be grouped together into phrases using either single quotes (') or double quotes ("). The difference is a function called *word stemming*. This means that a search for one word will include all words with the common stem being searched for. A search for **spend** would include words like "spending" and "spendthrift." To use word stemming, use the single quotes. To disable word stemming, use double quotes.

Let's do another search. Here, we'll search for **"Louisa May Alcott"** (we have to put it in quotes because Reference.COM defaults to the Boolean modifier *or*, and we don't want to have to slog through every scanned message that has Louisa or May or Alcott in it).

The results page looks like Figure 7.8.

It looks a lot like the Deja News results page, doesn't it? The date the message was created, the score for the message, the subject of the message, the e-mailing list or newsgroup to which the message was originally posted (e-mailing lists are noted in green, newsgroups in red), and the author of the message.

You're probably getting the idea that Reference.COM looks a lot like Deja News. It does. What really sets it apart is its capacity for e-mailed queries.

TIP

> *Remember your defaults. Deja News's quick search query defaults to* and, *meaning that a search phrase without any Boolean modifiers is assumed to have* and *between each word. Reference.COM's quick search query defaults to* or, *meaning that a search phrase without any Boolean modifiers is assumed to have an* or *between each word. Keep the difference in mind when you're using the two services.*

E-mailing Queries To Reference.COM

This is it. This is the kind of thing that makes you feel nice and geekish. Reference.COM can actually run searches by e-mail and send the results back

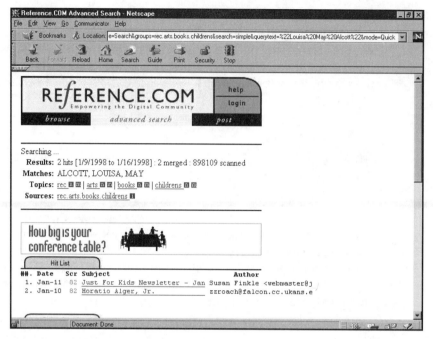

Figure 7.8   The Reference.COM results page.

to you, a lot like the listserver archive searching that we discussed in Chapter 6. Even cooler, Reference.COM automatically runs searches and sends you the results on a regular basis. While you must register to use this feature, both the registration and the service are free, and the registration process itself isn't that intrusive.

The Basics

Once you've decided to register, you have two options to use this service: using Reference.COM's online form for initial queries, or carrying out all queries from your basic e-mail account.

Using The Online Form

Reference.COM has an online form that allows you to select your initial queries. To get to this form, click on Login at the bottom of the first page of the Reference.COM site. Then enter your user name and password. This brings you to a search page similar to the initial Reference.COM main page. Click on User Profile, the green tab immediately beneath the search field box. This brings you to a page where you can edit your password and e-mail address. Halfway down the page, you will see a list of your current queries (if any) and another green tab, Add Query. Click on this tab to add a query.

The Add Query page has several fields, as you can see in Figure 7.9. The first field allows you to name your query, and the next two lines let you choose whether your request will be passive (return search once) or active (continually search and e-mail results over a time period you select). The next six fields let you define which terms you want to search for in the different parts of a Usenet post, including the Subject, Author's Name, and Organization.

Using E-mail

Prefer to edit your requests directly from your e-mail account? Then remember this e-mail address: **email-queries@reference.com**. This is the address to which you'll send all your queries. All message activity will take place in the body. You don't have to use a subject for these messages if you don't want to.

Queries are structured just like they are in the regular search box, only you're sending them by e-mail, so you must specify what the computer needs to do. The keyword in the case of searching is *find*. So if you want to find the names Dave Stewart and Annie Lennox in an e-mail message, you'll send this in the body of the e-mail message:

```
Find "Dave Stewart" AND "Annie Lennox"
```

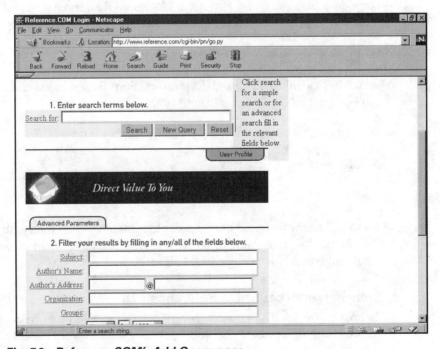

Fig. 7.9   Reference.COM's Add Query page.

Reference.COM will e-mail you the results of the search, along with the first 10 lines of each search result (it will give you only the first 10 lines of up to 25 search results, so try to be as specific as you can). Each article will have a unique identification number. To retrieve the entire article, send the command *get* with the identification number to **email-queries@reference.com**. For example, if we wanted to get message number **04_1996&771112**, we would send the following command

```
GET 04_1996&771112
```

and the article would be e-mailed back to us.

Less Basic Basics

You can filter searched messages by date using the *where age* command. For example, say we wanted new references to NAFTA. We could send an example like this:

```
Find IRS where age < 3 days
```

That would send us those articles containing the word "IRS" that were less than three days old. You could also use **>3** for more than three days, **=3** for exactly three days, and so on. You could even find references to IRS on an exact date:

```
Find IRS where date = 1-Oct-1997
```

Search by field, like you do with Deja News? Sure. Both subjects and newsgroups can be searched easily. For subject, try this:

```
Find IRS WHERE SUBJECT CONTAINS hearings
```

And for newsgroup, try this:

```
Find "Bob Marley" WHERE NEWSGROUP CONTAINS music
```

All that is pretty neat and much easier to remember than the symbols used in Deja News, but being able to create a user account and run active queries is what really makes Reference.COM shine.

Creating An Account On Reference.COM

To create queries that you can run regularly, you have to first establish an account with Reference.COM. You do this by sending your e-mail address and password in the body of a message to **email-queries@reference.com**, like this:

```
REGISTER Crow@biteme.com PASSWORD goldbot
```

This creates an account for you. Now you want to create a query. You do that using the command *define query <queryname> as find <queryphrase>*. When you want to define a query, you have to resend your username and password. A message defining a query might look like this (note the *user* beginning the name and password information).

```
USER crow@biteme.com PASSWORD goldbot
DEFINE QUERY Servo as FIND "Tom Servo" OR "Joel Robinson"
```

Now to run that query, all you have to do is send your user information and the *run query* command, like this:

```
USER crow@biteme.com PASSWORD goldbot
RUN QUERY Servo
```

Wait, it gets cooler. You can define how often you want to run a query—automatically—and have the results sent to you by e-mail. (Note: This sends you reports of only new messages, not rehashed old ones over and over again.) The way you do this is with the *every* command.

```
USER crow@biteme.com PASSWORD goldbot
RUN QUERY Servo EVERY 2 DAYS FOR 6 MONTHS
```

Every two days for six months, Reference.COM will run the query Servo through its database and send you a report. You can retrieve articles automatically by using the *get* command as described earlier. If you ever want to stop using a query, send a *deactivate query* command to **email-queries@ reference.com**, like this:

```
USER crow@biteme.com PASSWORD goldbot
DEACTIVATE QUERY Servo
```

This is a great way to keep up with topics that you're interested in over the long term, and to do ongoing research without investing a lot of time and energy.

Between FAQs and archives, we've shown you a lot of ways to find the information you need. But if you still can't find what you want, you're going to have to take it to the newsgroups.

Taking The Usenet Plunge

Enough with the archives and FAQs. Let's talk to some real people.

There are corners of Usenet that are gracious and civilized, offering lively discourse and dishing up food for thought. There are those places that you will access with ease and enjoy immensely, and will visit often. They'll make you a better person and leave the world a better place to be.

Then there are those places that make those scandalous daytime talk shows look like PBS.

The mechanics and basic rules of posting to newsgroups are not much different from those of participating in e-mail lists. But because Usenet is public and prone to more public involvement, there are special perils you have to watch out for and things of which you need to be aware. Let's talk about them.

Usenet Will Not Do Your Homework

This should go without saying and probably does for most of you. But we should put it down in print that despite what the miracle pundits of the information superhighway say, Usenet was not built to do your homework for you. If you post anything like the following message, you're going to get flamed. Heck, you're going to get toasted to a crisp. Beware.

```
Hi
I'm doing a report on zippers.
Please send me 500 words on the history of zippers.
Thank you
```

If you need zipper history, ask for pointers, ideas, and feedback—but don't ask folks to do your homework.

Look Out For Trolls

Trolls are no longer just rock munchers who live under bridges looking for unwary goats—instead, they're alive and well on Usenet.

A *troll* is a newsgroup post specifically planted to cause discord. (By the way, it's not named after the mythical beast, but rather after the fisherman's practice of dragging bait through water in hopes of attracting fish.) Trolls range from the wildly obvious (posting "Kittens suck!" on **rec.pets.cats**) to the more subtle (posting a graphic description of a capital crime on several newsgroups).

Don't fall victim to a troll. If someone posts something outrageously wrong or inflammatory, just ignore it. They're just trying to get your goat.

On the other hand, don't plant trolls either. It's difficult by definition to post an innocent troll, but you could come close. For example, say you wanted to get Biblical opinions on abortion. If you posted a message to **talk.abortion** that read something like, "I'm trying to find all the reasons abortion is a sin," you would probably cause an uproar, even though you were posting on a topic covered by the newsgroup. A better way to do it would be to rephrase the question ("I'm trying to find all the Biblical arguments against abortion.") and try more scholarly newsgroups, like ones devoted to Bible study.

Don't Be A Spammer

Spam, besides being pork shoulder and ham, is also the stuff on the Internet that nobody likes. It's either a post that's sent to hundreds of different newsgroups, or a post that's sent over and over and over again. There is enough real traffic on the Internet that spam places a burden on the machines carrying newsgroups.

Spams are not limited to the commercial realm. Anyone can be a spammer. A bit worried? Take this easy quiz. If you answer any one of the questions with "yes," then you are a spammer. Change your ways—you're wasting folks' time and money.

Do you regularly:

- Send your research message to several dozen or hundred newsgroups? Did you just send your latest question, "Why do we breathe?" to 6,000 newsgroups, including **alt.fan.air-supply**?

- Post your research message to newsgroups that only fit the topic you're researching through a painful contortion of logic? (For example, posting your question about Los Bros Hernandez's "Love and Rockets" to **alt.fan.peanuts** because they're both comics?)

- Send out chain letters asking people to invest $5 for a possible return of $50,000?

Beware Of Posting Requests

Newsgroup messages can get archived, forwarded, printed out, posted, and otherwise moved around. That's why, if you want folks to take a survey, send a postcard, or otherwise communicate with you in your research effort, it might be dangerous to ask them to do it through Usenet.

We're not saying don't ask questions on Usenet. What we are saying is that if you want a minimal amount of information that several hundred thousand people could give you—like an e-mail giving last name and state of residence for a survey—be careful where you ask for it. You may find that your newsgroup posting has joined the ranks of the electronically undead, the message that just won't die. Six years after your research project is completed, e-mail messages will continue to trickle in as your message is found in archives, forwarded, reposted by well-meaning folks, and used as an elementary school project.

For those kinds of questions, use a World Wide Web page. You have much more control of it, and when the project is over you just take the page down.

If you must post a research need to Usenet, put an expiration date on it so folks know when to quit circulating it. That way it has at least a fighting chance to die a natural death.

Moving On

As you see, newsgroups are a lot like mailing lists, only much larger and noisier.

Between the newsgroup searching sites mentioned here and the FAQ and archive listings, you should be much more comfortable with the idea of using Usenet for timely research needs.

Mailing lists and newsgroups were easy enough to explain, but are you ready for the biggest research tool in your toolbox? Its traffic increases daily and its media coverage dwarfs that of mailing lists and newsgroups. Ironically, it's the youngest technology of any we'll discuss in this book, although some of the parts may feel like "oldtimers."

Are you ready to check out research tools on the World Wide Web?

CHAPTER 8

Other Research Tools Accessible From The Web

If you've ever watched the first season episodes of "Gilligan's Island," you probably noticed how the Professor and Mary Ann were treated in the theme song. They're referred to as "and the rest," even though they were the two coolest characters on the show.

We feel as if we're doing the same to fans of Gopher, Finger, and Telnet by lumping the programs into this one chapter as "other research tools," but our reasoning is sound—far better than that of the "Gilligan's Island" producers, we're sure.

When the Web came along a few years ago, it shook up the Internet's potential for organizing and presenting information. Although there were fundamental applications, such as e-mail and newsgroups that it could not displace, there were other functions of information presentation—Gopher, Finger, and Telnet—that it did threaten.

Since that time, Gopher and Finger have been declining gradually in popularity, as has Telnet in many cases. It'll be a long time before they disappear completely, however, and you should know how to use them and how they work differently from the Web in general, just in case.

I Want My FTP

If the Gopher fans are mad, the File Transfer Protocol (FTP) fanatics are probably furious, because we don't intend to cover FTP sites at all in this chapter.

FTP allows users to access large file archives and download the files in which they're interested.

Unfortunately, even with the FTP file search tool called Archie, searching for a file with FTP can be a hopelessly frustrating task. Many major sites, such as oak.oakland.edu, now have Web gates into their FTP archives; and others, such as the TUCOWS site, seem to be built with only the Web in mind. We have no doubt this trend will continue, so let's leave the standard methods of using FTP to the history books.

If you want material that's found on an FTP site, it's easy to access it through your Web browser. There are also a number of search engines that make searching FTP possible (we'll be talking about those in Chapter 11).

TIP

You've found a Web site that is attached to an FTP archive, and you want to download something on the site. What are you going to do? Simple. Click on the item. You'll probably get a dialog box asking what you want to do with the file. Choose to save it to your hard drive, then pick the directory in which you want to save it.

Gopher

Gopher, named after the cuddly mascot of the University of Minnesota where it was developed, is in many ways the granddaddy of the Web. Gopher servers organize information into menus, like the one in Figure 8.1.

Move your mouse to the item you want and boom!—it's on screen. Gopher servers can organize textbooks, binary objects like graphics or sound files, and even computer programs in this kind of easy-to-understand menu sequence.

Pros For Gopher

Gopher presents its information in a format anyone can understand—that of a menu. Its linear format leaves little to guesswork—menu choice A takes you to menu choice B, which takes you to article C, and so on. Gopher enables this simple system without a lot of fancy graphics, so information can be loaded and transferred quickly.

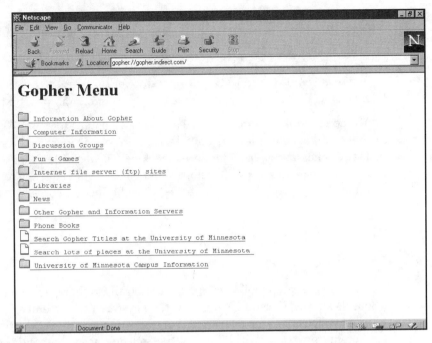

Figure 8.1   A Gopher site menu.

Cons For Gopher

Gopher was created for a UNIX, pre-Navigator, pre-Serial Line Internet Protocol/Point-to-Point Protocol (SLIP/PPP) environment, and it shows. The linear format is restrictive in the way it links documents together, and most Gopher servers don't handle graphics and other multimedia data well. (Gopher can carry graphics files and the like in its menu but not display them as inline images as can Navigator.) And, at the risk of beating a point into the ground, some of the stuff you find is old news—there are some Gopher servers out there that need a good cleaning.

Searching Gopher

Gopher servers have a tremendous advantage as linear tools in that they're linked together, and you can access several at once with the Gopher search tools. The primary tools with which you can search Gopherspace (Gopherspace is like cyberspace but consists of Gopher sites only) are called *Veronica* and *Jughead*.

Veronica And Jughead?

What is this, the Internet or a comic book? Ostensibly, Veronica stands for *Very Easy Rodent Oriented Net-Wide Index to Computerized Archives*, and Jughead stands for *Jonzy's Universal Gopher Hierarchy Excavation and Display*. However, we think you'll agree that these acronyms are a bit of a stretch.

The comic book tradition started when a search engine tool for FTP was developed and called Archie, a takeoff, we suppose, on the word *archive*. When the first Gopherspace search tool was developed, it was called Veronica. Finally, another search tool was developed and called Jughead. They're great programs—they just have weird names. (But the instant someone develops a search tool called Big Ethel, we're outta here.)

Veronica

Veronica is a search tool developed to search all Gopherspace document titles. Sounds simple, doesn't it? It is, but the key word to remember here is *titles*; Veronica doesn't index every word of every document, just the titles. (This is different from some World Wide Web search engines, which index every word of every page they come across.) This makes searching a tricky proposition.

On the Web, Veronica is accessed from a Veronica server. Here are two for you to try. To get to these, press Ctrl+O to open the location box, and then type the site address starting with **gopher://**.

- *Veronica at NYSERNET*

  gopher://empire.nysernet.org:2347/7

- *Veronica at PSINET*

  gopher://veronica.psi.net:2347/7

TIP

*When you pull up most Web pages, the preface of the page is **http://**, like **http://www.yahoo.com**. When accessing a Gopher site, it is **gopher://**.*

The Searching Process

When you connect to the Veronica server, you get a screen that looks like Figure 8.2.

Veronica supports the kind of Boolean phrasing discussed in Chapter 6. The words *AND, OR,* and *NOT,* in capital letters, are the Boolean operators. In addition, words can be grouped as a phrase within quotation marks—"*Riverdale*

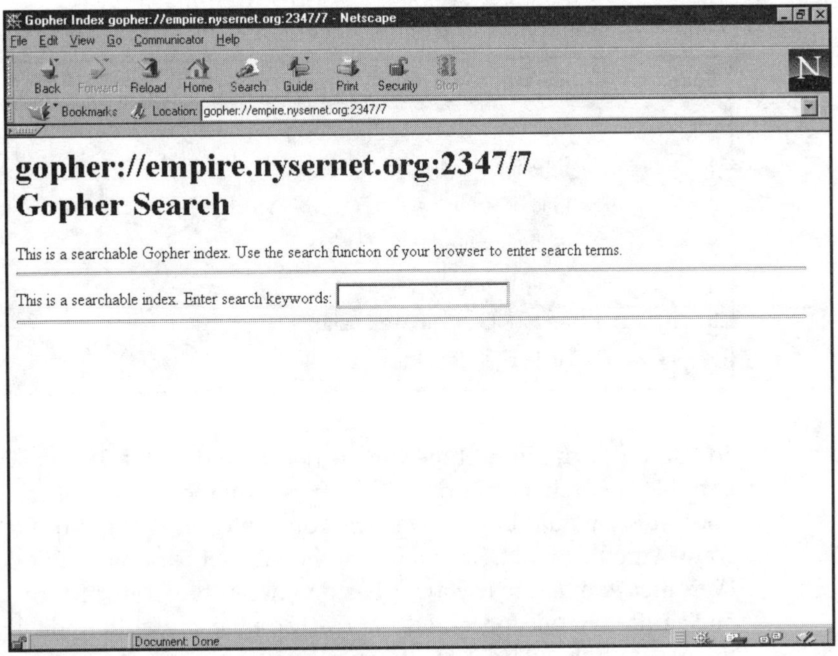

Figure 8.2   Veronica server menu.

High"—and Boolean-linked terms can be grouped within parentheses—*Betty AND (Archie OR Moose)*.

Veronica also supports an asterisk as a wild card at the end of a word; it won't work properly if placed at the beginning or in the middle of a word. For example, the query *moo** will pick up moo, moot, moon, moosebreath, and so on.

The default Boolean operator for Veronica, like Deja News, is *AND*. The query *Betty Reggie "Mrs. Grundy"* will be treated like *Betty AND Reggie AND "Mrs. Grundy,"* and you'll find items that have Betty, Reggie, and Mrs. Grundy in their titles.

Specifying Gopher Type In Searches

Gopher documents do not have headers—like subject and date—as do newsgroup postings and e-mail messages. However, Gopher documents can be broken down into specific types, and you can use Veronica to search for types with the -t modifier. Table 8.1 lists the main types of Gopher documents:

TIP

When specifying the Gopher document type you're looking for, make sure you use the proper case. In document types, g and G are not the same thing!

Table 8.1 Main types of Gopher documents.

Code	File type
0	Text file
1	Directory (not individual files)
4	Mac HQX file
5	PC binary file
g	A GIF image
h	An HTML image (Web page)
I	An image other than a GIF file

To use the -t modifier, type this: *-t type code keyword*. If you wanted to find Graphics Interchange Format (GIF) files with the word *computer* in their titles, your query would be *-tg computer*. You can even string types together if you want; Veronica will treat them as if they have the Boolean *OR* between them. (Veronica is mean that way; it has one default operator for regular searches, and a different one for -t modifiers.) *-tIg computer* would find GIF files or other images with the word *computer* in their titles.

Specifying Results Limits

Veronica also lets you specify the maximum number of items to be found, by using the -m modifier. For example, *-m4000 Jughead* will return 4,000 search matches, if there are that many available, for the word Jughead. (Without this modifier, the top limit for returning matches is usually about 200.) There is no limit to the number of items you can specify using -m.

Can you mix the -t and the -m modifiers together? Sure, but you have to give them each their own hyphen—they're picky that way. *-tg -m500 puppy* would find you up to 500 GIF files with the word *puppy* in their titles.

TIP

For the sake of example, we put the -t and -m modifiers at the beginning of the string, but they can be placed just as easily at the end of a search phrase.

Once you've done a search with Veronica, you'll get a results page that looks like Figure 8.3.

Click on what you want, and the document appears in your browser window.

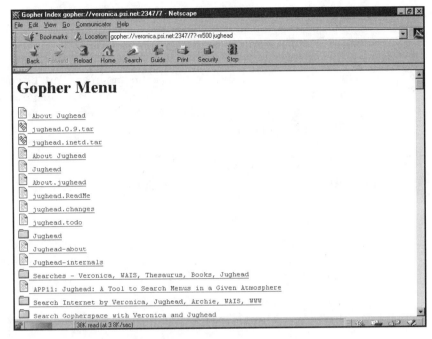

Figure 8.3   Veronica search results.

TIP

Warning! Many Gopher sites were created before Web designers split huge files down into smaller, more easily navigated files, so some of the documents you access will be very long.

Coping With Long Files

When confronted with a long file and a growing sense of frustration, make use of Ctrl+F (for Mac users, use Command+F). This pops up a little Find box that enables you to search for a text string within a Web page. It's handy when you don't feel like slogging all the way through a particular document. But don't use Ctrl+F until the page has finished loading. It's entirely possible that the text you're looking for is on the last line of the loading document, and Ctrl+F won't be able to find it until the document is completely loaded. What happens if it's not loaded and you try looking for it? You'll get a "text string not found" error, which will really frustrate you.

Jughead

Jughead is a search engine similar to Veronica, but without Veronica's scope. Jughead was designed to index high-level menu items: It indexes more the "menus of menus" than individual documents in a menu. Be sure you know the extent of a Jughead program's search capabilities before you use it. A high-level-menu Jughead is good for doing general research when you're trying to find information collections.

Searching With Jughead

Jughead searches just like Veronica with two exceptions: The first is that the -t and -m modifiers don't work. The second is two additional modifiers—the ?all and the ?limit modifiers.

- **?all** Returns all the results for the search of a particular keyword. (The usual limit is 1,024 results.) For example, *?all Avalon* will return all results for a search of the word Avalon.

- **?limit#** Limits the number of results returned. For example, *?limit50 Avalon* will return 50 results for a search of the keyword Avalon.

Trial Gopher Sites

With this overview, you should be able to work your way around Gopher and its search tools. Here are a couple of sites to get you started:

- *Gopher Jewels*

  gopher://cwis.usc.edu/11/Other_Gophers_and_Information_Resources/ Gopher-Jewels

  This site gives you some of the best remaining sites in gopherspace and some good tips on how to navigate them. However, you will find several locations that have not been updated since the early 90s, including the Library of Congress's Law Collection and Rice University's Government, Political Science, and Law gopher. Most sites will have a warning at the top of their menus, but be on the look out for the "file last updated" note on others.

  Several of the Gopher Jewels are still valuable, including the Comprehensive Epidemiological Data Resource (CEDR), which is updated more frequently online than in print. Just use common sense using these older tools: Labor statistics from a particular year are archives that are not likely to need updating, whereas a weather forecasting site will need constant attention.

■ *University of Minnesota Gopher*

gopher://gopher.micro.umn.edu

This is where it all got started, and you can find some priceless information on their gopher, from bookstores around the world to a stunning array of recipes (try the pumpkin scones!). Be sure to look over the "Other Gopher and Information Servers" section to find gophers around the world.

One particularly useful option is the Voice of America Newswire/News and English Broadcast, available on the UMN gopher or at **gopher:// gopher.voa.gov/11/newswire**. Like most news services, VOA displays a strong perspective but is a good example of the utility of a regularly updated gopher—you can get well-organized news from Hollywood to the Congo without waiting for a lot of graphics to load.

■ *University of California-Irvine*

gopher://peg.cwis.uci.edu:7000/11/gopher.welcome/peg/GOPHERS

The folks at UC-Irvine do a good job of weeding out dead sites from this collection of gophers from Africa and the Pacific Rim to the United States and Canada. While a few may be outdated, this is a worthwhile site if you are a gopher user looking for hard-to-find global news.

Now let's go from the organizationally sublime to the slightly ridiculous—a neat little tool called Finger.

Finger

Back in the dark days before SLIP/PPP connections, most folks had UNIX accounts. They dialed into UNIX machines to connect to the Internet. There wasn't much in the way of graphics, and the typical nongraphical UNIX interface can be quite intimidating.

Still, clever users managed to inject humor into the interface with Finger. Finger was designed originally to let users check on the last login of other users. When you Fingered a user's e-mail address from a UNIX account, you'd get information about that user's last login, whether they had any unread e-mail, and so on.

You'd also get the contents of a text file called ".plan" (the quotation marks indicate a hidden file on the UNIX system). Originally the .plan file was just that, for plans. Academic users put their research plans or interests they were pursuing in this text file. Eventually the .plan file evolved into an art form, containing weekly trivia, diatribes, pages of quotes, and anything folks could think to fit into a text file. In a way, they were a precursor to World Wide Web pages as personal expressions.

Security concerns, firewalls, and aliases have made Fingering more difficult than it used to be. Still, there are some neat tricks to do with Finger, and it's an interesting way to get regularly updated information on topics from trivia to baseball.

Finger Gateways On The Web

You access Finger through a Finger gateway on the Web. Here are two for you to use:

■ *Finger Gateway With Faces*

www.cs.indiana.edu:800/finger/gateway

Just use the following instructions, and you can while away the hours trying out everyone's e-mail addresses. This Finger gateway has "faces" in that it supports images returned with any Finger text—photos of the author, the insignia of the host (a university mascot or company logo, for example) and other pictures.

■ *Finger!*

www.amherst.edu/~atstarr/computers/finger.html

Another good Finger site with a comprehensive explanation of Finger and some good samples and gateways.

When you access one of these gateways, you get a screen that looks like Figure 8.4.

Just type in the e-mail address you want to Finger. Your results screen will look like Figure 8.5.

Some of the e-mail addresses you try won't work. Some sites have disabled Finger, some sites are behind a firewall, and some addresses are not complete enough for you to use Finger properly. For example, someone might have the address of fred@fictionalexample.com. If anyone tried using the Finger program on that address, Finger would not work, because Fingering was not allowed on that account. E-mail sent to fred@fictionalexample.com would get to its proper destination, however. America Online, Prodigy, and CompuServe addresses are not Fingerable.

So don't expect Finger to work on every e-mail address. However, we're including a few for you to play with because we don't want you to be disappointed.

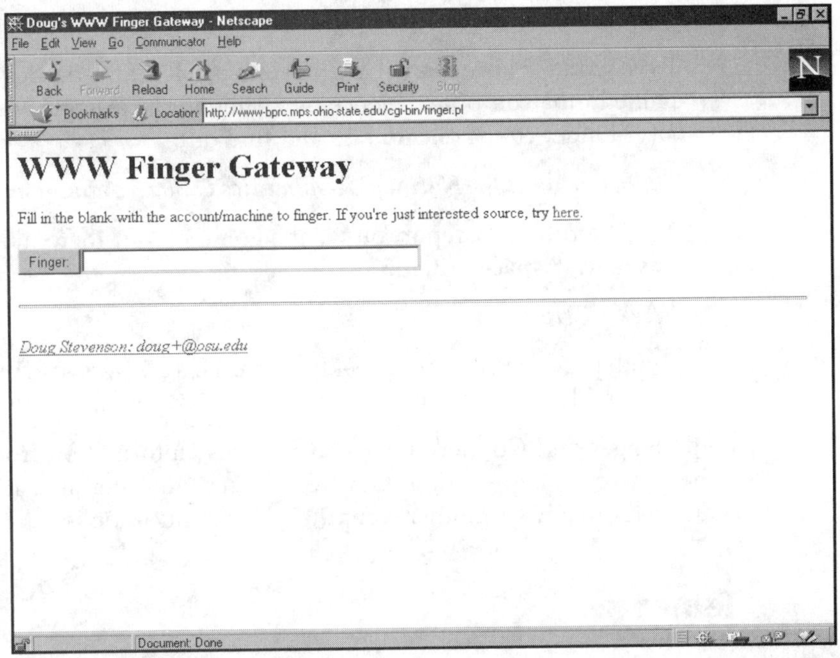

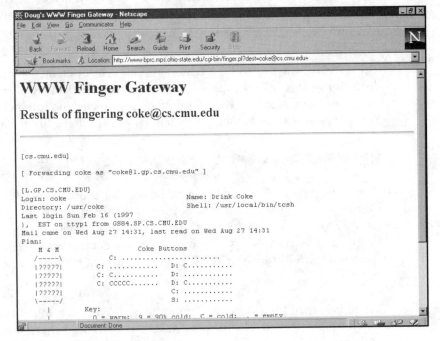

Figure 8.4   Finger gateway screen.

Figure 8.5   Finger results screen.

■ *Coke Machine on the Net*

Ever wonder how many cans of soda are left at a particular soda machine in the computer science department of Carnegie-Mellon University? Finger **coke@cs.cmu.edu** and find out.

■ *Daily Events at the National Aeronautics & Space Administration (NASA)*

To get a full daily report on what's going on out there in space, Finger **nasanews@space.mit.edu**.

■ *Weekly Trivia*

Cyndi presents you with weekly trivia. This address also includes other Fingerable e-mail addresses. Finger **cyndiw@online1.magnus1.com**.

While Finger and Gopher allow you to access information from other machines, there's an application that treats your computer as if it's a terminal connected directly to another computer. This application is called Telnet.

Telnet

Telnet connects you to a remote computer. By using Telnet to log in to a remote site, you can use the site as if your computer were connected directly to it. That means better control of the site, but at the same time it means fewer graphics because you are connecting to a remote site as a "dumb terminal"—no graphics, just text.

There are two ways to access a Telnet site. One is by opening your Telnet application (or whatever Telnet application you're using, such as NCSA Telnet) separate from Navigator. The easier way to do it is to click on a Telnet site from a Web page, which will automatically launch your preferred Telnet application.

Put Some Telnet In Your Tank

Check the Preferences options, under Edit, and then choose Navigator, and make sure you have your preferred Telnet program listed under Apps. If you don't have it listed, you're not going to be able to Telnet. If you don't have a Telnet application you can always pick up EWAN for Windows at **www.lysator.liu.se/~zander/ewan.html**; or NCSA Telnet for the Mac at **ftp.ncsa.uiuc.edu**.

Telnet is known for its gaming applications; players use Telnet to connect to environments called Multi-User Dungeons (MUDS) where they can play Dungeons-and-Dragons—type games. Other sites emulate popular books like *Dune* or *The Lord of the Rings*. These are great fun, but Telnet also has its serious side and can be used in many great ways for research, such as accessing card catalogs, information services, and search indexes.

Researching With Telnet For Windows Users

If you don't have a Telnet site to click on within the Web, here's how to open a Telnet session. If you're not using EWAN (Emulator Without A good Name), we can't help you, but pay attention anyway. You might learn what you need to know.

1. Launch EWAN.

2. Select File|Open. A pop-up menu of preselected sites appears.

3. Pick the New option on the right-hand side of the screen. A dialog box opens, asking for:

   - **The name of the site.** Use any name you want; this helps you select it from the dialog box later.

   - **The network address or host name.** The host name is the series of words separated by periods; for example, **news.mindspring.com** is a host name. When it's given as words, it's the host name. When it's given as a string of numbers separated by periods, it's the network address. For example, if we wanted to Telnet to **martini.eecs.umich.edu 3000**, then the host name would be martini.eecs.umich.edu. However, if we wanted to Telnet to **111.1121.243.31 3000**, we would connect using the network address. The number after the words or the string of numbers is the port number.

   - **The port number.** If there isn't a number after the host name, make sure the button next to Telnet is clicked on. If there is a number, like 3000 in the preceding example, then make sure the Custom button is selected and the number 3000 is in the box next to it.

4. Once you do this, click on OK and watch the red light at the bottom right portion of the screen. When it turns green, you're connected. Sometimes you have to wait a couple of minutes to get anything on the screen. If you wait a few minutes and don't get anything, press the Enter key a couple of times. When you're connected to a site, you can usually begin using its resources immediately. Sometimes, however, you'll have to use a login name and password. These are usually noted for you before you log in.

Researching With Telnet For Mac Users

If you don't have a Telnet site to click on within the Web, here's how to open a Telnet session. (If you're not using NCSA Telnet, we can't help you, but pay attention anyway. You might learn what you need to know.)

1. Launch NCSA Telnet by double-clicking on the NCSA Telnet icon.

2. Select File|Open or press Command+O.

3. A dialog box appears, presenting you with the following fields:

   ■ **Host/Session Name.** Enter the IP name or number of the host computer. This is the word part—or the string of numbers separated by periods—of the Telnet address. When it's given as words, it's the host name. When it's given as a string of numbers separated by periods, it's the network address. For example, if we wanted to Telnet to **martini.eecs. umich.edu 3000**, then the host name would be **martini.eecs.umich.edu**. The number after the words or the string of numbers is the port number.

   The port number follows the host name or IP number and a single space. If there isn't a number after the host name, that's okay. Some host computers offer Telnet services on "nonstandard" ports, and you'll have to know which port it's on in order to connect successfully.

   ■ **Window Name.** Enter the name you would like to give the session or leave this field blank. Naming the window is optional, but it is designed to help you identify a particular window when you have multiple Telnet sessions open.

4. Once you do this, click on the Connect button and wait a few seconds for the connection to be established. Sometimes you'll have to wait a couple of minutes to get anything on the screen. If you wait a few minutes and don't get anything, go to the Connection pull-down menu and select the session's title. It will then tell you the status of the connection and whether there is a problem with the connection, and allow you to abort or continue.

Some Telnet Sites To Try

Here are some sites for you to experiment with. Have fun!

■ *The Library of Congress*

   locis.loc.gov

   This site provides access to card catalogs, legislation, organizations, and copyright information (see Figure 8.6).

■ *The University of Michigan Geographic Name Server*

   martini.eecs.umich.edu 3000

   Type in your city's name or ZIP code, and see what happens.

■ *National Football League (NFL) Information Online*

culine.colorado.edu 863

Moving On

With the conclusion of this chapter, let's stop a minute. Catch your breath. Pat yourself on the back. You now know a lot about how to squeeze everything you can out of the basic Internet functions: newsgroups, e-mail, Gopher, Finger, Telnet, and the Web. Better yet, you know how to do it using Navigator.

From this point, you've learned how to pull information to you—how to go out on the Web and get what you need. In the next chapter, we're going to look at "Push" technology—specifically Netcaster—how news and information in which your interested can be brought to your desktop.

Let's get to it!

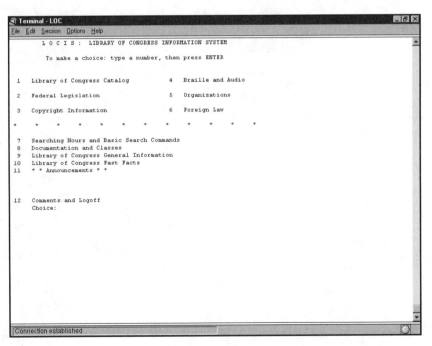

Figure 8.6   Access lots of useful information at the Library of Congress.

CHAPTER 9

Push Technology: When Push Comes To Shove

By now you've realized how many tools are out there on the Internet and that the scarce resource is not tools but *time*. You've made some headway into your research on global climate change, but you're also becoming aware that the carpet is desperate for a vacuuming and the kids are giving both you and the computer the evil eye. If only there were a way to get some of the resources delivered to your desktop instead of hunting through Web sites and newsgroups.

What Is Push?

Also called *client-side pull*, *push* is a good start to balancing the information/ time dilemma. Think of push content as the online version of television or radio broadcasting: Apart from selecting the channel, you don't actually surf through the content to find what you are looking for. Rather, you choose a station with a format you find generally appealing (rock, adult contemporary, news, sitcoms), and the station producers send, or push, the content your direction. You still have to listen to or watch the program, but chances are the producers have narrowed down the topic enough that you'll find most of it interesting.

Push does the same thing for the Internet. You choose a "channel" or format that fits your needs—entertainment news, sports reports, technology updates— and the push content provider sends that channel's content to your push client

131

software. While you still have to read the articles (the way you would have to listen to songs or watch a news broadcast), you don't have to spend three hours sifting through search engine results to find them.

TIP

> *You should treat push content as a handy supplement to, rather than replacement for, the other tools in your toolbox—every service doesn't have access to every news source, and relying solely on a push provider can limit your options unnecessarily.*

Why Use A Push Content Service?

While no one tool will completely remove the time-consuming nature of research, push services can remove some of the randomness associated with wading through huge virtual stacks of text and multimedia documents.

Imagine you are writing an article on affordable horse care in U.S. metropolitan areas. You belong to a couple of horse-oriented mailing lists and have visited newsgroups dealing with horse care. You also realize that the type of questions you want to ask are so broad that they would either be a source of irritation to the other members or generate so many responses that your mailbox would collapse. You're willing to spend some time on the different search engines to find some resources, but you're afraid you won't get a full picture of what's out there.

Using a push content service may help you cover some of your bases, since the content providers may deliver articles or interviews that are either too ephemeral to appear on a search engine or may not appear relevant the way they are posted in the search results.

Selecting Push Content Services

There are currently two different types of push content services: those that require you to install client software and those that use utilities built directly into Communicator.

Client-Based Services

A *client-based service* relies on software that you must install before receiving push content.

PointCast

www.pointcast.com

PointCast (see Figure 9.1) is probably the most well-known of the client-based push content providers. To use PointCast's services, just go to the Web site and click on "Download the PointCast Network" to get the free client software.

After you download and personalize the software, you will begin receiving Web content directly on your computer without having to surf for it. PointCast provides a list of its content partners on its site.

Browser-Based Services

Netscape Communicator's push service, Netcaster, eliminates the need for you to install special software to receive push content and allows you to browse

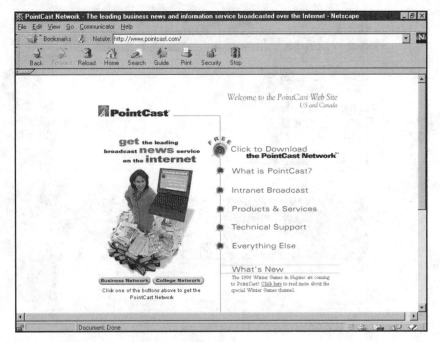

Figure 9.1   The PointCast Network.

offline (see Figure 9.2). While some other browsers allow you to do this too, Netcaster has added benefits that you should investigate to experience push content at its best.

In addition to eliminating the need for special software, another major benefit of Netcaster is the cross-platform availability of its channels. Because Netcaster channels are based on HTML, you can access them whether you are a PC or a Mac user. Netcaster also has a feature called Channel Finder that enables you to select channels to which you want to subscribe directly from a master list on the Netscape site. This feature cuts down on the time you spend hunting for a major or mainstream site. We'll briefly discuss how to add a channel using Channel Finder. For a more in-depth discussion of Netcaster and all of its features, be sure to check out the *Official Netscape Communicator 4 Professional Edition Book* by Phil James and Tara Calishain.

Netcaster keeps track of the channels you've selected in the My Channels list. To add a channel using Channel Finder, go to the Channel Finder list, as shown in Figure 9.3, and select a channel that looks worthwhile.

Click on the button for that channel, and a *descriptor card* pops up. You can either double-click on the card or click on the Add Channel button to view the preview information about that channel. A preview screen appears, and you

Figure 9.2   Netscape's Netcaster.

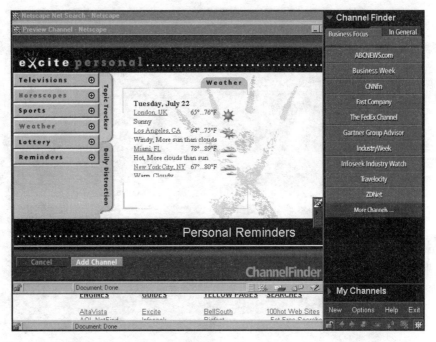

Figure 9.3   Netcaster's Channel Finder.

can decide whether to click on Add Channel or Cancel based on this window (see Figure 9.4).

If you decide to add the channel, Netcaster gives you additional options for its display through a properties dialog box as shown in Figure 9.5. Some of the features include how you want the name displayed in your list, the URL (which should already be entered), how often you want the display to be updated, cache size, and how you want the channel to appear on your desktop (as a standard window or a *Webtop*—see the following tip).

TIP

> *You may see references to "Webtops" in your push content searches. No, this isn't an arcane term for a Netsurfer's hairdo. Instead, it's an arcane reference to what your computer screen's desktop or workspace becomes after Web content is pushed into the unused space. In other words, instead of looking like a standard desktop, your screen only has the channel's content and not the usual backdrop or navigation bar you're used to.*

Think this is great? It gets better—in fact, Netcaster allows you to turn any Web site into a channel. So if your interests are more diverse than the preset

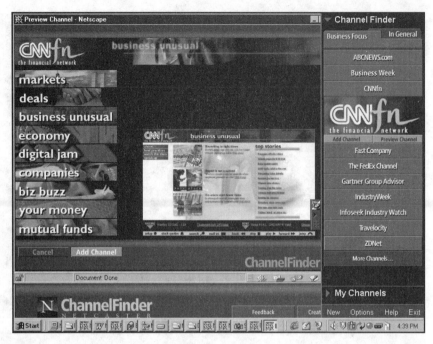

Figure 9.4 *Netcaster's channel preview screen.*

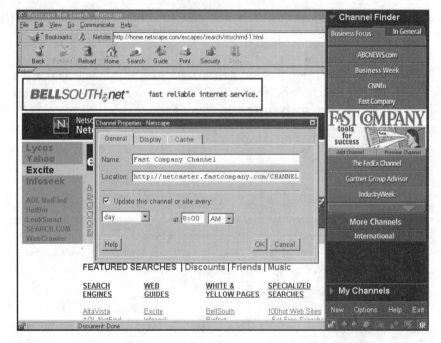

Figure 9.5 *Choosing channel properties.*

channels, you can choose another Web site to be pushed to your desktop on a regular schedule without changing servers. But how do you go about setting this up?

Believe it or not, creating a client-side pull site out of any Web site is simple with Netcaster. Go to the Netcaster drawer, and click on Add. The channel dialog box pops up immediately, and you can set your properties the same way you did by going through Channel Finder. The major difference is that you have to enter the URL yourself. Click on OK once you're finished, and you are ready to go. Accessing any of your channels is as easy as accessing a document on your hard drive—just go to the Netcaster drawer, select the My Channels button, and click on the channel you want to display.

Which Service Should I Use?

Not all push content services are created equal, and considering the amount of information available on the Internet, you should select one that does a good job of filtering.

Finding Push Content Sites

There are dozens of push-focused sites—or *channels*—out there, from business-oriented content providers to community-action organizers. Following are just a few of the better ones.

Business-Focused Channels

These channels are just a sample of what's available for anyone interested in business. And remember, they are also ones that are specifically designed with push content in mind—we've not included a lot of other fine sites that you can add yourself using a service such as Netcaster.

CNN Financial Network

www.cnnfn.com

A smart and well-organized site, CNN Financial Network (CNNfn) is one of the preset channels you'll discover on the Netcaster Channel Finder list. It is also a source for much of PointCast's financial information. CNNfn gives you immediate access to pressing financial stories, news about domestic and international markets, and insights into business-related issues such as travel and investment trends.

Business Wire

www.businesswire.com

If you want to keep up on the nation's headlines, Business Wire is a great place to try out a little client-side pull (see Figure 9.6). The headlines are updated frequently throughout the day, and the site itself gives you access to additional business-related information such as trade shows, corporate profiles, and IPOs on the Net.

Money.com

www.money.com

Money magazine's Web site is another great resource for business information, particularly since it creates in-depth stories that may not be found in more newspaper-styled sites. In addition to global business stories, Money.com gives you tips on how to make the Internet work for you, whether your concern is saving for college or planning for retirement.

Nikkei Net

satellite.nikkei.co.jp/enews/

Nikkei Net (see Figure 9.7), an online business service from Japan, gives you angles into global business that you might not find in the American press.

Figure 9.6   Business Wire.

Figure 9.7   Nikkei Net.

Available in English or Japanese, it features updates on the Tokyo market, summaries of the Asian business scene, and analyses of high tech, auto, and other sectors.

Management Express

www.anbar.co.uk/management/express.htm

This site explores issues relevant to managers and management researchers. Management Express journalists review best practices, management theories, and new tools from around the globe, presenting them to you in an easily readable and fast-loading format.

News Channels

For more general news stories and resources, consider integrating a couple of these sites into your routine.

The New York Times On The Web

www.nytimes.com

Where would news hounds be without the not-so-Gray Lady? You don't have to sacrifice your copy of *The Times*, even if you are stuck behind your computer for hours on end. You'll find everything you expect in the online version of *The Times*, with the added bonus of not getting any newsprint on your fingers.

South China Morning Post Internet Edition

www.scmp.com/news/

One of the leading papers in Hong Kong, the *South China Morning Post* (SCMP) requires free registration and is amenable to being turned into a push content site. SCMP provides you with stories from Asia and the globe, along with world stock market updates and three-day weather forecasts (see Figure 9.8).

Toronto Globe And Mail

www.GlobeAndMail.CA/

The Toronto Globe and Mail, Canada's national Web site, features news stories, Canadian national issues forums, and investment information. The site includes extras such as career advice, birth and death announcements, and online personals.

Sports Channels

If the amount of sports available on TV just isn't enough to keep you up-to-date, check out the following sites.

Figure 9.8   South China Morning Post.

The Sporting News

www.sportingnews.com

Customizable, filled with sports stats, stories, and daily updates, *The Sporting News* includes live audio and Fantasy League features as well (see Figure 9.9). You can display the site itself as a channel, or else opt to have just the scores displayed on your desktop.

ESPN Sports Zone

ESPN.SportsZone.com/

As you might expect, ESPN brings you a site packed with sports stories, scores, and insights from across the sports world from basketball to auto racing. Not limited to the professional arena, Sports Zone also gives you the latest on personal health and fitness. You can also tailor the real-time SportsTracker to your sporting preferences.

Launch.net

www.launch.net

Whether you're a dedicated balloonist or a distant fan, Launch.net, as shown in Figure 9.10, will introduce you to new material every day. Balloon basics are a

Figure 9.9   The Sporting News.

Figure 9.10 Launch.net takes you everywhere.

good place to start, but you can also find out about piloting opportunities, flights in Luxembourg, or the closest long jump competition. Since the site is created by professional balloonists, it will be well worth your consideration as a channel on your computer.

SportsZine

www.sportszineuk.co.uk/

Everything you ever wanted to know about rugby and cricket but were afraid to ask. SportsZine covers the interesting but oft-neglected-in-America sports such as rugby, European football (soccer), cricket, scuba, and windsurfing. You'll also find live chats and interviews with sports celebs.

Family Channels

Give your children even more stimuli online.

Disney.com

www.disney.com

As you may expect, the Disney.com site includes a lot of coverage of its movies and toy tie-ins. But don't let this deter you from trying it as one of your channels—there are plenty of activities to do on and off of the Web, including seasonal crafts for the family, tips on how to manage the ups and downs of childrearing, and a "Kid's Channel" with games and puzzles for the younger set. You'll also find a comprehensive listing of the other Disney-related sites on the Net.

GRIPVision

www.gripvision.com/

Produced by high school students for high school students, GRIPVision is an excellent resource for young adults and parents alike (see Figure 9.11). Students will find information about careers, financial aid for college, and social "rants" from their peers. Parents will get a good insight into life in high school and their kids' concerns about peer pressure, family challenges, and academic concerns.

United Nations CyberSchoolBus

www.un.org/Pubs/CyberSchoolBus/

Whether you read it in English, French, or Spanish, you'll find a world of information on the United Nations CyberSchoolBus. The CyberSchoolBus is kid-oriented but pulls no punches—it tackles concerns such as poverty and

Figure 9.11   GRIPVision.

land mines in a direct but not over-the-top manner. The site also has a quiz section, facts about the Model United Nations, and an online bookstore.

Tiger Watch

user.aol.com/tigertrail/index.htm

Concerned about the environment or just want to introduce the kids (and yourself) to these gorgeous cats? Tiger Watch presents all kinds of information about tigers, their natural environment, and efforts to improve their chances of surviving. The site is packed with photos and includes a special kid-oriented page for the younger set of tiger-philes.

Travel Channels

If you're planning a trip or just want to imagine you are, these sites will take you there.

Travelocity

www.travelocity.com

Sponsored by SABRE, Travelocity lets you buy airline tickets, rent your car, and book a hotel room in over 70 countries. The format is straightforward and includes FareWatcher, a low-airfare alert service, and Kroll's "Top News" for top travelers, a warning system for international travel destinations.

The Trip.com

www.thetrip.com

While The Trip.com is tailored for business travelers, any frequent traveler will enjoy the bonuses on this site (see Figure 9.12). In addition to the expected flight, rental car, and hotel reservations, The Trip.com gives you real-time flight tracking, tips on travel comfort (ever wondered about the best way to pop your ears during descent?), and help with tracking all of your frequent traveler points.

InfoHub Specialty Travel Guide

www.infohub.com/

When the average travel site doesn't fit your needs, surf over to InfoHub to investigate more exotic climes around the world. You can search the tour gallery or look through travel destinations from Antarctica to backwoods North America. There are also theme-oriented pages including history, holiday, and gourmet food-oriented vacations. You can also find transportation, accommodation, and financial aid tips—whatever your travel destination.

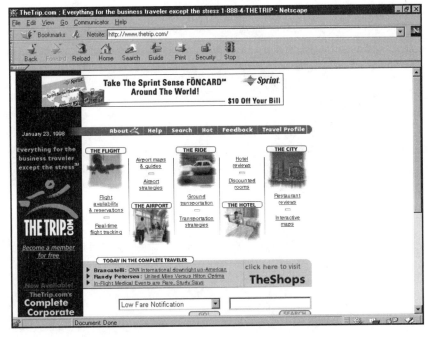

Figure 9.12   The Trip.com.

Diversified Travel Management

www.tourandtravel.com/

No service charges, retail and wholesale tickets, and customized trips are only the start. Not content with the Antarctica? Try hopping a freighter. Better yet, hook up with the Clergy Travel section and get going on the tour of your choice.

Moving On

You can see from this glimpse into push content provision that there is a lot of information to be had on the Web—far more than any service provider can push at you—no matter how hard they shove. This means that sometimes you have to take the Web into your own hands to get what you need. What's the best way to do this? We'll start with a general overview of the Web in the next chapter.

CHAPTER 10

The World Wide Web

In the nine previous chapters, we've talked a lot about using the Internet as your research toolbox. We've gotten into what helper applications you can use, what plug-ins can help you make the most of your surfing experience, and so on. We've given you ten friendly tips for Internet research. You've gotten a good grounding in how the basic Internet tools of mailing lists and newsgroups can make your research more thorough.

But now we're getting into the Web. And the Web is a lot less straightforward than those other tools. It has nooks and crannies and pages that run the gamut from pure research to pure drivel. This is an exciting, scary, and interesting place.

We decided that before we dropped you headfirst into it with a discussion of search engines and how to find specific research things on the Web, we'd start you off with a brief chapter on how to use the Web to make your life easier by *getting local*, *getting package information*, and *getting informed*. By the time this chapter ends you'll know how to get a weather report for your city, how to track a UPS package online, and even how to get some of them there Consumer Information Reports without sending an SASE to Pueblo, Colorado. Not only are these interesting tricks if you're trying to find out what happened to a shipment or if you want to know if it's going to snow when you go on your ski trip, but it'll give you a grounding on how to use the Internet for practical, everyday information, in addition to more esoteric research.

Let's start out by getting local.

> **TIP**
>
> *Three cheers for horsing around! In addition to research and mundane information gathering, be sure to spend some time on the Internet just "horsing around." Pick a hobby or a subject you're interested in and just wander around on the Web awhile, going from link to link. Not only will you learn something, but you'll see how other folks are organizing their Web pages, the links that lead you from information point to information point, and where popular hubs of interest are. (If you are researching skydiving and all the skydiving pages put one page as first on their list for really good skydiving info, you know that it's probably the best resource available online.)*
>
> *There is a lot to be said for structured, focused assignments. But don't forget that you can also learn a lot by just playing around. Give yourself time for each.*

Going Local

If you live in a big city, finding local information on the Internet is no problem. Places like CitySearch at **www.citysearch.com**, Digital City at **www.digitalcity.com**, and Sidewalk at **www.sidewalk.com** cater to larger cities like Houston, Atlanta, Seattle, and even the Raleigh/Durham area of North Carolina. So if you're from a midsized city, you might be disappointed to explore those places and find that they don't contain anything on your city.

Take heart. There are two more sources for "meta-information" on your town, in addition to scads of more specific town information. Let's start with the meta-information sources: City.Net and Yahoo! Get Local.

Get Meta: It Pays

When we say "meta-information," we mean that information about all aspects of a city is gathered at this one particular Web page. City.Net is sponsored by Excite, which is a search engine. Yahoo! Get Local is sponsored by Yahoo!, which is a subject-based catalog of Internet pages. (We'll get into the differences between those two things in Chapter 11.)

Both these services gather lots of information about a particular town or state and put it all in one page. Very handy. We'll look at City.Net first.

City.Net

www.city.net

City.Net starts at the top of the world and gives you the option of going to any one of several continents. The U.S. pages start at **www.city.net/countries/ united_states/**. You have the option of choosing a general U.S. site (such as the

FestivalFinder site of music festivals in the U.S., or one of several government sites), a U.S. state, or one of the largest U.S. cities that runs down the right-hand side of the screen.

Click on a state. We'll click on North Carolina. As you see in Figure 10.1, clicking on a state gives you a similarly organized page, with a map of North Carolina at its top, general NC resources along the middle, and a list of cities at the bottom of the page.

This is a superbly organized site, especially if you're looking for general NC resources or you live in a midsized to large city. It is far from complete, however. It doesn't contain anywhere near the number of actual cities in North Carolina, and it lists only a fraction of North Carolina's 100 counties.

If you live in a small city or want to get information on a small city, you might find that Yahoo! Get Local does the job better for you.

Yahoo! Get Local

local.yahoo.com/bin/get_local

Yahoo! Get Local isn't as pretty as Excite, and its pages aren't as nicely laid out. But since it can operate via ZIP code, it covers more territory.

At the first Get Local page, you'll have the option of either plugging in a ZIP

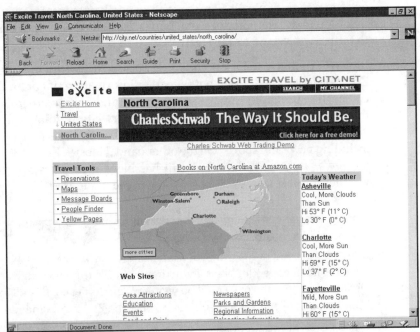

Figure 10.1   Looking at North Carolina via City.Net.

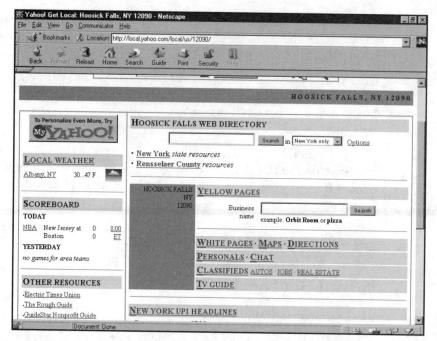

Figure 10.2   How it is in Hoosick Falls.

code or clicking on a state name. Clicking on North Carolina in this case doesn't get you a map of North Carolina and general state information, but instead links you to dozens and dozens of North Carolina cities, from Barium Springs to Little Switzerland to Tar Heel.

If you do want to enter a ZIP code, Get Local returns with the city to which the ZIP code is assigned, along with weather information (if not for that city, for a city in close proximity), sports scores, news, and links to other information on that county, city, or state. Of course, not every city is going to have the same amount of information. Beverly Hills (90210, natch) has a lot of information, including news and sports. On the other hand, Hoosick Falls, New York (12090) has fewer resources, though it still has New York news and sports, and a weather forecast from Albany, as you can see in Figure 10.2.

What If You Don't Know The ZIP Code?

Obviously, if you're checking out a city with which you're familiar, you're going to have a ZIP code. But what if you're going on a trip and you want to learn a little more about the city you'll be visiting? You don't see it listed in the Yahoo! Get Local city listings, and you don't know the ZIP code. What do you do?

Let's take as our hypothetical example Frying Pan Landing, North Carolina.

For some reason, you are going to Frying Pan Landing. Frying Pan is not listed in the Yahoo! Get Local city list, so you need to find out the ZIP code to enter it at Get Local and get the city information that way.

Your next stop should be the US Postal Service site, at **www.usps.com**. (Most of the time, agencies associated with the government, like the U.S. Postal Service, have a .gov at the end of their Web site address, instead of .com. In this case both usps.com and usps.gov will get you to the postal service.)

Once there, open this Web page: **www.usps.gov/ncsc/lookups/lookup_ ctystzip.html**. This page will let you put in a city and state, and will return the ZIP code for that city. (If a city has more than one ZIP code, you'll get the list of all ZIP codes applicable to that city.) Go ahead and type in Frying Pan Landing NC in the box and click on the "Process" button. We'll wait.

Did it work? Aha! No, it didn't, did it? You got a message that Frying Pan Landing couldn't be found in the database. Note that the error message says that some city names are not recognized for mail delivery purposes. Or, we might just be pulling your leg.

But we're not; there really is a Frying Pan Landing. You don't have to take our word for it, though. Here's how you find out. Click on File|New|Navigator Window. Another Netscape Window will open up, leaving you with the ZIP code lookup in one window. Go to the new window, the one that doesn't have the ZIP code lookup. Now open the URL for MapQuest at **www.mapquest.com**.

Click on the Interactive Atlas link. From here you'll go to a new page that gives you the option of entering a business name, address, ZIP code, and so on. You can also just enter the city and state of the area you're trying to locate. Go ahead and enter Frying Pan Landing in the City: box and NC in the State: box. Then click on Search.

MapQuest will generate a map, and look...there's Frying Pan Landing. It's also surrounded by several other cities, including Gum Neck, Gum Neck Landing, Jerry, and Buffalo City.

Now, here's where having the two Navigator windows open comes in handy. Switch back to the USPS window, and try to get the ZIP codes for the other cities; you may not get any of them. In that case, return to the MapQuest window and use the Zoom Bar on the right-hand side of the screen to zoom out a bit. You'll see more cities around Frying Pan Landing to try in the USPS database.

We will not keep you in suspense: try Swanquarter NC. It's not next door to Frying Pan Landing, but it's close enough so that getting that ZIP code and using it on Yahoo! Get Local will get a lot of useful information. Plymouth, NC will also work.

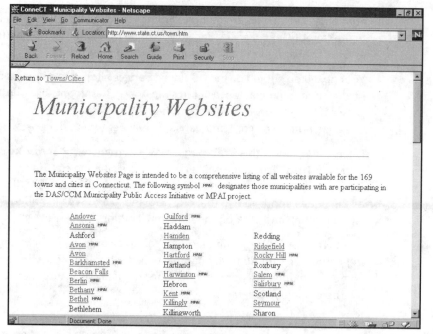

Figure 10.3   Connecticut is wired!

Of course, you don't have to use a meta-site to find everything you need to know about a city. Some state pages have lists of cities that are accessible online. (Connecticut is an excellent example of this; as you can see in Figure 10.3, the state site has a comprehensive list of cities and their Web presences; the page itself is at **www.state.ct.us/town.htm**.)

What if you don't want to know everything there is to know about Port Arthur, Texas? What if you just want to know the weather? There are a few places on the Web where you can get very specific information. This is where knowing the ZIP code really comes in handy.

ZIP Code-Based Info

ZIP codes are very handy, and for a lot more reasons than putting one on a letter. Several places on the Web make information available based on ZIP codes. These are only a sample.

The Weather Underground, at **www.underground.com**, can give you plenty of current weather information from your ZIP code, including temperature, sunrise and sunset, and even the phase of the moon!

If you trek over to Prevue at **www.prevue.com** and enter your ZIP code, you'll get local cable listings. (This doesn't work for every ZIP code, though—only the 22 million cable viewers that Prevue covers.)

Maybe Fluffy's been chewing on the mouse again. Time to find a vet. Do it with VetSearch at **www.vetsearch.com/search.html**. Enter your ZIP code and you'll get a list of the vets in your area, along with links to Web pages if they're available.

Are you a compulsive coupon cutter? Check out HotCoupons at **www.hotcoupons. com**. Entering your ZIP code will get you a listing of categories, including household, home improvement, and professional services (see Figure 10.4).

If you want to do a little good in this old world, check out SERVEnet at **www.servenet.org**. Entering your ZIP code will list the volunteer outlets and opportunities in your area.

Finally, the online Gazetteer at **www.census.gov/cgi-bin/gazetteer** is a prime place for census information. Enter a ZIP code and you'll get population data, census information (did you ever wonder how many people were actually *in* Swanquarter, North Carolina?), and access to an amazingly detailed map.

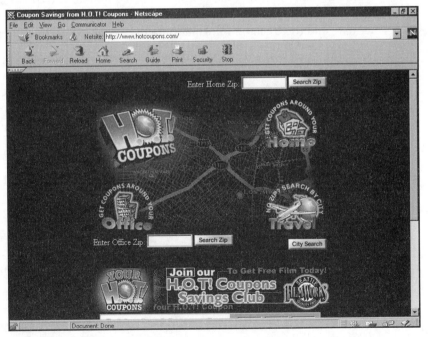

Figure 10.4   Cutting coupons the online way with HotCoupons.

Okay, now you know how to get a weather report, maps—even coupons for your corner of the world. Let's talk a little now about getting package information, so you don't have to hang around waiting for your UPS box to arrive.

Getting Package Information

We include this section because package information can be a tedious and mundane procedure offline, and it's a good example of how the Internet can be used for very regular, everyday stuff, and not necessarily for esoteric research.

Did Aunt Martha get that fruitcake you sent her? Did that birthday present you sent to Uncle Fritz get there yet? If you shipped your package via UPS, FedEx, DHL, or RPS, you can find out online.

UPS

www.ups.com

You can track your packages with UPS by clicking on the tracking button on their site, and entering the tracking code. If you like, you can also send e-mail to **totaltrack@ups.com** with the tracking number in the subject or body of the e-mail, and the tracking information will be sent to you by return e-mail.

UPS provides you with other online resources, too. By entering information about a package you want to ship, you can get a cost estimate from the "Quick Cost Calculator." And if you don't know where to drop off your UPS package, use the drop-off locator. By entering your address or ZIP code (gosh, that little thing comes in handy) you'll get a map of authorized UPS drop-off locations.

FedEx

www.fedex.com

FedEx also offers a lot of information, including a package tracker, drop-off locator, and a rate finder. FedEx also offers a couple of extras, including an online application for a FedEx account and free software that enables you to do a lot of the shipping administration details on your own computer.

DHL

www.dhl.com

DHL does a lot of international shipping, and it shows. The home page includes service bulletins (from Italy and Egypt when we looked at it) that alert you to possible delays in international shipping. DHL's tracking system allows you to track up to 10 packages at a time.

DHL, as an international shipper, also has a neat pull-down menu covering every country to which it ships. Each country listing includes import guidelines, demographic information, and even a flag of the country. (Uh-oh...we're straying dangerously close to real research here.)

RPS

www.shiprps.com

If you're shipping a lot of something, you might be using RPS. It has plenty of online information, including package tracking (Web-based or e-mail), time of transit estimation, and package rates. You can also request that a proof of delivery be sent to you complete with the image of the consignee's signature!

Are you feeling informed yet? Hopefully this chapter is showing you that you don't have to treat the Web like this big, weird, alien THING. Instead there's plenty of information that we can use in our day-to-day lives.

The last stop on our tour of the Internet-as-useful-everyday-device is the consumer arena.

Getting Informed

Are you using the best of everything? Are you getting your money's worth? Do you know the best ways to repair your flooded home, teach your kids how to make the most of a budget, buy the best car? You need consumer information, you old consumer you. Let's take a look at a few places that you can get really informed. We'll start with that bastion of knowledge out in Pueblo, Colorado—The Consumer Information Center.

The Consumer Information Center

www.pueblo.gsa.gov/

You've probably seen those commercials that encourage you to send for a free catalog from The Consumer Information Center. We feel a little guilty, actually, telling you about the Web site, because we're afraid that if everyone finds out about it there won't be any more cool commercials.

Oh well, you come first. Anyway, the Web version of the CIC has over 200 booklets available, covering subjects such as health, federal programs, children, and small business (see Figure 10.5). The booklets that are online are

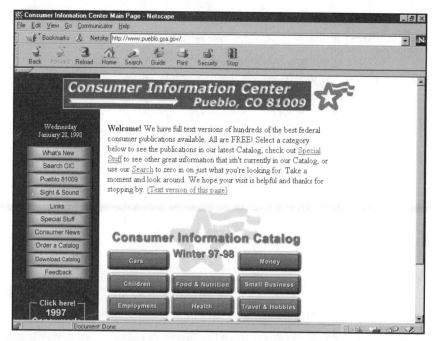

Figure 10.5   You don't have to write to Pueblo to get CIC booklets anymore.

text-only, so you might be missing out on some illustrations. However, you can order printed copies of booklets. (Many are free, some are between 50¢ and $2. Only a few are more expensive than that.) Of particular interest is the *Consumer's Resource Handbook*, which gives you extensive information and contacts for help with consumer problems and complaints. You can see the 1997 version at **www.pueblo.gsa.gov/1997res.htm**.

Consumer Product Safety Commission

www.cpsc.gov/

If you have kids and you want to know more about the toys they're playing with and the safety devices you've bought for them, you definitely need to check out this site. This consumer information site has a variety of materials, including publications (including child safety reports and instructions on how to hold a "Baby Safety Shower") and kid-oriented materials—like a comic book on bike safety.

The real highlight of this site, however, is the recall list. The CPSC keeps an on-going list, dating back to 1990, of recall press releases and information. You can even search this information. You'll get far more recall notices here than you would in the general media, so it's definitely worth checking out periodically.

Consumer Reports Online

www.consumerreports.org/

Though some of this site is pay-oriented, you'll get a lot of free information online. Want to learn how to set up a home office or a stereo system? You can find out here. There's also a freely accessible recall list that you can search or browse by category. If you decide you like the site and want to join, it costs $2.95 a month for unlimited access, with a discount for yearly subscriptions and current *Consumer Reports* subscribers.

Finally, if there hasn't been enough information in these three resources to suit you, we encourage you to check out Consumer World at **www. consumerworld.com**. Consumer World is a meta-site that provides information from several different places, including scam alerts, company information, news outlets, and editor's choice listings.

Moving On

Now perhaps a little of the mystery and esoteric nature has been taken out of the dealings with the Web. You've learned that you can use the Web for simple, day-to-day things that make your life easier.

Unfortunately, these simple day-to-day things aren't going to mean much when you have a report due on plate tectonics or the digestive habits of the camelopard. For that you're going to have to get into search engines, which are the backbone of finding things on the Web. Turn the page, and let's look at the leaders of the pack.

Part III

Specialty Information Resources

CHAPTER 11

General Searching On The World Wide Web

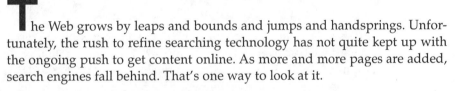

The Web grows by leaps and bounds and jumps and handsprings. Unfortunately, the rush to refine searching technology has not quite kept up with the ongoing push to get content online. As more and more pages are added, search engines fall behind. That's one way to look at it.

Another way to view the explosive growth of content on the Web is as a prod to companies to develop better search technologies. As time has passed, some amazing search and retrieval technologies have evolved on the Web.

TIP

*If you're one of the folks who has never opened a Web page except by clicking on a hyperlink, here's a new skill for you: Ctrl+O for Windows users, or Command+O for Mac OS users. This key combination opens a box into which you can type the page location where you want to go. (You can also use this command to open an HTML file on your hard drive.) Do your fingers hurt just thinking about all that typing? Here's another hint. If the page to which you are going is a native (HTML) Web page (not a Gopher or another type of site), then you can dispense with the **http://** and just type the page name directly. Typing **http://www.yahoo.com** and **www.yahoo.com** will get you to the same place. Over time this hint will save you a lot of keystrokes.*

General Search Resources

The largest general search resources are divided into three categories:

- **Search Engines.** These collections index complete Web pages or page titles without filtering or adding materials selectively. Sometimes they index Usenet posts or locations of Gopher sites as well. They usually don't review the material they've indexed—they leave it all in the database for you to search through. This is the place to go if you want the largest possible selection of raw material to search.

- **Preferred Engines/Edited Search Engines.** These collections add material selectively and review sites based on content. Some preferred and edited search sites prohibit listings of certain topics, such as pornography.

- **Hierarchical Indices.** These sites have a subject listing not unlike a card catalog, which allows you to browse subject listings instead of searching for specific keywords (though that's usually an option, too).

Search Resources Galore

Our least favorite question when helping someone with Internet research is "What's the best overall search resource?" The loyalties that have sprung up around the various search resources rival the Mac-Windows-DOS-UNIX-OS/2 operating system debates. Everybody's got a favorite. Some folks swear by AltaVista. Others like HotBot. Still others eschew search engines completely and prefer a hierarchical index like Yahoo!, and on and on and on. Ideally, you should stay flexible enough to experiment with new technologies as they hit the Web and to use the proper search resource depending on which problem you're researching. But the important thing is that you use what you like. The only "best" search resource is what's best for you.

Helping You Along: Spiders, Shoppers, And Other Agents

Do you think that Internet search engines are run exclusively by hand, with hordes of employees traveling to every submitted site, gathering the pages, and indexing them manually? Good grief. That would be boring, tedious work, wouldn't it? Let the computer do it.

And so it does. Most search engines and indexes use a computer program called a *spider* to index Web pages. Also called a *robot* or a *crawler*, a spider "crawls" through the Internet to a site, gathers and indexes the pages the site contains, and takes the information back to a central database. It's considerably faster for a spider to do the work than a human, and it's much less tedious for the human.

A spider is part of a larger category of Web and Internet programs called *agents*. Finding the authoritative definition for an agent is like trying to find spitcurls on a frog. For the sake of this section, let's consider an agent to be a software program that either directly or indirectly facilitates your Web experience through the gathering, comparison, and organization of information.

Most agents nowadays are behind-the-scenes types, like spiders and other Web crawlers. However, others exist, like agents that compare prices for you, and ones that ask for your tastes in music and movies. These agents compare your responses with those of other people and then make recommendations of music and movies you might like. As time goes by and agents get more sophisticated, they'll be invaluable research partners. Let's take a few minutes to get to know one or two of them.

TIP

If you want an in-depth discussion of agents and their incredible potential, check out Fah-Chun Cheong's Internet Agents: Spiders, Wanderers, Brokers and 'Bots, *by New Riders Publishing.*

Shopping Agents

You're writing an article on the latest offerings by female singer/songwriters. A new *Sly and the Family Stone* tribune album has just come out and you want to buy a copy, but you want to pay a good price for it. So you call a whole bunch of music stores and find out how much each of them is selling it for, then you pick the one that's the closest and has the best price, and then you go buy it.

Tedious. Wouldn't it be great if comparative shopping could be done automatically? (You probably know where we're going with this.)

BargainFinder Agent, at **bf.cstar.ac.com/bf/agent2.html**, is just one example of a *shopping agent*. BargainFinder asks you for the title of a CD and the artist, then goes shopping at a list of music stores on the Web, getting the price for the CD and a link to the site that carries it. Once the list of stores and prices has been generated, it's very easy to determine the lowest price.

The system still has a few bugs, however. Not all CD stores are eager to be comparison-shopped, and so they have blocked access to the BargainFinder agent. Sometimes, when the Internet is especially busy, the agent can't get through. Still, it's an excellent early example of a technology that will only get better as time goes by.

Recommendation Agents

Firefly (see Figure 11.1), a *recommendation agent* at **www.firefly.com**, takes a different tactic from BargainFinder. Instead of hunting down prices for a CD you specify, it gets information on your likes and dislikes, and compares your profile with that of other people in its database. Then it looks at the people who match your tastes, and makes recommendations to you based on their likes and dislikes. The CDs are also available for you to purchase online. This is a great way to get ideas when reviewing music or writing a story about music and musical groups.

The more time you spend telling Firefly what you like and don't like, the more precise the recommendations get, theoretically. For the most part we found that was true, though we got a laugh when Firefly recommended Igor Stravinsky and Janis Joplin on one page, and later recommended Charlie Parker and Led Zeppelin.

Although this is a commercial application, the possibilities for it as a research tool are mind-boggling. If you're an eighth grader researching science topics,

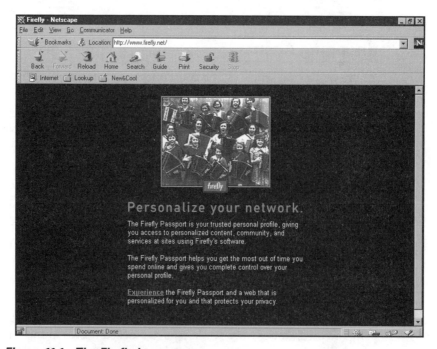

Figure 11.1 The Firefly home page.

and you use a Firefly-like recommendation agent, it could get your age, your course of studies, Web sites you have seen and liked or disliked, and your personal interests, and then recommend Web sites where you could research your homework. You would be tapping the knowledge of all the previous eighth graders who had used the service to help them with their homework through learning of their likes and dislikes.

Pretty neat, huh?

A Word Of Counsel About Agents

Agents are the next step in making the most out of the Web and the Internet, but they aren't a substitute for human intelligence. The day when a computer has as much ingenuity to attack a research problem as you do is a long way off. Treat them as tools, not as crutches.

An Overview Of The Best Search Resources

Instead of telling you which is the best search tool, we're going to give you an overview of the best general search resources. Of course, giving detailed instructions on using each one of these things would easily take up the rest of this book. Instead, we're going to give you the basics: acceptable Boolean logic, interesting and unique features, and a few extras.

Search engines index entire sites and their pages. When we give you a description of each search engine, we're also going to test each engine with three searches: the two words "zoo" and "giraffe," the name of Monty Python animator Terry Gilliam, and the phrase "continental drift." While we will not

A Word About Metasearches

A *metasearch page* is a Web page that searches several search engines at once. (Software is available that does this too, such as Quarterdeck's WebCompass.) While this can save some time, it isn't always what it's cracked up to be. The junk/treasure ratio is the same, for example, leaving you to sift through a larger heap of results to find what you're looking for.

Furthermore, metasearch pages don't always support advanced options of the engines they use to search, which means you might not be able get as specific as you'd like. Metasearch pages can be a real time saver, but don't use them in place of carefully considered and well-executed research. If you're interested in learning more about metasearches, check out **metasearch.com**, Dogpile at **www.dogpile.com**, and Inference Find at **www.inference.com/ifind/**.

evaluate all search results for relevancy, the result numbers should give you an idea of each site's scope of pages. Remember, no two search engines have the same collection of pages, so if two pages have the same number of results, it's not a guarantee that they're the exact same results.

AltaVista

altavista.digital.com

AltaVista (see Figure 11.2) reminds us of a pickup truck. It isn't flashy, and it won't win any design awards, but it's solid and reliable and will always get you there. With a large database of indexed materials, it's an essential addition to your toolbox.

Table 11.1 summarizes the Boolean operators used by AltaVista. These operators work a lot like the ones used in Deja News. Play around with 'em for a while.

Parentheses tell the search engine in which order to perform your query. For example, here are two queries that are worded exactly the same but have different parentheses:

```
bacon or (lettuce and tomato)
(bacon or lettuce) and tomato
```

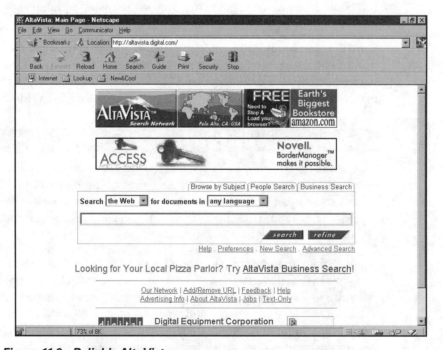

Figure 11.2   Reliable AltaVista.

Table 11.1   AltaVista's Boolean operators.

Description	Operator	Example
For simple searches:		
To include words	+	+ tomato +lettuce +bacon
To exclude words	-	+tomato -lettuce
To group words	" " or ;	"BLT sandwich" happy;chef
To search for wildcards	*	baco* finds bacon, Bacos, etc.
For advanced searches:		
Boolean operators	AND, OR, NEAR, NOT	
To group words	" " or ;	
Grouping the query	()	

The first looks for documents that include the word bacon or the words lettuce and tomato. The second looks for documents that include the word bacon or lettuce, and the word tomato.

Neat Stuff

AltaVista supports *constraining searches,* which search only a certain element of a Web page. This is like the Veronica search we discussed in the Chapter 8 that would look for only certain kinds of Gopher documents. The constraining term should be lowercase and should be followed by a colon. The constraining searches work in either simple or advanced searching. Table 11.2 is not an exhaustive list but does include the most common terms.

Table 11.2   Constraining search terms used by AltaVista.

Term	Function	Example
For Web pages:		
host:	Matches pages with a certain hostname	host:www.mindspring.com
image:	Searches for images only	image:blt.jpg
link:	Matches pages with at least one link to the URL you specify	link:www.allen.com
title:	Searches only the text of a Web page's title	title:Tara's BLT Page
For Usenet posts:		
from:	Searches from header only	from:blt@sandwich.com
subject:	Searches subject header only	subject: "I want a BLT"
newsgroup:	Searches newsgroups only	newsgroup:alt.fan.blt

The Bookmark Blues

An easy habit to get into when you're researching is to bookmark (Command+B or Ctrl+B) every Web page you find that looks interesting. Unfortunately, this practice leads to a fat bookmark file and potential frustration whenever you have to slog through it to find what you need. To avoid this problem, follow a few rules: Bookmark in groups as much as you can. The Yahoo! and Netscape sites both contain easily accessible groups of search engines; bookmark these sites instead of each search engine site. If you're not going to be using a major site often, don't bookmark it; you'll be able to find it easily enough later. If you use a page infrequently, but aren't sure you'll be able to find it later, take the four-click test: Does it take more than four clicks of your mouse to get from a general search resource to the page you're using? If it does, bookmark it.

Extras

Digital is bringing its AltaVista search technology to other places, including your computer. Click on the products button on the front page for more information.

Benchmarks

The results in Table 11.3 give you an idea of the scope of the AltaVista searches.

Excite

www.excite.com

Excite (see Figure 11.3) puts the "hyper" in hyperlink. With over 50 million Web pages indexed as of this writing and a friendly style, Excite is a good place to jumpstart your search for those rare resources.

Note that "weighting" search words increases their importance (see Table 11.4). Ordinarily, Excite assumes that all the words you're searching for are equally important. But with weight on a word, Excite looks for an instance of that

Table 11.3   AltaVista search results.

Search Words	Number Of Results
"continental drift"	4,991
zoo AND giraffe	52,955
"Terry Gilliam"	4,585

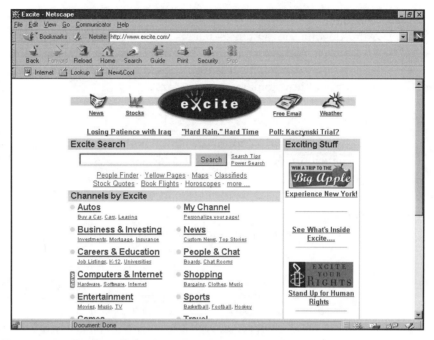

Figure 11.3   Excite reflects its name.

word first and gives pages that contain that word a high place on your search results list. You can even weigh more than one search term—the higher the number, the heavier the weight. For example, *Dilbert Dogbert^3 Catbert^9* tells Excite that Catbert is the most important search term in this query, with Dogbert a distant second and Dilbert last.

Table 11.4   Boolean operators used by Excite.

Description	Operator
For simple searches:	
To include words	+
To exclude words	-
To group words	" "
For advanced searching:	
To include words	+
To exclude words	-
To group words	" "
To weight words	^number

Neat Stuff

After posting the top ten search results, Excite generates a few words related to the topic you are searching. You can then check off any of these words to add to your search. This feature comes in handy if you are having a hard time figuring out how to narrow your search.

Extras

Excite carries the concept of one-stop shopping a bit further with a bevy of extras, including city.net (an information database covering major cities) and a people finder.

Benchmarks

Table 11.5 gives you a good idea of the scope of the Excite searches.

> **TIP**
>
> *If we've said it once we've said it a million times, and if we've said it a million times you're probably sick of it, but we'll say it again. Be specific. The more specific you are, the less time you'll spend looking through the stones to get to the diamonds.*

HotBot

www.hotbot.com

HotBot (see Figure 11.4) combines a large database with an extremely easy-to-understand interface. Though the simple interface precludes some advanced searching—you can't search for proximity matches (finding words close to each other) or partial words—this is a great search engine if you want to go, search, and get out.

Simple Searches

Simple searching in HotBot consists of a pull-down menu. Instead of typing in Boolean operators, you can choose to search for:

- **All words** (like the Boolean AND).
- **Any word** (like the Boolean OR).
- **A phrase** (like using "quotation marks").
- **A URL**.
- **A person** (This uses simple proximity searching. A search on the name Dorothy Parker would find those two words in any order—either Dorothy Parker or Parker, Dorothy.)

Table 11.5   Excite search results.

Search Words	Number Of Results
"continental drift"	2,060
+zoo +giraffe	844
"Terry Gilliam"	2,250

- **Date range** (last week, month, etc.).
- **Continent** (general continents, with North America split into domain type).
- **Media type** (image, audio, video, Shockwave).

Advanced Searches

If you don't like the simple interface of HotBot, click on the SuperSearch button underneath the Modify button. The expert option allows the use of some Boolean logic and also allows for limiting searches by domain name, specific dates (day, month, and year), and extra media types such as VRML and ActiveX.

Benchmarks

The results in Table 11.6 give you a good idea of the scope of the HotBot searches.

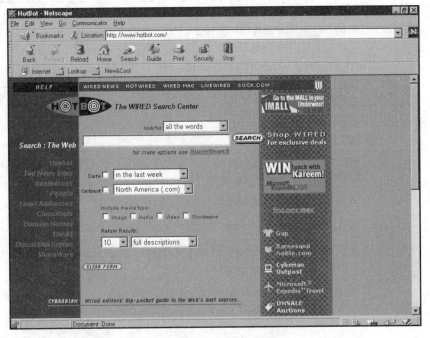

Figure 11.4   HotBot's easy-to-understand interface.

Table 11.6   HotBot search results.

Search Words	Number Of Results
phrase: continental drift	4,509
all the words: zoo giraffe	2,262
the person: Terry Gilliam	4,282

TIP

Don't underestimate the value of a well-turned phrase; keep shifting your words around until you get the results you want. Last fall Tara was searching the Internet for demo information on the computer game "Destiny." (She can't do research all the time, you know.) The word "Destiny" by itself brought way too many results. "Destiny demo" didn't work, either. However, "demo for Destiny" did the trick—and let her know that no demo was available at that time. Ah, well...back to "Colonization."

Infoseek

www.infoseek.com

One of our favorite sportscasters often uses the phrase "Whoa, Nelly!" We suspect you might let out a couple of "Whoa Nellys," too, when you see what Infoseek (see Figure 11.5) has to offer. Unfortunately, the database isn't as extensive as some of the other search engines out there, because this site goes all-out to make everything you need easily available.

Simple And Advanced Searching

Table 11.7 summarizes the Boolean operators used by Infoseek for simple and advanced searches.

Neat Stuff

When entering search words, a menu lets you check off what areas of the Internet you can search. They are:

- **The Web.** Webspace.
- **Usenet Newsgroups.** Archives of Usenet postings.
- **Company Directory.** Home pages, contact information, and stock ticker information by company.
- **News.** News stories from the past month.

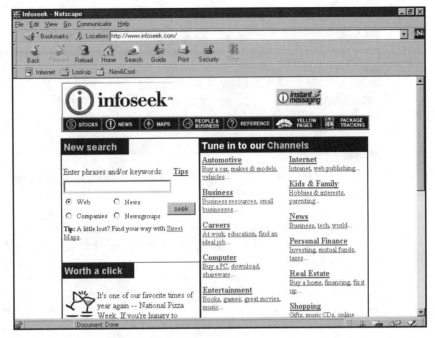

Figure 11.5   Whoa, Nelly! It's Infoseek.

Extras

Infoseek offers a lot of extras. Among them is a browsable topic index, a link to the BigYellow Yellow Pages, and personalized news. You can also check out Infoseek Worldwide, available in 10 different countries and written in the indigenous language.

Benchmarks

The results in Table 11.8 give you an idea of the scope of the Infoseek searches.

Table 11.7   Boolean operators used by Infoseek.

Description	Operator	Example
To include words	+	
To exclude words	-	
To group words	" "	
To find words between the words	-	**Louisa-Alcott** finds both Louisa Alcott and Louisa May Alcott.
To find words within 100 words of each other	[]	**[little wives]** finds Little Women and Good Wives, among other things.

Table 11.8   Infoseek search results.

Search Words	Number Of Results
"continental drift"	858
+zoo +giraffe	645
"Terry Gilliam"	50,103

TIP

Don't get stuck in a rut. We're assuming that you'll at least experiment with all the search resources in this chapter, but eventually you'll settle down to using one or two most of the time. That's fine, but be sure to periodically break your habits and try a different resource. These search engines are constantly refining, updating, and enhancing their tools. Don't miss out on their offerings just because you enjoy your old habits too much.

Snap!

home.snap.com/

A relative newcomer on the scene, Snap! (see Figure 11.6) gives you an extra twist on searching the Web by allowing you to refine your search by subject category in addition to performing whole-Web searches. You can enter a word and select a subject field such as Computing, Travel, and Shopping from the scroll bar to narrow your search.

Extras

Snap! gives you special search functions to find software, yellow and white page listings, e-mail addresses, and online events. For example, to find multimedia software for your PC, click on "Software" under the initial search field box. You will then be transferred to a page with three fields. Enter your word in the first field, choose a category (multimedia) from the second field (a scroll bar), and a platform (Windows) from the third. Click on "Go" and voilà! You're off to the races.

You can also browse the links in each section by pressing "Directory" right above the search dialog box and then clicking on the topic of your choice. The main page also has a special weather search function—just enter your ZIP code and Snap! returns both next-day and five-day forecasts.

Benchmarks

You can see Snap!'s performance in Table 11.9.

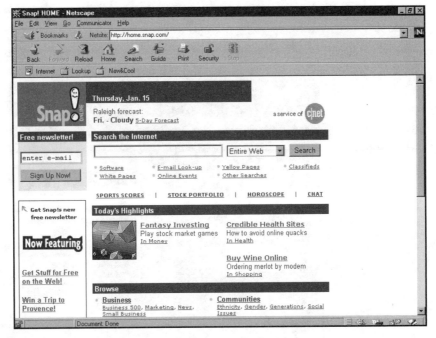

Figure 11.6   Snap! lets your refine your search.

Lycos

www.lycos.com

We have fond memories of Lycos (see Figure 11.7) from the first days of Web browsing. Lycos maintains a distinction to us as the older search engine that's made a smooth evolution into today's much more competitive world of search engines.

Simple And Advanced Searching

Check out Table 11.10 for the Boolean operators used by Lycos.

Table 11.9   Snap! search results.

Search Words	Number Of Results
"continental drift"	860
+ zoo + giraffe	59,460
"Terry Gilliam"	50

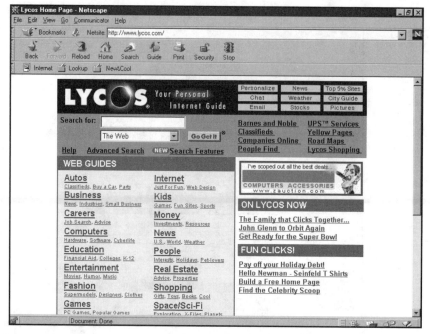

Figure 11.7   Old-timer Lycos has kept itself up-to-date.

Neat Stuff

By clicking on Advanced Search, you can narrow your search to sites, sounds, or pictures.

Extras

Lycos also has a ton of extras, including Point Communications's Top 5% Sites of the Web, CityGuide, a browsable topic list, and a People Find page. You can even track your UPS package or favorite stock from this site.

Table 11.10   Boolean operators used by Lycos.

Description	Operator	Example
To add words	+	
To exclude words	-	
For an exact match	.	**moon**. gets moon, but not moonlight, moonstruck, etc.
For searching word fragments	$	**moon$** gets moonlight, moondance, etc.

Benchmarks

Table 11.11 gives you a good idea of the scope of the Lycos searches.

Send yourself some mail. If you find a site that has a lot of information you need, sometimes it's better to mail it to yourself than to try to write it all down. Under the File menu in Netscape Navigator, choose Mail Document. A mail window pops up with the Web page as an attachment. Type your e-mail address in the To: field, and the page will be routed to your mailbox. You can even save a Web page to your hard drive.

Northern Light

www.nlsearch.com/

Northern Light's basic functions are similar to the other search engines—enter a term and limit it to the World Wide Web or search all online resources. An additional constraining resource is Northern Light's "Special Collection," which offers over 1,800 online magazines, newswires, and other resources not accessed by other search engines (see Figure 11.8). This collection is fee-based, but may be worth the investment if you are searching for hard-to-find information. Be sure to look out for special Features of the Week, such as free access to some special collection articles when accessed through the Northern Light site.

Extras

After Northern Light returns your search results, you can choose from special "folders" listed to the left of the results listing. Clicking on one of the folders automatically brings you to a page with a more narrow selection of URLs related to your term. For example, a search on arthritis may return folders such as "Lyme Disease" or "Autoimmune". Click on a folder to see the subset of URLs you find most relevant to your needs.

Table 11.11   Lycos search results.

Search Words	Number Of Results
"continental drift"	588
+zoo +giraffe	213
"Terry Gilliam"	550

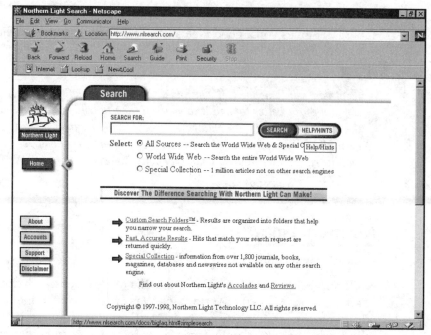

Figure 11.8   Northern Light also offers a fee-based Special Collection of resources.

Benchmarks

The results in Table 11.12 demonstrate the depth of Northern Light's resources.

Open Text Index

index.opentext.net/

The Open Text Index (see Figure 11.9) has a simple interface—just type in a few words, use the drop-down menu to indicate whether you're searching for all the words in any order or the phrase, and you're off. While this simplicity may appeal to bare neophytes, we think you'll find the power search a more flexible, appealing option.

Table 11.12   Northern Light's search results.

Search Words	Number Of Results
"continental drift"	3,114
zoo AND giraffe	2,144
"Terry Gilliam"	2,629

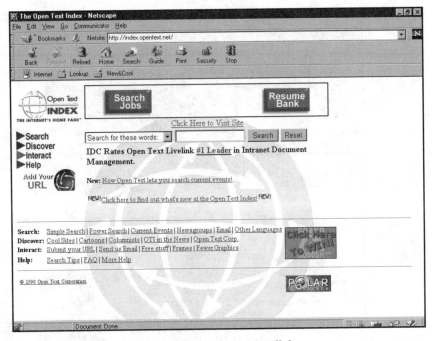

Figure 11.9   The Open Text Index gives you simplicity.

Advanced Searching (Power Search)

Open Text's advanced searching looks a little like a stack of HotBot query boxes. As you see from Figure 11.10, you enter your search word or phrase in the blank box, use a pull-down box to indicate where to search for it (whether that be Anywhere, Page Summary, Page Title, First Level Headings, or URL), and use another pull-down box for Boolean operators—AND, OR, BUT, NOT, NEAR, and FOLLOWED BY. NEAR looks for the search word within 80 characters either before or after the search word on the previous line. FOLLOWED BY looks for the search word within 80 characters after the search word on the previous line.

If you're not comfortable with Boolean phrasing, don't use more than a couple of the pull-down boxes; you can't use parentheses to group Boolean expressions, and the computer will read the expression you enter strictly from left to right. If you rely heavily on grouping your search expressions in parentheses, then using several pull-down boxes could change the meaning of your search.

Extras

Open Text's extras include an e-mail address search, Cool Sites, Cartoons, and Columnists, among other things.

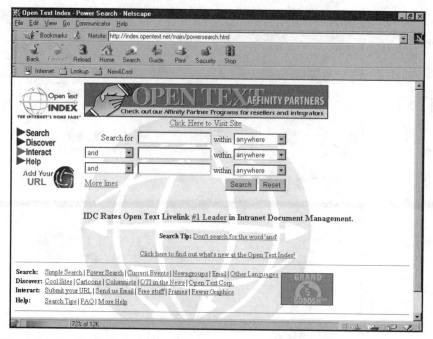

Figure 11.10   Open Text Power Search.

Benchmarks

The results in Table 11.13 give you a good idea of the scope of the Open Text searches.

Table 11.13   Open Text search results.

Search Words	Number Of Results
search for this phrase: continental drift	296
search for all the words: zoo giraffe	167
search for this phrase: Terry Gilliam	133

Do You Want To Go Backward?

Sometimes when you're doing research, you may want to take a step in a different direction—or even do a 180-degree turnaround. If you can't find the information you need by performing a forward search, pick the one or two sites that have come closest to what you need and do a backwards search on them. A backwards search finds all the sites that link to a URL you indicate.

The easiest way to do this is with WebCrawler. Click on the Special icon at the top of the WebCrawler screen, and choose Backwards Surf on the screen that follows. Type the URL of the page in the box, and WebCrawler searches its database and returns a list of the pages that link to the URL you entered.

WebCrawler does have a fairly small database, so you might want to backwards surf using AltaVista's constraining keyword, *link*: Go to the AltaVista search page and type **link:(URL)** and it'll give you a list of all sites linking to the Web page you indicate. This is a great way to find sites that are compilations of the kind of information you're looking for or sites with similar information. You can do this with HotBot, too...just choose "Links to this URL" in the "look for" pull-down menu.

WebCrawler

www.webcrawler.com

Ah, WebCrawler, WebCrawler, how fondly we remember thee from when thy URL was on an academic site and about three zillion characters long. (Now it's a much-easier-to-remember—**www.webcrawler.com**.) Unfortunately, what used to be the greatest search engine on the Internet has not aged well—it has a small database and its search returns are limited. However, if you're searching for a popular topic or set of keywords, this might be a benefit since you'll have fewer results to choose from. Furthermore, WebCrawler (see Figure 11.11) goes out of its way to be friendly and easy to use.

Searching

WebCrawler uses the Boolean operators AND, OR, NOT, ADJ, and NEAR/X. ADJ searches for words next to each other; *brass ADJ giraffe* would find brass giraffe, but not giraffe brass. NEAR/X, where X is a number, finds words within a certain number of words to each other; *ankle NEAR/10 spur* would find ankle's painful spur, ankle spur, and so on. Table 11.14 shows a few other Boolean operators.

Table 11.14   Other Boolean operators used by WebCrawler.

Description	Operator
Phrases	" "
Grouping the query	()

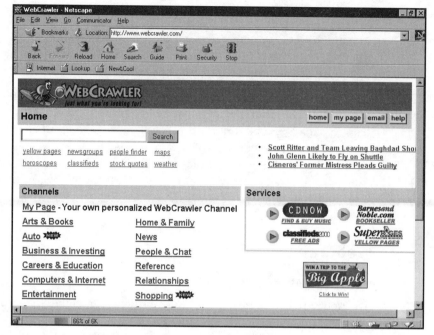

Figure 11.11   WebCrawler is still a friendly place.

Neat Stuff

Clickable buttons at the top of WebCrawler's screen add some neat function-ality to WebCrawler, including backwards surfing and random URL jumping.

Extras

WebCrawler has a variety of extras, including a Best of the Net section and a browsable topic list.

Benchmarks

The results in Table 11.15 give you an idea of the scope of the WebCrawler searches.

Table 11.15   WebCrawler search results.

Search Words	Number Of Results
"continental drift"	105
Zoo and giraffe	84
"Terry Gilliam"	123

Edited Search Engines

Edited search engines are the ones that filter materials before you see them. They may choose to exclude sites that contain objectionable material, or they may choose to include only sites that they consider good. They use a variety of criteria to judge possible sites, including quality of material on the site and the amount of material available on the site.

Magellan

magellan.mckinley.com

The largest and best of these sites is Magellan (see Figure 11.12). In addition to a regular database of sites, Magellan also includes a database of reviewed sites that you can search separately. You search by keyword and can narrow your search by searching for the quality of sites. (Magellan rates sites by giving them one to four stars; you can indicate in your search that you wish only to see sites that received better than two stars.)

You can also look for the green light—Magellan's indication that the site is viewable by an all-ages audience. Over and above that, Magellan strives to

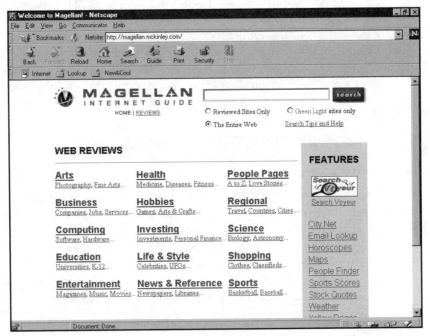

Figure 11.12   Magellan is the biggest and the best edited search engine.

keep its database family-oriented by refusing to list material that relates to hate groups, pornography, or pedophilia.

Its search options are very much like the others we've been talking about—include words with a plus sign (+), exclude words with a minus sign (-).

Magellan offers you some time savings if you're searching for a common topic by pre-reviewing sites so you don't have to. However, if you're looking for something obscure, this is not the resource you should be using. Go elsewhere.

Hierarchical Subject Indices

Hierarchical subject indices focus on giving you a browsable topic list, not on indexing all the words of a Web page. The most famous index on the Internet is probably Yahoo!, but two other good ones are The Argus Clearinghouse and the Virtual Library.

The Argus Clearinghouse

www.clearinghouse.net

This index is unusual in that it doesn't list individual site resources. Instead, it's an index of topical guides—sites that compile information on one particular subject or idea. Remember when we told you it was better to search a specialty index when you're searching for a very specific topic? You probably thought to yourself, "Great, but where do I find the specialty indexes?" Argus is a good place to start. Topic guides are rated and free of charge to end users (it's one of the requirements for inclusion in the Clearinghouse).

The World Wide Web Virtual Library

www.w3.org/vl/

The WWW Virtual Library (see Figure 11.13) is one of the oldest things on the Web. It was created in 1991 to keep track of the development of the Web, which had just been created by Tim Berners-Lee. (And if "He created the World Wide Web" isn't a *Jeopardy* answer one day, we're gonna be miffed.) You can view the topic list in alphabetical order or by library category. You can even get a "top ten topics" listing. Some of the entries are short, and some are mind-bogglingly extensive—the subjects are maintained by volunteers so what you get may vary a little, but it's still fun to poke around and see what you might turn over.

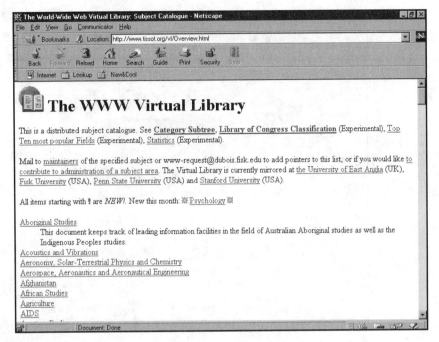

Figure 11.13   The World Wide Web Virtual Library.

Yahoo!

www.yahoo.com

Yahoo! (see Figure 11.14) represents one of the first attempts that we know of to index the Internet, and it's the one we still turn to when we have a quick question or want to search for a company's Web site. That's its primary strength; everybody knows about it, and practically everybody is sure to have their site listed with Yahoo! Over time it has spun off other sites. (The kid's version of Yahoo!, Yahooligans, is at **www.yahooligans.com**. Yahoo! Canada, as mentioned elsewhere, can be found at **www.yahoo.ca**, and so on.)

If you need a fast take on where a popular company is online, or an overview of sites, Yahoo! is a good place to start. You can't find everything here, but you can find enough so that it's a good way to start searching.

Yahoo! offers a search box that uses the Boolean AND, so drop a few words in there and see what happens.

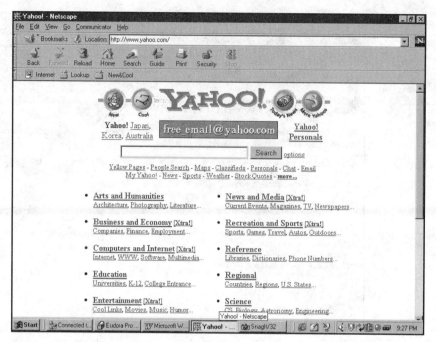

Figure 11.14   Yahoo! is great for finding companies.

TIP

A word of warning: If Yahoo! can't find what you're looking for in its database, it automatically goes to AltaVista and searches there. This can get annoying, especially when you're searching for something that could yield bunches of hits on a large general search engine. Watch the status bar at the bottom of Navigator. If it says "av.yahoo.com contacted, waiting for reply...," then Yahoo! has gone to talk to AltaVista. Click on Navigator's Stop button if you don't want search results from AltaVista.

Yahoo! also has many, many extras, including a good group listing of search engines and other lookup-type resources like phone book indexes. Just because of the groupings of resources it has, it's probably worthy of a bookmark.

Moving On

The size and complexity of the Internet can be confusing, and that's using a nice word. The search engines designed to take some of the complexity out of using the Internet can also be confusing.

The best way to approach using these sites is to just work with them. Experiment. Play. Horse around. Enter weird word combinations like *lobster AND "roller coaster"* and see what happens. Get familiar with the interfaces, and don't be intimidated by the sheer amount of material you may find.

One day it will pay off. Your mom, a technical librarian, will call you and say, "I can't get to the Government Printing Office!" You'll cruise over to Yahoo!, do a quick sweep for the GPO, and find the URL she's using. You'll try to use it and it won't work for you either. So you'll go over to AltaVista, do a search for + *"Government Printing Office" +GPO*, look at a couple of URLs, check one that works, and in a few minutes you'll be poking around the Federal Register and reading the URL off the screen to your mom. Your mom will thank you profusely. And you will feel extremely cool.

Of course, being your mom, she'll brag on you. So then your cousin calls wanting help with a report on stocks she's doing for her Economics class. Then your spouse will want help finding trademark information for his corporation. Then your third grade teacher—no, we're just kidding, but you'll find as you help people (and yourself) that the questions will get tougher, and a lot of them will focus on very specific kinds of research.

The next few chapters cover specific research needs—from domestic and international government information online to resources for finding people and businesses to resources specifically for student-types. Let's start out with Uncle Sam.

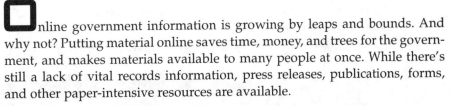

CHAPTER 12

Domestic Government Information Online

☐nline government information is growing by leaps and bounds. And why not? Putting material online saves time, money, and trees for the government, and makes materials available to many people at once. While there's still a lack of vital records information, press releases, publications, forms, and other paper-intensive resources are available.

Government information online puts some real punch behind the old saying, "Knowledge is power." Now, more than ever, there's an unparalleled opportunity for the citizenry of this country to participate in a real democracy—by and for the people—online. If your research requires census information, press releases from the White House, a summary of how your Congressional representative voted last year, or (eek!) a tax form, this chapter is for you.

> ### TIP
>
> *Please note that while all of the resources in this chapter provide government information, they are not all maintained by the governing bodies. Keep that in mind when considering information you acquire from them.*

Government Information By State

Most states maintain comprehensive Web sites that have tons of information about political leaders, state agencies, and updates on issues that are important to that state. The amount and variety of information available from site to site may make your first foray confusing, but a little patience will yield enough data to give your daughter's seventh grade essay on Texas state symbols an A+, or get you that grant to further analyze the distribution of plant species in the Colorado Rockies.

Reaching Individual States

You can go to most states' home pages by typing **www.state.*pc*.us**, where *pc* is the two-letter postal code of the state you're looking for. For example, try Alaska by typing **www.state.ak.us**, or Wyoming by typing **www.state.wy.us** (see Figure 12.1). If you do a quick survey, you'll find that most state home pages carry a core of information on the names, addresses, and e-mail addresses of the governor, lieutenant governor, Congress members, as well as contact information for many state-level departments and agencies. The depth of coverage and searchability varies quite a bit, however, as does the emphasis on details such as natural resources, tourist information, or business opportunities.

Take, for instance, the Kentucky home page at **www.state.ky.us**. It offers information ranging from state park locations to educational and business opportunities (see Figure 12.2). Suppose you are doing research on a story about business development opportunities in Kentucky and upstate New York and

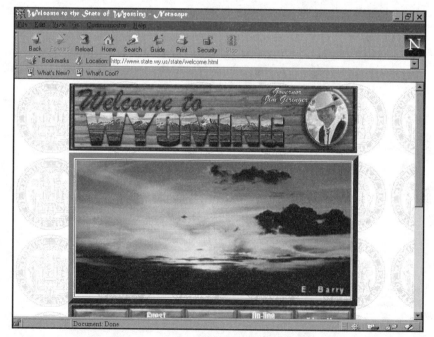

Figure 12.1 Check out the great state of Wyoming...online!

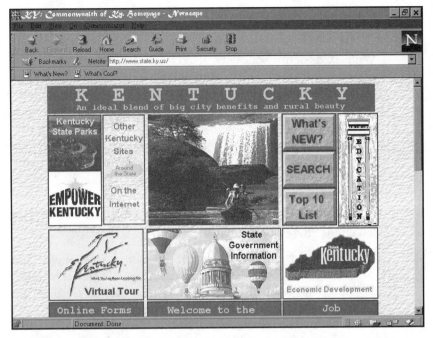

Figure 12.2   Kentucky has a huge amount of material online.

want to see which state has the most attractive incentives. You can go to the Kentucky site, click on Kentucky Cabinet for Economic Development, and pull up the Strategic Plan for Economic Development online. Then you could go over to New York, at **www.state.ny.us**, click on Citizen's Access to State Government, and navigate the Empire State Development section.

Most state sites also feature legislative bill tracing options, which allow you to check the status of a bill passing through the legislature with one or two mouse clicks. For example, North Carolina's Web page, at **www.state.nc.us** gives the lowdown on bills, committees, ranking members, and meeting times and places under the North Carolina General Assembly heading.

As another example, Colorado (**www.state.co.us**) is constructing a section that promotes citizen access to state government by offering everything ranging from voter and car registration to current events postings and state tax schedules. Can you imagine a citizen having access to so much information without having to set foot in long bureaucratic lines?

Compilations Of State Information

Individual sites are great, but sometimes you want the whole enchilada. Luckily there are some great sites that let you do extensive state browsing without typing in lots of URLs.

National Conference Of State Legislatures
www.ncsl.org

While parts of this site are targeted toward state legislators and staff, students of state government will find invaluable information about policy making and citizen involvement on every page. Resources include state-federal issue summaries, analyses of controversies such as health care and budget reconciliation, and information about individual state legislatures. The site is fully searchable by keyword, including the large policy issues database that covers everything from education and agriculture topics to fiscal planning and labor debates.

The Library Of Congress, State, And Local Governments Site
lcweb.loc.gov/global/state/stategov.html

Part of a larger Library of Congress presence, this site includes links to the National Conference of State Legislatures and Public Technology Inc., as well as maps of all states and Washington, D.C. Another excellent resource for students of economics and the political process is the University of Virginia Regional Economic Information System (REIS) link on this site. REIS catalogs several variables of economic data for metropolitan, county, and state areas from 1969 to 1994. Variables such as personal income, farm expenditures, and part-time employment levels can be viewed by location, variable, or year.

Now that you know how to get to the state resources online, how about trying to hook a fish that's a little bit bigger? Say, the size of an entire country?

Finding Federal Government Resources Online

Ever tried to find out the results of that Environmental Impact Survey the EPA, the Bureau of Land Management, and a host of oil companies were squabbling over? The Internet can help. But a warning: Be careful! Even though the federal government is positively huge, and government sites are almost an online embarrassment of riches, getting really specific at first cut may not be helpful because resource listings can be hard to find at a micro-level, and because there are so many departments and so many agencies and so many organizations. (We know this breaks one of our friendly suggestions for Internet research, but consider this the exception that proves the rule.) Instead of getting as narrow as possible right off the bat, try a couple of the following compilations first for the smaller federal institutions; then try individual institutional pages for larger agencies like the IRS and the postal service.

Agencies

Eek! There are zillions of federal agencies on the Net! How do you find the one you need? We have never been able to find the one site that has a comprehensive and friendly overview of the federal government online, but the following come pretty close.

FedWorld

www.fedworld.gov

FedWorld is accessible as a regular Web page or through Telnet or FTP. This site has a generous amount of data on the Supreme Court via its FedWorld/FLITE Supreme Court database, which allows a full text or name search of 7,407 Supreme Court decisions from 1937 to 1975. But that's only the beginning! You can also get information on the U.S. Customs Service, whether for travel tips or to report smuggling, online tax forms complete with instructions, and instant access to FedWorld's bibliographic database of over 1.6 million government documents dating back to the 1920s. For a fee you can also use the Davis-Bacon Act database of wage/job information.

The Government Information Exchange (GIX)

www.info.gov

This site not only connects you to the Federal Directory and Yellow Pages, but it also can direct you to Electronic Shopping Networks and Intergovernmental Collaboration sites. Some of these intergovernmental topics will take you off-site, so don't be disconcerted when you see the farewell message from GIX. You can return with a click of Navigator's Back button and continue to look through job listings, health tips, and a comprehensive list of federal agencies organized by agency name (CIA, FDIC) or service category (benefits, grants).

Infomine

lib-www.ucr.edu/govpub

This enormous site is bound to please even the person researching the most arcane subject. Well-organized, the contents of this site are searchable by subject, keyword, and title; or you can go to the Table of Contents and press the relevant letter or number of your issue heading, from Accounting to Zoology. Infomine also posts new additions from the past 20 days in a special What's New? section. And you won't find only federal resources here—indexed sites include state and international level government documents as well as documents largely unrelated to the political and economic scene. Be prepared for

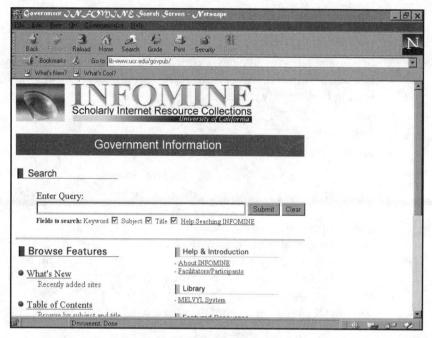

Figure 12.3   Infomine's resources are too extensive to absorb in just one visit.

Infomine's size—trying to see every listed document in one sitting is a bit like trying to look at every Smithsonian exhibit in one day (see Figure 12.3).

Federal Bulletin Boards

fedbbs.access.gpo.gov

The Federal Bulletin Boards is a free bulletin board service set up on the Web by the Superintendent of Documents at the U.S. Government Printing Office. You can download all file documents for free, and the service also runs on FTP and Telnet modes. Files are available on agencies and departments as diverse as the Food and Drug Administration, the Department of State, the Merit Systems Protection Board, and the Federal Labor Relations Authority. You can also get Congressional committee reports and Supreme Court opinions and files.

U.S. Business Advisor Search Of GovBot Database

www.business.gov/Search_Online.html

If you have a particular interest in government and business relations, try this site. You can insert query terms into the search engine and limit the number of documents you want retrieved. Two of the most attractive features of this site are the questions-and-answers section and the how-to section. Under questions and answers you can readily find answers to common business challenges straight from the source agency—the Small Business Administration, the Social Security Administration, or the Federal Communications Commission. Or you can go to the how-to page and find out how to get disaster assistance, business forms, or passports, again from the agencies in charge of those concerns.

Government Information And Research Links Site

www.podesta.com/links.html

Want to find out how much money was allocated by the Bureau of Land Management to local governments for tax-exempt lands? You could also find out about the Emergency Review Team on the Wild Horse and Burro Program or explore the Forest Service's Public Involvement in the National Environmental Policy Act page. This site also has downloadable extras, such as the multimedia version of the Northwest Forest Plan, complete with running instructions. Even above and beyond the land management links, this is a great site for databases, statistics, agency press releases, and general information about federal agencies.

The University Of Michigan Documents Center

www.lib.umich.edu/libhome/Documents.center/govweb.html

The University of Michigan is something of a legend in the areas of data collection and storage, and this site, like Infomine, will probably be a bit overwhelming at first. The Federal Government section has subheadings from general information (bibliographies, budgets, grants, historic documents—you name it) to Agency Directories. The site is pretty well-organized, and if you give yourself some time, you should be able to find most of what you want on this site—even in areas beyond the U.S. federal government, such as international organizations and local citizens' guides. Some areas are searchable by an onsite engine, such as the Bibliographies of U.S. Government Publications section. Plug in a keyword, title, author, or date and, voilà!; you'll land enough data to keep you busy for the next several months.

A Few Examples Of The Larger Government Sites

You're probably saying to yourself right now, "All these indexes are very interesting, but I want to get my mitts on some real information!" Well, strap yourself in and let's take a little tour of some major federal fogdogs in cyberspace.

The U.S. Senate

www.senate.gov

The Senate site allows you to explore the Senate directory by state or name, and puts you right on a senator's home page if she or he has one. Like the state sites, each senator's page contains a core of information that includes office location, telephone, fax, and e-mail information, internships, and a biography. Other highlights include procedures for U.S. military academy nominations, Washington, D.C., tours, and ordering information for U.S. flags. The main section of the Senate site also includes leadership, class membership, committees, history and artwork, and how to visit the Senate while in session.

The U.S. House Of Representatives

www.house.gov

Similar in structure to the Senate site, the House site also includes a section called "Empowering the Citizen," which gives you the Code of Federal Regulations, National Performance Reviews, and the "Washington Waste Watch," which will direct you to agency sites and online help.

TIP

When writing to the president or to one of your congressional representatives, you must include your name and a physical return address to assure any type of response, and form letters on e-mail generally generate a "thank you" note from an autoresponder rather than an actual human. Some congressfolks are more likely to read and respond to their e-mail than others. When you feel strongly about a particular issue, your best bet is still to make contact the old-fashioned way—via phone or paper letter.

The White House

www.whitehouse.gov

The site shows you how to contact the president and vice president by e-mail or regular mail. There's also the "White House for Kids," a tour guided by Socks, the White House cat, and aimed at the primary school set. There is also an Interactive Citizens' Handbook (see Figure 12.4) that allows you to search this site and a Government Information Locator Service that, when completed, will allow you to find all government information, on or off the Internet.

TIP

*If you want to keep up with the day-to-day activities of the White House, you can get White House press briefings via the White House summaries list. This list provides daily summaries of White House press releases. To subscribe, send a message to **majordomo@reeusda.gov**. In the body type **subscribe wh-summary**. (If you're thinking that this looks like one of the mailing lists we covered back in Chapter 6, you're right!) Back issues and specific documents are available as well.*

Figure 12.4 **The Interactive Citizens' Handbook on the White House Web site gives you lots of links to federal resources.**

The Internal Revenue Service

www.irs.ustreas.gov

Structured in a newspaper format, *The Digital Daily*, this site lists tax statistics and information, how to file electronically, an IRS newsstand, and printable forms and publications.

The U.S. Postal Service

www.usps.gov

Another narrowly targeted site, the USPS contains a ZIP+4 search engine, addressing tips, postage rates, and even State Department passport information. If you send a lot of overnight mail, you'll also be interested in their online Express Mail tracking service.

The Social Security Administration

www.ssa.gov

The SSA has a lot of neat features. You can run a Personal Earnings and Benefits Estimate statement, find out about Disability Redesign progress, and learn how to report Social Security fraud; there's even background on the agency itself. The site is available in Spanish as well as English.

Social Security Death Index

www.ancestry.com/ssdi/advanced.htm

This site is a boon to genealogists everywhere. Using a person's name you can establish his birth date, when and where he or she died, and final benefit payment information.

Keeping Up With The Clintons (And The Gingriches And The Gores...)

You now have the tools to find out about the big institutions in your state and at the national level—thousands of documents concerning who did what and how it should be done. But another consideration is keeping an eye on day-to-day changes and breaking stories in the world of politics and governmental concerns. It's easier than it used to be, thanks to the Internet. There's a variety of materials available to keep you informed about what's going on in Washington and around the country. These are just a few.

The Federal Register

www.access.gpo.gov/su_docs/aces/aces140.html

A publication of the Government Printing Office (GPO), the Federal Register lets you select an issue and research it thoroughly while getting the most up-to-date information available. You can search sections (Presidential Documents, Reader Aids, Proposed Rules, etc.) and use Boolean functions and wildcard characters. You can even choose the amount of material you want to look at with each search, up to 200 documents at a time.

C-SPAN

www.c-span.org

Want to augment what you've found on the Senate and House sites? Go to this site while the Congress is in session and get live House and Senate audio (see Figure 12.5). C-SPAN also posts the latest information on election campaigns, Congressional activity, and political debates. Another audio feature is the Weekly Radio Journal. If you think you've missed an interesting article from a month ago, the site maintains an easily accessible features archive.

Figure 12.5   C-SPAN: Congressional news straight from the horse's mouth.

CNN/Time All Politics

www.allpolitics.com

This site offers information about current government issues from "Best Bytes" news briefs to full-text headline stories. While not as comprehensive as the other government servers, All Politics is strong on up-to-the-moment issues and breaking stories from Washington. The site also has a variety of games that allow you to have fun while learning about issues such as campaign strategy, the elections process, and Congressional procedures. A Special Reports section has more in-depth coverage of major stories such as the presidential fundraising probes.

Getting Involved

This isn't exactly within the realm of "research," but we don't feel it would be fair to write a whole chapter on government information online and not give you a few pointers on how you can get involved. We can't all be Jimmy Carter, but we can be active in our government's processes. It's our responsibility as citizens to participate in deciding the policies of our country, whether it's researching a speech to give to your town council or sending a letter to your senator. The Internet removes the excuse of "it's too hard" or "there's no information," so grab that mouse and get going!

Political Parties Online

Ever wondered about your party's platform? Ever been curious about what Ross Perot really means by "reform"? Wonder no more—many parties have a presence on the Net, and most of these sites outline their platforms, rules, and histories. Of course, there are over a dozen parties on the Internet and what follows is just a sample of what's out there. The inclusion of these four is by no means meant to slight the other parties on or offline, but as you're probably seeing by now, the Net is so vast that you have to limit yourself to small bites at a time.

The Democratic Party

www.democrats.org

Updated daily, this site features News Flashes, scheduled candidate photo ops, and issues involving the Democratic party community. And in the interest of getting you involved, the site makes it easy to join the Democratic National Committee (DNC), volunteer, or register to vote on the Get Active! page. The Democratic Party page also gives you the opportunity to subscribe to DNC online news, which will send press briefings and releases directly to your e-mail box. They also elaborate on issues critical to the Democratic party and post speeches by important Democratic political figures.

Republican National Committee

www.rnc.org

Interested in a different perspective? Visit the Republican party's Main Street location. The RNC site includes commentary on political players, the RNC platform, and opportunities to subscribe to several Republican mailing lists. The GOP newsstand on site includes, News Releases, Congressional Session reports, and RNC "Talking Points." This site also has an array of links to politically related Web sites.

Libertarian Party

www.lp.org

The Libertarians have a particularly strong outline of their party's philosophy, historical roots, and positions on different issues. They also list membership information and current activities, and they have an onsite quiz that lets you evaluate your ideological position on a political map. Additionally, the

Libertarian party dedicates a page to detailing the party's position on censorship on and off of the Net, and gives links to related sites and the Libertarian party archives.

The Reform Party

www.reformparty.org

This site details the principles of reform which are the basis of the Reform party, featuring online headquarters and state-by-state information (via a click-sensitive map or text lists). You can quickly find the locations of state offices, phone and fax numbers, and the composition of executive committees and meeting agendas. Like the other parties, the Reform party lets you know how you can lend your support through volunteering or registering as a member, but it takes the interactivity one step further. The Interactive Gallery allows you to participate in an online chat room, download images, send in your feedback, and get audio and video clips.

Getting The Skinny: Political Information And Activism Online

Want to kick-start your journey into political activism? Take a gander at these sites.

Vote Smart

www.vote-smart.org

Vote Smart is a self-described "one-stop shopping center for political information," and the site is researcher-assisted (complete with an 800 number). Candidate speeches, gubernatorial, congressional, and state legislative races are all listed by state. Biographical and contact information is included for state legislators, and if that isn't enough you can also find out about political campaigns, issue information, and educational and reference resources. Vote Smart also has the buzz on over 13,000 political leaders (see Figure 12.6). The Links Where You Can Participate section gets you in the mood for active citizenship by giving you quizzes, opinion polls, and access to newsgroups. And if you're feeling a bit too serious, you can look into Vote Smart's archive of political humor and campaign satire.

eVote

www.evote.com

eVote makes it easy for you to receive both the latest information on political issues and get involved. After you scan its 24-hour coverage of U.S. federal

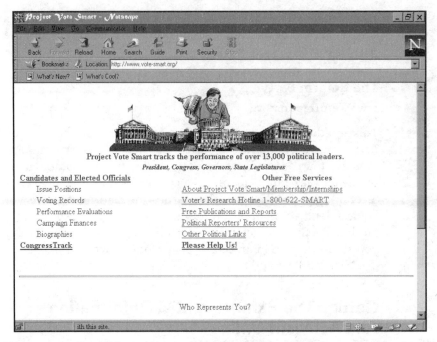

Figure 12.6   From biggest to smallest, Vote Smart has information on almost all of the presidential candidates.

and state government news, you can cruise over to the eVote Conference Center and sound off on the scandal of the day. Looking for some numbers to back up your school report? eVote has a polling station which achieved the first Internet polls to yield results as accurate as the more traditional national polls. You'll also find an Election Library and dozens of political cartoons to pass the time between major votes.

Zipper

www.voxpop.org/zipper

Not entirely sure who your elusive second senator is? Wondering what ever happened to that congressperson from District Four? Zipper gives you immediate access to this information with an 85 percent accuracy rate. Just put your ZIP code into the query box, and Zipper will give you information on your senators and representatives. It also shows you how to send an Internet telegram (Netgram) to a whole Congressional committee, and you can sound off on a controversial issue on the Weekly Views page.

The Electronic Frontier Foundation
www.eff.org

This site does not readily fit into any of the above categories. A nonprofit organization dedicated to protecting free expression as well as responsibility in media, the EFF maintains current news and archives on freedom of speech and privacy issues. As controversial as these subjects are, we can't discount EFF's importance in preserving the freedom of cyberspace. After all, one of the reasons that the Net is so useful for finding and using information is that there are so few restrictions beyond common courtesy on what you can post and circulate. Be sure to drop by (see Figure 12.7).

Contacting The Government Online

As you can already see from this chapter, an increasing number of political and administrative officials are getting online contact addresses. Most of the sites, such as the Senate, House, and White House, have pages with their members' e-mail addresses. If you still can't find what you're looking for, try one of these.

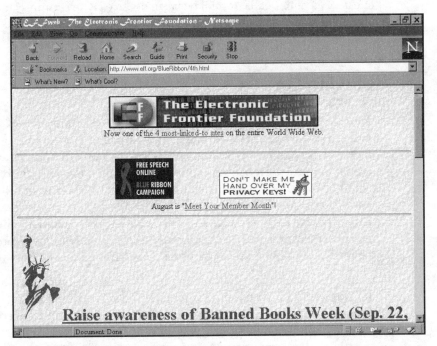

Figure 12.7   Check the Electronic Frontier Foundation to keep up with the state of freedom on the Internet.

ACFC Congressional E-mailer

www.erols.com/afc/acfc/em-cong.htm

You can e-mail House and Senate representatives, president or vice president from this straightforward site. Remember that all messages will be sent from your e-mail address. Not sure how to approach a legislator by e-mail? This page has brief tips on effective communication with your political leaders.

Mr. Smith E-mails Washington And The Media

www.mrsmith.com

Want to e-mail Washington? You'll find e-mail addresses for every member of the 105th Congress, organized by state, along with addresses for the president and vice president. There is also a text copy of the U.S. Constitution. And if you feel strongly about an issue and want to tell the world, you can e-mail most of the major print media from this site as well, including newspapers and magazines dealing with subjects from art and travel to politics and economics.

Between these two sites and the lists embedded in the state and federal pages, most if not all of your bases are covered. But again, e-mail is not always as effective as phone calls or mail because it's so easy to compose and to handle, and in some ways it is impersonal. So while you can get all kinds of information online, you may have to do your lobbying the old-fashioned way.

Moving On

So now you're well on your way to becoming the community expert on state and national affairs, and you have a good idea of how to find out about the FDA's latest nicotine regulations. What's more, you can find out what's on the agenda of the next House subcommittee meeting on business reform, and you can e-mail the chairwoman to let her know you'll be there with bells on. You've got the facts, you've got the access, and you're getting involved at home. But there's more to the world than the United States. What about that human rights resolution that was being considered in the United Nations? And what were the results of the 1996 presidential elections in Zimbabwe?

Some of the major compilation engines we just explored, such as Infomine, the University of Michigan Documents Center, and the Library of Congress site, can help get you started in the right direction when you need to do your searching internationally. And you certainly learned some activist techniques and about the international relations planks of U.S. party platforms on the Freedom Page and Vote Smart. But why not extend your virtual reach overseas? Get up, grab that passport you got with the help of the U.S. Postal Service site, and get ready to explore international governments and organizations!

CHAPTER 13

International Resources Online

The Internet can bring the world to your door, but take note—before you get your heart set on downloading a nifty image of that village you visited on your honeymoon in the Czech Republic, remember that not all countries are online and the amount of information available from those that are online varies widely. The depth and extent of coverage continue to increase rapidly, though, and the majority of nations now have basic Internet access. So, while not all countries offer the extensive level of access that the United States does, most have at least e-mail access and several more are rapidly adding Web resources.

So what's out there? Let's take a look!

International Governments Online

Most governments have some presence on the Web, even if it isn't on their own official site. Some international organizations, such as the United Nations, maintain different levels of information about member states, while other sites are clearinghouses for subject matter that mentions most, if not all, nations at some point. With a little time and patience, the following indices yield some interesting data.

United Nations

www.un.org

The United Nations (UN) site contains a broad range of general information about the UN itself as well as its member states. In addition to explaining the UN's history, statutes, and organs, the UN page includes a calendar of conferences and meetings, audio-visual services, and publications information.

The UN site is an excellent place to go if you are unsure of a country's legal status—for example, the former Yugoslavia is officially known as "The Former Yugoslav Republic of Macedonia." There are also databases onsite that require registration and allow free access for two months (such as the Treaty Databases) and others which have extensive samples but require subscriptions for more in-depth coverage (the Monthly Bulletin of Statistics, for example). Still wondering about that human rights resolution? The full text of the Declaration of Human Rights is carried onsite, as are regional updates on the status of various rights and development initiatives.

CIA World Factbook '96

www.odci.gov/cia/publications/nsolo/wfb-all.htm

This incredible resource gives a comprehensive survey of every country on this shrinking blue planet. While the style tends to be dry, the information available is quite thorough and well-organized—as may be expected from an intelligence agency. You can gather background information on countries through historical synopses as well as encyclopedic information on major revenue sources, population, birthrate, geographical position, and the like. A bonus for serious researchers or those without large blocks of time is that much of the information is now available for download.

Electronic Embassy

www.embassy.org

Electronic Embassy (see Figure 13.1) is an excellent source of links to country information straight from the old horse's mouth. The site is particularly helpful if you are a business person trying to get savvy about local commerce and trade, the press and culture, and education and travel. Non-U.S. embassies on the Web are indexed in alphabetical order by country name, but here's where the differences in Web access become apparent. For example, the Central African Republic has a page with only a listing of the embassy's physical location, phone number, and fax. Brazil, however, has an official embassy site and an e-mail connection. And Israel has several official Web sites, leading from the Embassy page to the Foreign Ministry in Jerusalem to the Consulate General in Chicago.

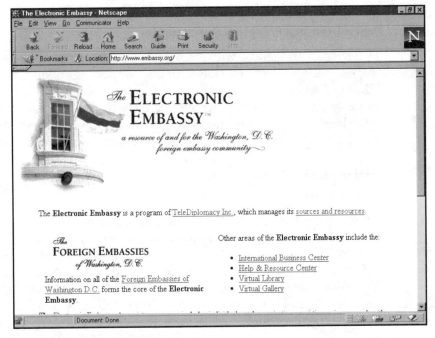

Figure 13.1   Electronic Embassy.

Electronic Embassy also has an International Business Center and a Help and Resource Center, which should handle a lot of your practical needs, whether you want to know how to do business with an international audience or just want to renew your passport.

The Web Sites On National Parliaments

www.soc.umn.edu/~sssmith/Parliaments.html

The Web Sites on National Parliaments page has links to national parliaments from the Estonian Riigikogu to the Ukranian Supreme Rada. Most of these links contain parliamentary history, electoral information, and current parliamentary compositions. Be sure to remember the "When in Rome" rule: Some of these sites have English translations, but others are in indigenous tongues only. The National Parliaments page also has links to supranational parliamentary institutions such as the European Parliament, the North Atlantic Assembly, and the Latin American Parliament. And just in case you really are curious about elections in Zimbabwe, the site has pointers to other sites which list recent election outcomes, embassy pages, and national constitutions.

Elections And Electoral Systems Around The World

www.keele.ac.uk/depts/po/election.htm

A terrific clearinghouse with an extensive index of links to general elections pages, this is not just for results, but also for postings of upcoming elections. Elections-related information, such as the Center for Voting and Democracy's page on proportional representation are also listed. You can check elections information by time frame or by country name, and each country has sublistings with notes about languages, other than English, that are available.

International Organizations

www.library.nwu.edu/govpub/idtf/igo.html

Sponsored by the GODORT International Documents Task Force and the Northwestern University Library, the International Organizations page is quick-loading and organized by alphabet. Low on bells and whistles but high on information content, you have access to hard-to-find organizations such as the Baltic Marine Environment Protection Commission (HELCOM) and the Universal Postal Union (UPU) in addition to the more common ones such as the Association of South East Asian Nations (ASEAN).

Rongstad's Worldwide Military Links

members.aol.com/rhrongstad/private/milinksr.htm

This page has over 1,400 links in topic areas ranging from the "U.S. Navy in Asia" to "Equipment, Weapons, Uniforms, and Insignia Contractors." Whether you are trying to find a specialty military magazine online or historical information from the Library of Congress Military Collection, this is the place to go. There are even links to military academies in the United States and abroad, and links to papers and discussions on controversial issues such as gays and unit cohesion in the military.

Galaxy World Communities

galaxy.einet.net/galaxy/Community/World-Communities.html

Along with extensive coverage of almost every nation with an online presence, the Galaxy World Communities site (see Figure 13.2) catalogs academic organizations, commercial sites, and discussion groups. You'll also find articles and collections about current events and academic issues as well as cartography resources and global events listings.

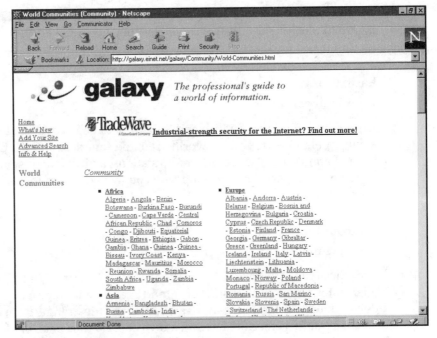

Figure 13.2   Galaxy World Communications.

Yggdrasil Pages

www.geocities.com/CapitolHill/6911

Don't let the unusual name scare you—this site is a solid collection of country Web pages. You'll find both independent and official pages of sovereign countries along with UN-affiliated sites. The strongest aspect of this site is its attention to international organizations, from defense-oriented groups such as NATO and PERC to humanitarian concerns such as the FAO and Green Cross.

World Links

Whether you're planning a vacation or preparing a dissertation chapter, sometimes you need detailed information on individual countries that isn't available on worldwide indexes. The following sites offer more in-depth information on a smaller region or set of countries than the previous indices.

World Tourism Organization

www.world-tourism.org

In addition to the usual tourist information, the World Tourism Organization site has articles about political and economic issues such as ecotourism and child prostitution. The WTO also contains postings about new regions opening up to tourism (and the controversies they generate) and special topics of interest to senior citizens.

Latin World

www.latinworld.com

Latin World gives you English and Spanish-language coverage of Latino-descent populations around the world, from the Americas and the Caribbean to Spain. Latin World also features radio stations, a virtual newsstand, breaking news headlines, and forums along with country-specific information and pictures.

Metropolis

www.metropolis.org

The official site of the World Association of Major Metropolises (see Figure 13.3) offers information in English, French, and Spanish about the management and development of large urban areas. Member cities range from Abidjan to Varsovie, and several cities have their own pages. While parts of Metropolis are still under construction, you can still find information about urban planning,

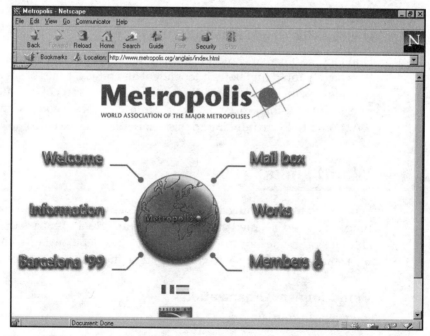

Figure 13.3   Get a perspective on many major world cities with Metropolis.

urban ecology and health, economic development, and social and cultural issues in the most populated regions of the earth.

Pacific Islands Internet Resources

www2.hawaii.edu/~ogden/piir/

This is probably the most comprehensive site on Pacific Island countries on the Web (see Figure 13.4). Again, the amount of information available online for each country varies widely, and you will get a lot more online about the Federated States of Micronesia than you will about the Republic of Palau. Sites cover issues from human rights practices and travel advisories to nuclear testing at Maruroa (French Polynesia) and ecotourism. The Pacific Island page also includes links to related conferences, seminars, and workshops as well as press releases and pictures.

MIT Caribbean Home Page

www.mit.edu:8001/activities/caribbean/home.html

This MIT Caribbean Home Page has alphabetized links to Caribbean country home pages. The topics covered are extensive, from the expected tourist and weather information to detailed links on academic institutions, sports,

Figure 13.4   Pacific Islands Internet Resources.

Caribbean-focused media, and Internet Service Providers. There are fun sections, too, like the Jam Session from the Caribbean and the Steelbands on the Web locator.

Yahoo! Canada

www.yahoo.ca

Yahoo! Canada is not exactly a regional index, but it is quite handy for exploring Canadian resources and is a critical indicator of the direction that Yahoo! is taking globally. Links are organized by subject, descending from the most general (Society and Culture) to the more specific (UniCan and the Quebec Referendum). Most entries have both French and English versions, and this Yahoo engine is tailored to popular Canadian—not American—activities and perspectives. So expect to find hockey highlighted under sports, not basketball. In addition, multiculturalism takes on a different meaning since Quebec's quest for independence is such a hot topic.

Eurolink

www.syselog.fr/eurolink/

Eurolink contains information on 16 countries, each with a keyword search. The overall site is available in French or English, and you just need to click on a country's flag, or scroll down in alphabetical order, to get to its engine. Each nation has information on its domestic servers, business and economy, country resources, and arts and sciences—you name it, it's probably there! Again, be aware that once you are at an individual country's site and out of the Eurolink main pages, you may not be able to get an English translation.

ASIALINK

www.syselog.fr/asia/

ASIALINK, like its European cousin, contains substantial information about the business, economy, Internet, and cultural resources available in that region. You'll also find translation resources and career opportunities in English or Chinese.

Russian Web

www.sitek.ru/~admcomer/xsu.htm

Not exclusively Russian, this site covers Web links from the former Soviet states in an alphabetically listed format. Russian Web accents computer and technology pages, but also contains links to political, health, and library-oriented sites.

Africa Online

www.africaonline.com

Beautifully organized and continually updated, Africa Online (see Figure 13.5) features extensive news coverage from around the continent, with a special emphasis on Kenya, Cote d'Ivoire, and Ghana. You'll find sections on computing, health and women's issues, along with the usual travel, arts, and commercial information. Africa Online also features the "Griot" section (a griot is a West African storyteller) with music, stories, history, politics, and cartoons from the continent. There is also an interactive Kids Only section with games, the Global Classroom, and magazines.

Arab World Online/Yahala

www.yahala.com

Yahala is broken into three subsections, each covering a different aspect of Arabic nations of the Middle East and North Africa. Subjects vary from the arts to government, and the education section has data on both institutions in the Middle East as well as those in the United States that focus on Arabic studies. The media sources that are available through this site are quite good, including some, such as the Lebanese News Wire, that are not readily available

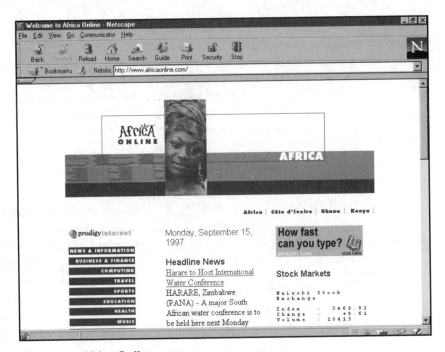

Figure 13.5   Africa Online.

elsewhere. Several links are in Arabic, and the site is searchable by either subject and keyword together or by keyword only.

> **TIP**
>
> *Unsure about your language skills and don't know how to get some practice? Or are you an avid reader of Hebrew but your browser doesn't support Hebraic script? If you have Windows 95 or Windows 3.x, run, don't walk, to Accentsoft at **www. accentsoft.com** and get up to speed in over 30 languages through its plug-ins.*

International Media Resources

So now, with all of this international data, you might wonder how you can get interesting, incisive analyses of all of the issues raised by different countries' sites. Who pulls it all together from a variety of perspectives? The international media, of course! Following is an overview of the international media that's out there.

NeWo News Resource

newo.com/news

NeWo starts with a click-sensitive map of the globe: click on a region and start your journey. NeWo also has general sources with strong global reporting sections, such as the *Christian Science Monitor, Jinn Magazine, Time WorldWide*, and special focus news sources like Science and the Environment. Many of the stories available through NeWo would not be carried, especially not so prominently, in mainstream U.S. papers. There are also news indices, references to media in languages other than English, and weather services.

OneWorld News Service

www.oneworld.org/news/index.html

OneWorld News Service (see Figure 13.6) carries stories from other news services and organizations, such as Amnesty International, in a newspaper format. You can get quick access to information on Oxfam's unique protest in London against land mines or on fair trade issues facing the World Trade Organization. You can select new stories by area (continent and country) or theme (such as aid and debt, or biodiversity and conservation). Best of all, OneWorld has a special reports section that uses multimedia such as text and photos, QuickTime movie clips, RealAudio interviews, and the Speakeasy newsgroup.

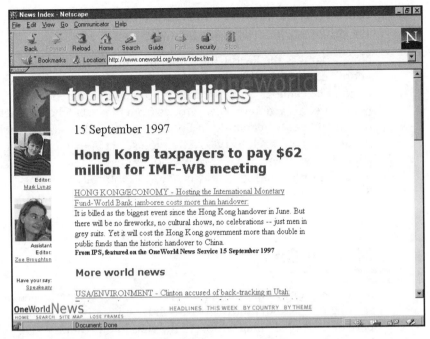

Figure 13.6   OneWorld News Service.

Small Hours/News

www.aa.net/~rclark/news.html

Small Hours has an outstanding collection of links to newspapers from around the world, particularly African newspapers. They also indicate the frequency of publication if other than daily, and whether that source is current or updatable (which is a problem in areas such as the former Soviet Union). Not all newspapers are online, but all of those listed have information on how to have the paper delivered to you by e-mail, or to your home or office. Some, such as Burma Net, are available through FTP. Small Hours also maintains extensive, searchable archives, but you should bear in mind that the graphics on some back issues may not work as navigation shortcuts.

Newslink

www.newslink.org

The incredible Newslink has over 7,000 news links to worldwide sources, listed by U.S., non-U.S., and campus newspapers. Newslink's Asian and Middle Eastern sections are comprehensive—carrying papers from Pakistan's *Dawn* to the United Arab Emirate's *Khaleej Times* (in English and French). The site is searchable and includes references to broadcast media networks as well, including some in non-U.S. areas.

United States Information Agency (USIA) Daily Washington File

198.80.36.136/products/washfile.htm

Now what was the Paris Club's announcement on debt relief for the world's poorest countries? And what is Clinton's record on Africa? USIA's Daily Washington File catalogs these and other hot news stories from the past 14 days, with a special section on news stories from the last 48 hours. Pick a topic or a region and get to searching in English, Spanish, Russian, French, or Arabic. Archives extend back to 1992. After you select your topic or region, the Web page kicks you over to a text-only Gopher menu, which will make downloading and printing stories rapid if not as graphically pleasing. There are also links to other news services, government departments, congressional servers, and major U.S. newspapers.

Moving On

Shrinking world, expanding Internet? You bet! As you can see, with the right starting points, the rapidly growing Internet can help you manage the quick pace of the global village. Most of the sites in this chapter give you historical, business, and cultural information about hundreds of countries, as well as information on transnational organizations. Several of the sites have interactive features, and the variety is enough to keep you up-to-date and even entertained.

But sometimes background information isn't enough. What if you want to get in contact with your second cousin in Argentina? Or perhaps you need the address for that nice young man you met in Rome—New York. Turn the page to find out how to get information from the white and yellow pages for the United States and abroad.

CHAPTER 14

Finding Folks Online

Sometimes your research needs are narrowly focused. They're so focused, in fact, you're targeting your efforts to finding one person. In most cases, a Web search engine won't help you if you're looking for contact information.

But help is just a few clicks away. Even if you are looking for someone who doesn't have an Internet account, you sometimes can get a paper address and phone number for them online. In fact, these resources are divided into two categories: (1) e-mail finders and white pages, and (2) paper address and phone number finders.

We'll be talking about how to find people online and offline as well as going over some genealogy resources.

TIP

Remember the Netiquette from Chapter 6? It applies to using online address and phone number finders, too. Most of these sites have features that limit your ability to generate mass mailing lists easily, but even so, making the Internet a fun and informative environment means each of us must exercise self-control. Don't send people unsolicited advertising, and don't use the information generated online to blindly cold-call potential contacts. Most of all, if it is difficult to find information about someone's phone number, paper address, or e-mail address, it's possible that person wants it that way for reasons of which you are not aware. Respect his or her privacy and move on to another project or contact.

Finding E-mail Addresses

So you're wondering if your best friend Peggy Smith from senior year at Pine Grove High School still lives in Lake Forest, Illinois—she'd be a great contact for the dissertation you're writing on shifting political perspectives in the Midwest. But you've moved to Colorado Springs, Colorado, and can't imagine how to find out if she's still there. What can you do? Use the Internet, of course! You can find out where Peggy lives, what her address and phone number are, and if she has an e-mail account. Start with some of these sites.

Four11

www.four11.com

Four11 has two search options—one for registered and one for unregistered users—and six directories—e-mail, telephone (both white and yellow pages), celebrities, maps, *netphone* (telephone software used over the Internet), and government. Unregistered users can do a basic search on someone's name, address, or domain name to find out street address, phone number, or e-mail address. If you register (it's free), you can expand your search to include the name of your old high school or college, see if someone else is online at the same time you are, so you can send them immediately, and add information beyond your name and address to your personal listing.

Just put Peggy Smith in the name boxes, and Lake Forest, IL, in the city and state boxes. Four11 will return her address if she still lives there. You can then click on Details to get her phone number, and click E-mail to see if she has a virtual address. And by the way, Four11 has a neat little feature called Smart Name, which matches whole names (Margaret, Robert) with common nicknames (Peggy, Bob). If Peggy has e-mail service, her address appears and you can click on it to send her a note from your Web browser asking for some information to help your dissertation research.

Internet Address Finder

www.iaf.net

What if you have someone's e-mail address but want to find out the proper name attached to it? Go to Internet Address Finder (IAF). While you can do a standard search using a person's name, organization, or domain (wild cards are allowed), the Internet Address Finder also allows a "backward" search from an e-mail address. Simply enter the person's address—for example, wow@domain.com—and press Enter. IAF will report the name and physical address for the account holder of that e-mail address, if it's available. IAF also is available in French, German, Dutch, Portuguese, and Italian.

Bigfoot

www.bigfoot.com

Still looking for Peggy and want to check another source? Bigfoot (see Figure 14.1) gives you simple (name) or advanced (location or domain details) search options and lets you search in English, French, Italian, German, Spanish, or Japanese. While most of the search details on Bigfoot are pretty standard, you should check it out if you tend to hop around a lot between Internet Service Providers, as Bigfoot gives you free forwarding for life with free registration onsite. (What it will do is give you an e-mail address at bigfoot.com and forward any mail sent to your Bigfoot address to your current ISP. This comes in handy, as you can just give out your Bigfoot address and be assured that your e-mail will reach you no matter where you go.) It also has Congressional address information and debate forums.

Usenet Addresses Server

usenet-addresses.mit.edu

If you've just finished reading Chapter 7 and want to know more about that nifty argument posted by Joe Public on a Usenet group but can't figure out how to get in touch with him, trot over to Usenet Addresses Server. This site obtains addresses from official Usenet group hierarchies as well as a few other alternative and special hierarchies, rather than getting information from phone books or demographic research organizations. You can search its information base by "arbitrary text" (using a part of a person's name or organization) or

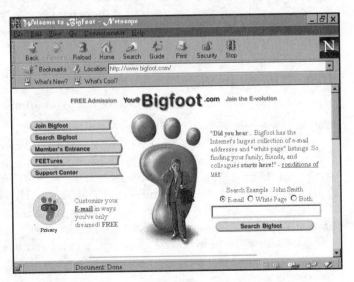

Figure 14.1   Bigfoot steps out with excellent resources.

by the standard given name, surname, organization, or isolated name (e.g., nicknames, initials, etc.). The Usenet Addresses Server includes old addresses, too—its address database goes back to 1991—which may clutter things up a bit but also allows you to cross-reference information about the names you bring up.

Special Needs: Finding College Internet Addresses

Finding out about student life at Cornell or admissions requirements at Northwestern just got easier. Many, though not all, colleges and universities have online phone books with departmental, administrative, and student address and phone number information. We haven't been able to find a comprehensive list of college phone books, but there are some nice university databases from which you can reach a university and check for a phone book at its Web site. Be aware, however, that some parts of many college servers are closed to those not actually logging in from their domain, so you may have to write to the school direct to find out some information. Nonetheless, these sites should give you a leg up on your quest.

Colleges And Universities

www.universities.com

This site allows you to search more than 4,000 colleges and universities worldwide using part or all of a school's name. For example, entering *Manchester* brings up four names, three of which have current links to different universities in England. You can click on any of these names to go directly to the home pages of the school, and the search will pull up relevant financial aid information where it's available.

Global University Web

www.artsci.wustl.edu/~jrdorkin/GUWeb/GUWeb.html

Global University Web (GUWeb) also lists hundreds of colleges and universities around the world but is organized by continent and country. Pick the country, and you get either an alphabetical listing of colleges or, in the case of nations such as the United States that have tons of schools, you can select by alphabet, Ivy League, or Military Academies and Colleges. GUWeb (see Figure 14.2) also lists the top 25 undergraduate institutions in the United States, as ranked annually by *U.S. News and World Report,* and lets you search information on the Educational Testing Service network. You'll even find an "Employment Arena" which lets you post your resume or browse the job postings of major companies onsite.

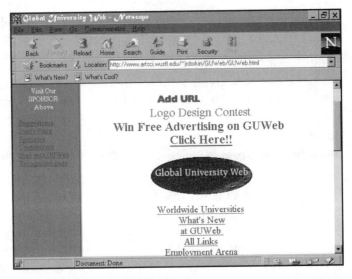

Figure 14.2 Global University Web.

Finding Phone Numbers And Paper Addresses

In addition to finding e-mail addresses for old friends and new business contacts, address finders can be used as virtual white pages for old-fashioned phone book information. (Yes, people do other things with their phone lines besides connect them to modems.) Of course, finding phone numbers on the Internet is faster and doesn't get newsprint ink on your hands, and a few of the finders have special features Ma Bell only dreamed of.

Yahoo! People Search

www.yahoo.com/search/people

People Search is a straightforward finder that uses Four11's database to let you look up phone information by inserting name and address information. You can find both e-mail and phone listings, and since it is text-oriented you'll find it is a speedy download when you're in a hurry.

Switchboard

www.switchboard.com

Switchboard gets its information from a company that researches demographic information around the country rather than from a phone book or other search company. You can find both individuals and businesses online by using names, cities, and states. Search results are strictly limited to eight at a time so that unscrupulous people can't gather many addresses to use in sales solicitation. If you use the free registration, you can get special features on your own account, including the Knock Knock option for your e-mail address: If someone wants to get your e-mail address from the Switchboard site, Switchboard will act as a messenger, giving you the stranger's own e-mail address and letting you decide if you want to give him or her your e-mail address.

Infospace

www.infospace.com

The huge Infospace lists individual and business addresses from the United States, Canada, and many other countries including Argentina, France, and Slovenia. In addition to the standard search by name, city, and state or province, you can click on the resulting phone number and dial the person's line if you have a touch-tone phone. Infospace has sections with yellow pages (business), blue pages (government), and fax number information, as well as a My Town touch-sensitive map to select a town visually. You also can use Infospace to look up e-mail addresses, or take a jaunt through the Infospace e-Shopping Center.

International Phone Books

Although some of the previously discussed sites let you look up addresses and other information in a few countries outside of the United States, none is as comprehensive as you might wish if you are trying to find an old friend in Angola or a colleague in Bosnia. We've found one source that has an impressive list of phone books from around the world, but remember: Just as the level of connectivity to the Internet varies from country to country, so do the completeness and ease of use of their phone directories. Don't expect consistency from one area to the next, even within the same continent or subcontinent.

The International Phone Book Directory

www.infobel.be/infobel/infobelworld.html

This directory was developed in Belgium and has an impressive list of phone and fax numbers from around the world. Some countries have only one or two entries, such as Yemen, while you lose yourself in the thousands of entries for the U.K. or U.S. Many countries have multiple entries that include 800 (toll-free), blue (government), yellow (business), white (individual), and fax directories.

How To Stay Out Of Online Directories

Just as many people choose not to have their phone number published in paper phone books or listed with directory assistance, you may want to ensure that your personal information does not appear on one of these finder services. Most of these sites respect your wish and will let you remove your information from their databases.

A few things to keep in mind: First, if you have an unlisted number through your regular telephone service and the online finder site gets its information from phone companies, then your name and other information should not appear; second, if you find your information on one, it may not be on another—check each one individually if you want to be sure; and last, if you want your name removed, look for instructions on each site—they do vary somewhat. We'll talk more specifically about this in Chapter 21.

Genealogy On The Internet

One of the reasons people search for phone numbers and addresses online is to research their family roots. This is a fascinating hobby that teaches you about family, history, and yourself. Perhaps your interest in tinkering with computer hardware came from your grandfather, who, along with his grandfather and his grandfather's father, was a watchmaker. Genealogy is a great way to trace these roots and find out more about yourself.

Though there aren't a large number of vital records online (yet), there are a number of projects going on to make more materials online. There are also thriving communities of genealogists who are constantly sharing family data and information.

The rules for genealogy etiquette on the Internet are the same as they are in the nonvirtual world. Be polite in your requests, give as much information as you have, offer to share, and if someone doesn't want to help you, don't press them on it. They have their own reasons, and it's not your place to judge them.

There are literally thousands of links online pertaining to genealogy. We cannot give you a comprehensive overview of them in this book, darn it. However, we have found four that should start your journey well.

NAIL
www.nara.gov/nara/nail.html

NAIL is an interactive database made available by the National Archives and Record Administration (NARA). NAIL contains more than 250,000 descriptions of materials, which is only a fraction of the holdings of NARA. (Just think what this database is going to look like a few years down the road!) A variety of material descriptions are available, from sound records, still pictures, maps, text records, criminal case files from the late 1800s, and case files for more than 50,000 Americans who enrolled in the Five Civilized Tribes between 1898 and 1914. (This is a must for people who have traced their ancestry back to Cherokee, Creek, or Seminole roots.)

Searching is simple—plug in your surname and see what comes back. This project has expanded to include resources such as descriptions of 1061 sound recordings of White House telephone conversations by Lyndon B. Johnson, and we can't wait to see how many more resources are added as time goes by.

USGenWeb

www.usgenweb.com

Wow. Hold on a minute. Wow. The goal of the USGenWeb, as it's stated in its white paper, is to "create a global library for genealogy research." And—wow. Enough with the wows, already! But we can't help it. This stuff is overwhelming. USGenWeb opens with an "image-map" of the United States. Click on the state in which you're interested. You'll go from there to state and local resources. There are also archives and links to other genealogy resources on the Web. The USGenWeb is expanding to include the WorldGenWeb, and if you're really excited about your ancestry you can "adopt" a country and help them put its resources online. The project was only started in June 1996, but we can already see it improving as time goes by.

Helm's Genealogy Toolbox

genealogy.tbox.com/

Matthew Helm built his toolbox to give genealogists a "one-stop shop" to find all the genealogy materials we need online. There are 10 main categories, including Genealogy Guides and Indexes, Surname Data, Groups and Associations, Genealogy Software, and Heraldry. The Toolbox has a FAQ for new users and an overview for more experienced online root-diggers. You can even search for surnames and other keywords using simple Toolbox search materials.

Cyndi's List Of Genealogy Sites On The Internet

www.cyndislist.html

How many sites do you think Cyndi's list includes? Three thousand? Nope. Five thousand? Nope. Try 23,200 links as of this writing, in over 70 categories. Though this site is not as easy to search as Helm's Toolbox, its scope makes it a must-see. (Pack a lunch, though—you're going to be here a while.) The categories are broken down as an easy-to-understand list, from Acadian, Cajun, and Creole to Western Europe. One of the nice features of this site is that each category has a note mentioning the last time it was updated. You don't have to investigate the category if it hasn't been updated since the last time you checked it, which saves you time.

Moving On

So now you're on your way to tracking down Peggy, and you're going to drop her a note over e-mail so that she has time to put your face with your name before you call her on the phone. Instead of slogging through dozens of phone books in your public library, it took you three minutes on the Internet to get all of the information you needed to reconnect with her.

But what if you guys hit it off really well and she invites you out to Lake Forest to check out her new computer store? And you know your suitcase is getting worn out from all of that traveling you did last year. Don't get up: turn the page and find out how to find businesses online and get a great set of luggage—or practically anything else—delivered to your front door.

CHAPTER 15

Finding Business And Professional Resources Online

Just as the Internet has changed the way people communicate and the way the government dispenses information, access to the Internet has changed the way businesses relate to each other and to consumers. While you won't find every business online, there is quite a range, from Kmart to Lexus to Ragu. This comes in handy when you need to do business research. You don't need to head over to the library to get contact information, press releases, and earnings reports—you can find them all online.

Business Information Available On The Internet

What kind of business information can you find online? Depends. Publicly held companies are legally obligated to disclose several aspects of their businesses, and much of that kind of material is available online. On the other hand, even small, privately held companies can have extensive Web sites and press release archives. The first place to look for these sorts of materials is a company's own Web site.

Finding Individual Companies' Web Sites

One easy way to find a major store or brand name is simply to try www.*name*.com, where *name* is the store or brand you're searching for. For example, Kmart can be found at **www.kmart.com**. You'll find a "Virtual Store" with products ranging from automotive to personal products, and an online copy of the store's circular if you'd rather shop locally than on your computer.

Of course, some brands will fool you—the fantastically funny Ragu site (see Figure 15.1) is **www.eat.com**—so if you don't get what you're looking for right away, try going to one of the search resources' business and economics pages. Yahoo's Business and Economy section is at **www.yahoo.com/Business_and_Economy**, and has a grand survey of major online stores and brands.

Databases And Expert Information

But don't stop there. What if you want information about general business trends, economic prospects in different states, or expert information on a particular resource? There are several databases online that give corporate information and expert advice for both businesspeople and consumers.

If you are interested in information about the business climate of a particular state, try the state pages discussed in Chapter 12. For example, North Carolina's page (**www.state.nc.us**) has a section devoted to the Department of Commerce, which tracks state economic trends, business incentives, special industry news (for example, film or technology), and strategic development plans. It also has a searchable database for businesses registered in North Carolina. Most states have similar pages.

And don't forget the granddaddy of consumer protection and business information: the Better Business Bureau, which is online at **www.bbb.org/council/main/index.html** and has information for both U.S. and Canadian businesses.

Figure 15.1   Ragu offers a lot of information on its Web site.

The BBB site includes a resource library, a dispute resolution center, alerts and news releases, and business and charity reports. You can even file a complaint online or find out about efforts to promote honest advertising.

Other useful sites are the U.S. Securities and Exchange Commission's home page (**www.sec.gov**) and EDGAR database of corporate information (**www.sec. gov/edgarhp.htm**). The SEC home page has a small-business section, news digests, SEC rule making news, investor information and fee rates, and feedback from the enforcement division. The EDGAR database automatically collects, validates, and indexes submissions by anyone who is required to file with the SEC. The database has searchable archives, a central key index and ticker symbol lookup, and customer filing retrieval tools. You have the option of downloading files by the Web or FTP.

Of course, the businesses themselves are also a good source of expert information. If you're doing research on ratites, an online emu farm might render some interesting information on the state of the emu industry. For more mainstream business concerns, try one of the following sites.

Global Entrepreneurs Network

www.gen.com

Global Entrepreneurs Network (see Figure 15.2) has a resource center with sections on Web page creation, design assistance, and HTML help. Additionally, GEN offers a set of "Success Tools." The set includes links to professional seminars and workshop calendars. You can also search the site and read up on

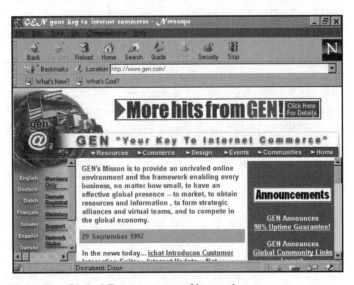

Figure 15.2   The Global Entrepreneurs Network.

breaking business stories, or connect to "Business Links," an impressive array of business-oriented pages. Global Entrepreneurs Network also offers a "Success Bookstore," which is library on business topics, education, and personal development. The site is translated into eight languages, and includes business chat rooms and forums.

Xplore Business

www.xplore.com/xplore500/medium/business.html

Another source of information is the Xplore Business site. Xplore connects you to sites such as the Chicago Board of Trade/Marketplex, which has tons of information on futures and options, the AgriMarket, EcoCenter, and the like. And if your questions run into the personal business realm, you can also get to Networth for the lowdown on mutual funds or to set up a personal portfolio. There is also a link to the U.S. Patent and Trademark Office, the perfect place to find out if someone else has already thought up a way to get those knots out of your shoelaces, and to get legal materials and copies of patents if they haven't.

TIP

*Sometimes you may want to get a corporation's own spin on things, instead of reading a story in a newspaper. Check out PR Newswire at **www.prnewswire.com** for an archive of press releases. There's also Business Wire at **www.businesswire.com**.*

Krislyn's Strictly Business Sites

www.krislyn.com/sites.html

Krislyn's Strictly Business Sites has the usual range of business categories (finance, management, taxation, etc.) but throws in a few extras that are hard to find elsewhere: bartering, technology transfer, and venture capital sources, for example. The site is updated frequently and has an onsite bookstore with titles, authors, prices, and, where available, reviews of leading business books.

Ideas Exchange

www.rimart.com

Ideas Exchange (Figure 15.3) is a site dedicated to inventors and entrepreneurs. Features include a New Products section, which helps inventors raise capital for their projects, and Inventors Corner and a bookstore emphasizing innovation and getting new products on the market. The most useful section, however, is the Experts Online section. Here you will find experts in business categories, such as intellectual property, business services, and product development, all of whom can help you with your questions or concerns, right online.

Figure 15.3   Ideas Exchange.

TIP

Want to get a stock quote straight from the horse's mouth? NASDAQ is online at ***www.nasdaq.com***. *You can also reach the New York Stock Exchange at* ***www.nyse.com***.

Professional Organizations On The Web

Whether you're looking for information on a specific trade for a report or you want to learn more about your own field, the rapidly increasing number of professional organizations on the Web are a great resource. Many national organizations have separate chapter or affiliate pages, and subjects range from sea urchin harvesting to criminology, on levels that suit everyone from high school freshmen to captains of industry. Most pages have chapter information, membership guidelines and requirements, lists of conferences, seminars, and symposia, organizational charter and rules, as well as related links and information on political and economic legislation in process. These collections should jump-start your research.

Association Network's Links To Associations On The WWW
www.assoc.net/assoc/aninews/alinks.htm

This is a straightforward list of links from around the United States, with an especially solid concentration of California companies. Thinking about starting an offbeat restaurant? Check out the Sea Urchin Harvesters Association link to find out global prices for urchin sales. Then you could head over to the American Homebrewers Association, which includes a newsstand and bookstore, an events calendar, and a chance to attend Beertown University if you aren't up to date on your beer styles.

Of course some of the links are more mainstream, though that doesn't make them less interesting. The Software Publishers Association has everything you ever wanted to know about anti-piracy initiatives, consumer education updates, and the latest on software development events. And before you sink your retirement money into a boutique inn when what you wanted was to have a host home, be sure to check out the Professional Association of Innkeepers International home. The site is completely searchable and includes conference information, an Innkeeper's library, and a link to the home page and archives of the newsgroup **rec.travel.bed+breakfast**.

Virtual Community Of Associations

www.vcanet.org

Organized by the Greater Washington Society of Association Executives, this site includes association information from around the United States. The site has a directory that is searchable by keyword or by alphabetized list, and each entry in the directory includes the URL and brief description of a professional association. For example, the Manufactured Housing Institute (Figure 15.4) has an entry that describes its mission and membership, and a link to its home page. You'll also find a resource center, calendar of events, and discussion area on the Virtual Community site.

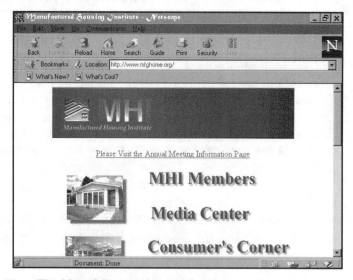

Figure 15.4   The Manufactured Housing Institute.

American Society Of Association Executives (ASAE)

www.asaenet.org

This society bills itself as the Internet's biggest searchable database of organization sites on the Web (see Figure 15.5). The Gateway to Associations is a directory of over 1,800 ASAE allied societies alphabetized by state. Each association includes leadership and contact information, and is searchable by association name.

You can also find a searchable directory of convention centers and bureaus in the United States, as well as an alphabetical listing of international ones (which is not currently searchable). You might also find the "Career Starters" links of current positions in the association and nonprofit sectors helpful if you're in the market for an entry-level position. This section lists descriptions, necessary job skills, and contact information for jobs paying up to $30,000 per year, categorized within the Washington, D.C., area and in the United States, generally. And if you've already started your career and want to get ahead, the ASAE offers subscription services to two job lists, one for the $30,000—$50,000 range and another for $50,000 and over.

You'll find a lot more than links on this site, though. You can also find the Association's Marketplace page, which includes a Buyer's Guide and Technology Solutions Directory. Curious about Clinton's position on the 401(k) legislation for tax-exempt employees? The Government Affairs page has updates, photos, background information, and more on political issues relevant to professionals in national associations and nonprofit organizations.

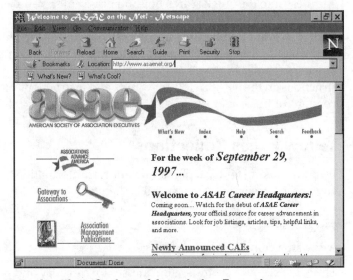

Figure 15.5 American Society of Association Executives.

Finding Offline Contact Information Online

Sometimes all you want is to reach out and bend the ear of a real human at a company without an Internet presence. The Internet to the rescue! First, a lot of the paper directories gathering dust under your end table have been put online. More importantly, however, instead of thumbing through hundreds of pages of dog-eared newsprint, the resources online let you plug in a name and get a number, address, or even a map with a few clicks of your mouse.

Toll-Free Numbers

The Internet can help you find 800 or 888 numbers without bothering an operator.

AT&T Toll-Free Internet Directory

www.tollfree.att.net

This toll-free directory allows two search options. First, you can browse by category using either the alphabetical listing or the specialty section (for travel and gifts). Still planning that dream vacation in Harare? Press the Travel icon, go to Category Listing, and press Hotel to find out if Holiday Inn has an 800 number, and if there's a franchise in Zimbabwe. You can also find out an 800 number for a kennel for Sparky to stay in while you're gone in January.

The second search option is a "quick search" by single or multiple criteria. Suppose you wanted to book tickets on American Airlines. Enter "American Airlines" into the quick search box and press enter. You'll get several numbers back, from the American Airlines Automated toll-free number to freight and packages. Want to compare fare prices? Look beside the phone numbers, press on the highlighted subject name beside American, and you'll get a screen with other companies in the same category (passenger airlines). There are also instructions on the new 888 toll-free prefix and instructions on how to get printed versions of this directory.

Yellow Pages Collections

If you're looking for local phone and address information for a particular store, any of the sites in this section will be helpful.

Zip2

www.zip2.com

This site lists over 16 million businesses by category and business name, area of a city or town, or by distance from a particular location (see Figure 15.6). Okay, you're in the market for an iguana, and you'd like to know where the

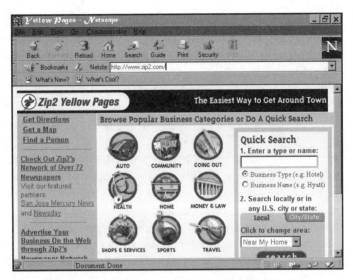

Figure 15.6   Zip2 lists more than 16 million businesses.

nearest pet shop is in Chicago, Illinois. You can enter "pet shops" in the Business Name box, along with the town and state. Zip2 returns 64 entries, and suggests that you narrow the search by "starts with" (one or more letters) or contains (part of a name, say "pet"). If you type in **gr** for "starts with," Zip2 returns one name; with "pet" in the contains category, it returns 33 stores in Chicago with the word pet in their titles. When you select a store, Zip2 gives you the name, address, phone number, and a map with the location of the store in Chicago highlighted. If your browser supports Java, you can even click on the map to get an interactive version.

There are two more features of Zip2 that are especially nice if you're unfamiliar with an area. You've just moved to a new neighborhood in a big city, or you're a tourist looking for a vegetarian restaurant and a great nightclub. Selecting the second option, area of a city, you can find out all of the different commercial establishments in a metropolitan area. Or, you could select the third option: Suppose you know you want to eat at Leona's Restaurant, but you don't know where the nearest club is to go dancing afterward. Specify the Leona's address and the distance you're willing to walk or take the train. It's a great night—say you'll walk a mile. Zip2 will show you the clubs or other commercial addresses within a mile of Leona's address.

BigBook

www.bigbook.com

This is another yellow pages directory that is equally thick on information. BigBook is searchable by name, category, and location, and returns both the number and names of establishments that fit your criteria. For example, searching under IBM, for name, returns 188 listings; searching under Chicago, for location, returns 96,669 business listings. But if you enter both IBM and Chicago, you get one listing—and it isn't even the Big Blue (it's a barbershop on IBM Plaza). So you won't find everything, but combining search terms can definitely make the load more manageable.

BigBook also has a map feature. You submit a street address and town, and BigBook returns a map of that area. Let's try another example. Say you pick 601 University Place in Evanston, knowing that you want to take your parents to see the Placement Center on Homecoming Weekend at the University, but you're a transfer student and don't know where all of the hotels and restaurants are. Insert the address, and BigBook will pull up a list of all of the businesses in the area around 601 University Place. Pretty soon you'll be able to do this in three dimensions for major cities—you'll get a 3D image, a 2D map, and a search frame of cities such as San Francisco, which has skyline features that make 3D mapping useful as well as fun.

Big Yellow

www.bigyellow.com

This site has four directories: residential, e-mail, global, and yellow pages. BigYellow is searchable by category and business name, and is especially useful for getting fax numbers in Asia and the Middle East. There are also Big Categories, which give you details on subjects such as dining out.

International Business And Contact Information

Speaking of faxing a contact in Sri Lanka, sometimes domestic-focus yellow pages aren't enough for finding out the location of a business or about doing business generally. There are several sites for finding address and phone and/or fax information, as well as broader information on doing business outside of the United States. The following are a few places that will help you get started.

American Computer Resource Inc. International Calling Codes

www.the-acr.com/codes/cntrycd.htm

This site has phone, fax, and address information for companies outside of the United States. Along with a standard alphabetical list of numbers for countries and areas within countries, the site provides long distance dialing instructions, access to its import/export library, and a list of other phone and address links.

MSU-Ciber International Business Resources On The WWW

ciber.bus.msu.edu/busres.htm

This is a phenomenal site for beginning research on overseas prospects, following up on leads, or doing background on foreign business climates (see Figure 15.7). Sections are broken down into categories such as News and Periodicals (contains over 78 links to international business media); Journals, Research Papers, and Articles (including some periodicals, such as the *Russian Business Law Journal,* which are out of print and available only as back issues); and International Trade information. Each entry has a brief synopsis of content and highlights.

Worldclass Supersite

web.idirect.com/~tiger/supersit.htm

What if you're starting up a company and want to find out how your competitors overseas are using the Internet to promote their products? Or maybe you're a businesswoman who wants to bid on Middle Eastern government tenders, and you're not sure where to begin. Once again, knowing where to go on the Web can stop you from having to slog through reams of paper at some government office or embassy desk. Try Worldclass Supersite on for size (see Figure 15.8). Worldclass has a stunning range of information for and about businesses, from feedback from the Japan External Trade Organization on doing business in Japan, to Frankfurt Digital Marketplace's high-tech database, to OOCL's interactive sailing schedule. Worldclass lists and analyzes 1,025 top

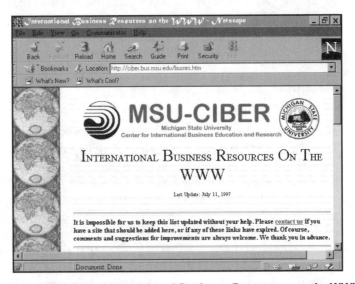

Figure 15.7   MSU-Ciber International Business Resources on the WWW.

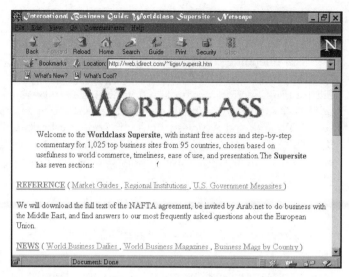

Figure 15.8   Worldclass Supersite lives up to its name.

business sites in 95 countries, and includes timely, critical business information as well as arcane tidbits, like how Xerox got its name.

Where's That Street Address Again?

So your interview is at 3:00 PM; however, it's 2:30 and you've lost the scrap of paper that had the company address and map. What might have been a disaster before the Web age is now just a matter of pulling up one of these map services, which will give you not only the address of a company, but a map for you to print out and take with you on the road.

Mapquest

www.mapquest.com

This site (see Figure 15.9) has several features: the Interactive Atlas, MoveQuest, TravelPlan USA, Personalized Maps, and Tripquest, all of which will make your life a lot easier. The Interactive Atlas allows you to choose the level you want mapped (national, regional, city, or street), and will label points of interest in the United States (personal, banking, lodging, and the like). You can plug in a ZIP code and select a category, say, dining, and a little plate and utensils symbol will pop up wherever there is a restaurant in that zone. You can even request the five points of interest that are closest to an intersection—for example, putting the street names "Halsted and Belmont" into the address box will give you the five restaurants in closest proximity to the intersection of those streets.

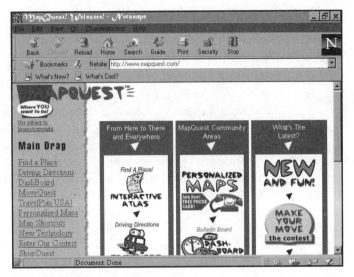

Figure 15.9 *Take Mapquest with you.*

The Tripquest section of Mapquest allows you to calculate the driving distances between two cities in the United States, Canada, and Mexico, and to get directions from point A to B. For example, if you want to drive from Chicago to Scarborough, Ontario, you can put "Chicago, IL" in the Starting Point box and "Scarborough, ON" in the Destination box, and press enter. Tripquest tells you that the total driving distance is 513.8 miles, and gives you detailed instructions on which interstate and provincial highways to take, how long each leg is, and whether a particular highway charges tolls.

LookupUSA

www.Lookupusa.com

LookupUSA is another great address finder for businesses and individuals. Using the American Directory Assistance section, you can type in a full name, two words, or a partial name with a wildcard (*) symbol (along with the city and state) to find a location. Suppose it's time to take Molly for a flea dip, and you've heard of a great shop downtown. Just put in the name, "Groomingdales," and the state and city (IL first, then Chicago), and press enter. Your search will yield two locations, and you can press View for either entry to get a full text citation for each one. You then have three options: press "Click here" for a complete business profile and ordering information; press "See this name on map" for a map complete with directions; or press "see credit rating" to see how well an establishment is doing financially.

U.S. Census Bureau's Tiger Mapping Service

tiger.census.gov

The U.S. Census Bureau's Tiger Mapping Service is a more research-oriented map service than the previous two. You can select any area in the United States and have a map drawn up for it by selecting any of the dozens of options. For example, if you wanted to know more about the geography around Colorado Springs, CO, all you would have to do is put that into the options box. The Tiger site will show you where the city is. But then suppose you want to know where the state boundaries are in relation to Colorado Springs, as well as water bodies, railroads, and census tracts, but you don't want highways or parks to be labeled. You'd just check ON boxes for features you wanted and OFF for those you don't, and then press Redraw. The map will be redrawn with the new features you selected. All maps are public domain, so there are no legal or copyright issues to worry about if you want to include them in a report or other works.

Finding Online Businesses

At some point most businesses will have an online presence, and many already do. Several business-only directories are cropping up, and these can help you sort out corporate information without having to wade through irrelevant materials.

Rexco's International Trade Resources

www.rexco.com/index.html

This site is a straightforward collection of links to businesses around the world. Categories include Global Trade Leads, Electronic Global Trade, Global Trade Organizations & Resources, and others. You can also take advantage of its online articles and educational materials while you're there.

SBE Business Link

sbe.d.umn.edu/resource/resource.html

A well-organized and searchable site, the SBE Business Link contains hundreds of links to businesses in fields including marketing, management, finance, and business law. You'll find additional resources for academics and practitioners alike, as well as postings about the latest trends in business and business-related research.

Resources For Getting Your Dream Job

You may not always want to use business resources to find a document filed with the SEC or to locate a good restaurant near the Roxy. Learning to use the Internet as a research tool may also land you the dream job you've suspected was out there but could never apply for in time. This section shows you how to make efficient use of your job hunting time, where to hone your interviewing techniques, and how to scope out a new city once you've signed on with a new company.

General And Domestic Job Hunting Sites

Start your research with these sites whether you want to stay in the United States or relocate abroad. Each of these sites has resources that will be useful to you regardless of your career goals: resume assistance, interviewing tips, relocation hints, and tidbits on how to get inside the mind of a job recruiter. Most sites have useful links to company sites and resources as well.

CareerPath.com

www.careerpath.com

This site lists over 210,000 jobs on the Net per month. Instead of posting direct company submissions, CareerPath.com (see Figure 15.10) allows you to search

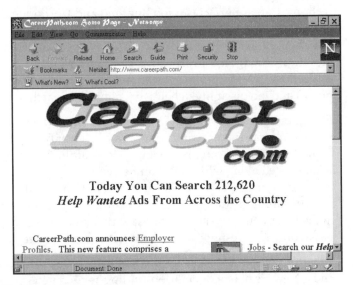

Figure 15.10   CareerPath.com.

the job listings of major national newspapers without the headache of piles of newsprint. You can search its help-wanted database by newspaper name, job category, or keyword.

For example, if you are a computer programmer who is willing to relocate to any major city, you could select the *Chicago Tribune, The New York Times,* and the *Los Angeles Times,* and then use the scroll bar to select a job category, submit a keyword, or both. It's a good idea to use both if you can—a selection of a job category in computers or a single keyword "computer" returns hundreds of job listings for just those three papers on an average week. Adding "programmer" to "computer" narrows your search to below 75 for most newspapers, saving you a lot of time if you are sure you want to be a programmer.

You can also select whether you want to look at this week's or last week's Sunday want ads. An e-mail account is not necessary to use the site, but if you have one you can register with CareerPath.com to have updates about the site sent to your e-mail box. Either way, the site is a free service. CareerPath.com also has a section for the Human Resources/Staffing professional, an especially good resource if you want to make sure that you or your company is making the best use of the latest technologies in the job placement arena.

The Monster Board

www.monster.com

This site gives you free access to over 50,000 jobs. Monster Board has two sections: Career Surfari (for job hunters) and Corporate Sphere (for employment and human resources professionals). Career Surfari has an online Career Search, the Resume Online, and an Employer Research section for doing background research on a prospective company. Monster Board's Career Search can be done by geographical location (single, multiple within region, international) and job discipline (chemistry, clinical research, etc.).

For example, a search on San Diego, California, and biochemistry yields 12 job entries. You can then narrow your search by specifying a company name and/or job title. Or, you can press View to look at the 12 jobs you found. Each job will be listed along with a job number, company name, location, job title, and a brief description of the position and requirements. If you've already posted a resume through Monster Board's resume service, you can place a checkmark in the box by the job(s) that interest you; then enter your resume number and password. Your resume will be sent to the appropriate people.

Other options on the Monster Board site include a keyword search of the site and a NewsSearch of over 40 job-finding-related newsgroups. Monster Board also offers you search shortcuts for particular locations (United Kingdom, Australia), and job categories (entry-level, outdoors jobs). The Career Center is an "interactive island" that lets you research employers before you go to your interview, and posts articles about top jobs, networking, minority resources, and so on.

CareerMosaic

www.careermosaic.com

This site gives you an alphabetized list of employers, and when you click on their names you are referred to their jobs pages. Alternatively, you can go to the J.O.B.S. database and enter a job description, location, and amount of records to return, and then press Search. Click on one of the job links returned to see a full description.

One of the best parts of CareerMosaic (see Figure 15.11) is the ResumeCM and Career Resources Center. ResumeCM lets you post your resume on the CareerMosaic site. You'll need to type in your name, address, and current job title, and then paste in an ASCII text version of your resume. After you submit it, you'll get a resume identification number—save it! You'll need it to delete or change your resume information later. Have questions about your resume or need background information for your interview? The Career Resources Center lets you research a company, join a professional organization, get the latest scoop on industries from architecture to non-profits, and find out what it will be like to relocate to Tucson.

The CollegeConnection section of CareerMosaic is handy whether you're still an undergrad or are a post-doc trying to take advantage of your university's placement options. Students at all levels can learn how to network on and offline, read over CareerMosaic's resume checklist, or find out about online

Figure 15.11   CareerMosaic.

job fairs. Special sections help you "Keep on top of trends" or negotiate a job in the health care field. Want a job in Brunei? CareerMosaic has Web sites for Asia (Malaysia, Indonesia, Singapore, Brunei, and Thailand), Australia, Canada, Japan, the United Kingdom, France, Hong Kong, and Spain, in addition to the United States.

Recruiter's OnLine Network (RON)

www.ipa.com

This site (Figure 15.12) primarily targets employment professionals and is the industry's largest virtual association. However, you can still get lots of job-hunting information and resume exposure on this site. RON accepts resumes and curricula vitae, careers services (trainers, publications, phone service, technology, and tools), and corporate histories. You can also search job postings by over 5,200 participating companies by keyword. Just put in a term, press Start Search, and you will get a brief display of location, job title, description, and a contact number—the most recent postings being displayed first. You can click on the brief display to get a full posting, which also includes e-mail information and compensation information.

The Internet's Online Career Center (OCC)

www.occ.com/occ/

This site lets you search job postings alphabetically or through a keyword search. You can also display companies by industry, state, or city, and there

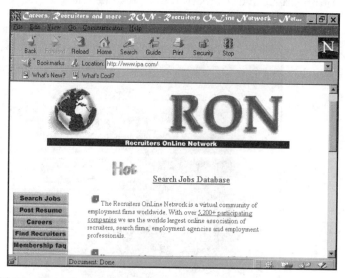

Figure 15.12   Recruiter's OnLine Network.

are separate pages for Medical/Healthcare careers (listed by hospital or health-related company) and Academe (via the Chronicle of Higher Education site).

OCC also has Career Fairs and Events, Agencies and Search Firms, and Cultural Diversity sections. The Cultural Diversity section includes Women's Career Resources (such as Women in Science and Technology, the Global Fund for Women, etc.) and Minority Career Resources (such as the American Indian Science and Engineering Society and the NAACP Career Conventions). OCC's Career Assistance section covers news about publications, laws, and outplacement questions, and the On Campus page gives students, business people, and faculty opportunities to interact via the Web, FTP, and Telnet.

Kaplan Career Center

www.kaplan.com/career/

This site (see Figure 15.13) has information on everything from resumes to getting out of debt; it also has interactive career games that will take you through a mock interview ("The Hotseat"), help you brainstorm career possibilities, and tell you how to get Career Counselor Job Search Software.

Kaplan's Career Selection page discusses the ins-and-outs of getting job experience, finding a career match, and addresses questions about personality tests. Kaplan also gives you strategies about the "Hidden Job Market," finding jobs that are not in the classifieds (through placement centers, government listings, networking, the Internet, and trade associations). You can then move on to the Resumes and Cover Letters section to get the latest on being specific about your experience and selling yourself to an employer. Once you've found

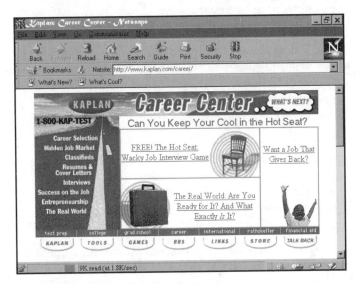

Figure 15.13   Kaplan Career Center.

a possible job and have gotten an interview, the Kaplan Interviews section gives you 50 practice questions and ideas about how to follow up and negotiate so you don't drop the ball on a hot prospect.

Kaplan doesn't abandon you after you've clinched the deal, either. You can go back to this site for Success on the Job tips (industry buzzwords, marketing tools, etc.), Entrepreneurship hints, and a survival guide to the Real World (getting out of debt, finding a place to live, relocating challenges, etc.).

First Steps In The Hunt

www.interbiznet.com/hunt/

This is a general Web guide to job hunting, which gives almost daily updates on articles on topics like marketing yourself, getting assistance with your search over the Net, and avoiding job scams. First Steps also lets you register your e-mail address so that you get notice of updates and its occasional Job Search Newsletter. The site also has a research section devoted to instruction on finding job opportunities over the Net (on sites such as the Unemployed Disc Jockey site, etc.), searching the Web, and making the most of matching services, job ads, staffing services, and job networks.

E.span

www.espan.com

Split into two "sides" for job hunters and recruiters, E.span (see Figure 15.14) is a comprehensive site that offers job searches, career information, and suggestions for human resources professionals. Jobs searches can be performed by keyword or by a customized search (keyword, company name, geographical area, educational level, managerial classification).

The E.span Career Companion takes you through your first job until you retire. The site gives you stock market tips, business indices, professional association information, personal assessment tools, and more. You can also get news from several media types and from around the world, and keep up to date with its technology and professional education sections.

The professional education pages are especially useful for finding online schools and distant education resources. A travel page tells you all you need to know about relocating—costs of living, real estate markets, rental markets, you name it! And just so you don't think that your professional life means you need to neglect your personal life, E.span gives you a good start for researching arts and culture, cooking, games, and "kids' stuff" in the Beyond section.

The Human Resources section has online recruitment tips, a resume database, and a human resources library. While this section is mostly targeted at people inside of the companies you're trying to get into, you can certainly find out a

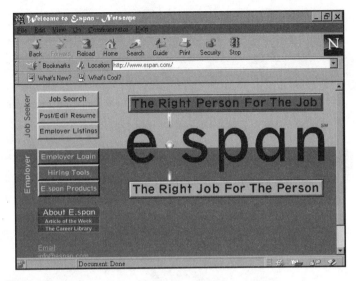

Figure 15.14   E.span.

lot of strategic information for background research and interview questions by looking through these pages.

America's Job Bank

www.ajb.dni.us

This is a public site that was established by the U.S. Department of Labor and the states' Employment Services Agencies. The Job Bank links the 1,800 state employment services offices, and there are usually about 250,000 jobs listed. None of the services require a fee.

Some of the features are standard for job search sites—looking for a job by keyword—but two others are largely unique to this site. The Menu Search lets you limit your search by occupation and location, and then gives you a list which includes the job title, location, salary, education, years of experience required, and whether it is part- or full-time. If you get multiple returns, you can have them sorted by state, city, title, and salary, according to the rank you choose. The Code Search page lets you search for jobs by occupation code, military code (with rank and branch), DOT code, or job number, plus location. You can also jump to state employment service Web sites, the job pages of employers' Web sites, or to private placement agencies.

NationJob Online Jobs Database

www.nationjob.com

This site lists jobs from around the United States, with a particular emphasis on the Midwest. No e-mail is required for the search engine. Specify location, education, duration, salary, and internship requirements, and then refine the results after you get the feedback. If you do have an e-mail address, you can get "P.J. Scout" to continue your job search for you while you're logged off. P.J. Scout will notify you by e-mail if any jobs matching your qualifications and interests are added after you leave the site. You can also search NationJob by specialty, company, or get the entire directory of companies available through this site.

International Job Hunting Sites

Trying to relocate overseas? Not even sure if they're hiring noncitizens in Belgium? Now you don't have to camp out on Embassy Row—just surf these URLs, and you'll be on an MD-11 to Brussels in no time.

International Job Search

www.overseasjobs.com/resources/jobs.html

This site has hundreds of links to employment resources in over 40 countries. The site includes a "flambe" of the week (hot site), which gives you the lowdown on issues such as whether the employer or agency affiliated with the site will help you with relocation and travel expenses, what the visa and residency requirements for that country are, or how complex the application and interviewing processes are. International Job Search includes regional listings (by country or continent), industry-specific job servers, business listings, and international job recruiters information. You can also find out about immigration issues in the United States, Canada, Australia, and the United Kingdom, or subscribe to the *Overseas Jobs Express Newspaper*.

Job Links

cip.physik.uni-wuerzburg.de/Job/job.html

This is a Germany-based international job information site. In addition to an array of regular, full-time jobs from around the world, Job Links has a list of opportunities in the international nonprofit sector, summer jobs, postdoctoral research positions, along with a listing of positions available through Global Academic Recruiters and specialty services like the Physics World Jobs Online. You can also find out how to subscribe to the Global JobServe and access its archives. There are excellent links to job research advice, from cover letters, resumes, interviews, and self-assessment tests, some of which are interactive. The site is available in English and German, and Job Links indicates whether a link is available in English or another language.

Overseas Job Express

www.overseasjobs.com/

This site is a must-see for anyone considering looking for or taking an overseas job. Not only will you find hundreds of job postings, you'll find critical information about green cards, visas, passports, and international employment conditions. You'll also read the latest on migration trends, how to use teaching English as a bridge to other jobs, and other articles of note for the global-oriented worker.

Moving On

By now you should be able to find out anything you ever wanted to know about doing business in Karachi or counteracting corporate espionage in Paris. The Internet is a fantastic resource for getting practical business information, whether you are an entrepreneur looking for a lead or a very hungry student searching for cheap eats or a good job in New York.

But occasionally even the starving student needs to research more than local diners and coffee shops. The Internet is also a practical and efficient resource for doing background research for a dissertation or finding obscure references to herbal remedies in the lesser works of Shakespeare. The next chapter will give you a way to augment your library card and help you make the most of the two days you have to finish that geology paper.

CHAPTER 16

Resources For Student Research

Picture this: You sit down in front of your computer, ready to type your essay on the controversy around Rutherford B. Hayes's election in 1876. Suddenly you realize you can't remember how many electoral votes were in dispute or what the final vote of the electoral college was. It's almost midnight, there isn't a library open in your time zone, and your professor is not sympathetic about extensions. No need to short out a flock of neurons—the Internet may be the student's best friend since cheap coffee and *Cliffs Notes*.

What's out there? So much that one chapter can't cover the depth, but you should be able to get a good idea here of the range of resources available for students from kindergarten kiddies through postdocs. Each of these sites has great links to pages with similar content, so once you find a page with your subject on it, you'll probably realize you have access to more information than you can use in one assignment.

Reference Indices

Sometimes all you want is quick access to a dictionary, a thesaurus, or *Bartlett's Quotations*. The following indexes have a range of standard reference resources, along with a few less common ones, and are a lot easier to search than your usual copy of the *Oxford English Dictionary* (OED).

Research-It!

www.iTools.com/research-it/research-it.html

This is a wonderfully simple collection of search engines attached to dictionaries, package shipping trackers, stock tickers, currency converters, and more. You can insert a word into the rhyming engine and get a list of words that rhyme with it. Just click on one of the words in the list, and you get the definition and an option to look it up in the site's thesaurus. There is also a language identifier: Insert a word such as *Verstehen* and press enter. The engine lists possible languages, in descending order from most to least likely. In this case, German, Dutch, and Afrikaans came up as the top three possibilities, with Latin at the end of the list. Research-It! also has a pronouncing dictionary, translators, French conjugators, and an anagram engine (insert a word or phrase and get a list of possible anagrams). And don't miss the "universal translator"—insert a word and it will be translated into every conceivable language.

Virtual Reference Desk

thorplus.lib.purdue.edu/reference/index.html

Purdue University's Virtual Reference Desk contains materials ranging from selected government documents (census data, code of federal regulations, Government Printing Office access, etc.) to information technology sources (Educom, Interactive Age, etc.) and map, travel, time, and date collections. Dictionaries comprise old standbys such as the *Oxford English Dictionary* (OED), *Webster's*, and some unique ones such as the LOGOS foreign language engine, the Free On-Line Dictionary of Computing (FOLDOC), and Usenet's College Slang.

Internet Public Library Ready Reference Collection

www.ipl.org:80/ref/RR

Ready Reference Collection (RRC) has a broad selection of general reference aids (almanacs, biographies, census data, and such). It also has a searchable roots surname list, UNICEF's Progress of Nations Index, instructions on how to cite electronic resources, and Morse code and phonetic alphabet tables. RRC also links to a searchable directory of nonprofit organizations on the Internet, and the biographies section covers topics from the complete list of popes to great Canadian scientists.

Dictionary.com

www.dictionary.com

This is an excellent source of dictionaries and language guides of every persuasion. You'll find *Webster's*, Strunk and White's *Elements of Style*, and the

New Hacker's Dictionary, as well as *Bartlett's Quotations*, and FOLDOC. This site also has *The King's English,* your opportunity to acquire painfully correct vocabulary, syntax, punctuation, and verbal arts and graces. Lost in the world of Internet-ese? Check out **whatis.com**, a complete glossary of Net terms organized by alphabet and topic.

Encyclopedias

If dictionaries aren't enough, and you need more detailed information about Zambian economics or Edward Abbey's life, online encyclopedias are a solution. Here are a couple.

FREE Internet Encyclopedia
clever.net/cam/encyclopedia.html

This encyclopedia collects macroreferences and microreferences and indexes them alphabetically. Macroreference sections include large topic areas from Africa/African-American themes to personal finances and zine indices. The range is quite eclectic. You'll find a list of African country home pages, the *Global Real Estate Guide,* and sci-fi and fantasy zines on one site. Microreference sections cover more specific topics such as environmentalist Edward Abbey's philosophy, the search for extraterrestrial intelligence, and the socioeconomic meanings of Zulu necklaces.

Knowledge Adventure Encyclopedia
www.adventure.com/encyclopedia/

This is a wonderful resource for the kindergarten to middle-school set. It's equipped with an encyclopedia search engine (see Figure 16.1). Knowledge Adventure includes a photo album section, which has pictures and descriptions of kid-friendly subjects such as dinosaurs, sea life, and space. There are also so-called jump-start interactive learning games, with settings from toddler to second grade, and field trip links to theater and laboratory pages.

Dictionaries

Several sites are dedicated to collecting every type of dictionary imaginable, from English-to-Halaka translators to the etymology of names. The following are a good sample of what's out there.

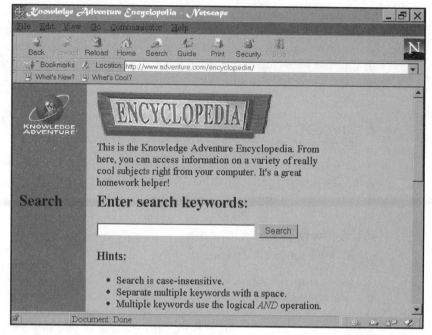

Figure 16.1 Knowledge Adventure Encyclopedia.

Dictionaries

math-www.uni-paderborn.de/HTML/Dictionaries.html

This site has English translating dictionaries (including American English to British English and the *Italian-English Hypertext Dictionary*), Swedish data terms, a biotechnology dictionary, and *The Dictionary of Scientific Quotations*. One of the more interesting and still-expanding sections is the etymology of names, which includes not only name origins but also fun explanations for why you should name your twins Melanie and Phoebe or Amy and May. On the practical side, it also has the INFOMEDICAL dictionary of information for patients and support groups, which includes facts about many diseases and contact numbers for more information and support.

OneLook Dictionaries

www.onelook.com

This has 169 dictionaries including science, sports, computers, religion, and much more. Access is simple: Pick a subject area and pull down the list of dictionaries under it. For example, to search for information about the disease lupus, go to the medical section and pull down the list. Select All Medical Dictionaries. This yields information about where the term was found, the percentage of times the word matched, and links to the term and the home pages of the dictionaries in which it was located. OneLook includes explanations of special terms used in dictionaries (modifiers, interjections, etc.) and a list of links to dictionaries not searchable with one of its onsite engines.

Wordbot

www.cs.washington.edu/homes/kgolden/wordbot.html

This is a robot-assisted page for looking up translations, definitions, synonyms, and so forth. Before you visit this site, however, be sure to turn off the link-underlining option, as every single word on Wordbot is a link. Go to Options, select General Preferences, then Appearances, and deselect Underlining. Click on any word on the site to find out its meaning. You also can enter a Uniform Resource Locator (URL) within the Wordbot site to have that page pulled up as a Wordbot page. For example, pull up an Italian page, change your dictionary selection to German, and look up the definitions for Italian words in German. You'll find this site an excellent resource if you want to augment your language classes by reading original-language texts but are uncertain about a few or many of the meanings.

WWWebster Dictionary

www.m-w.com/dictionary.htm

This one has a simple search engine that gives you complete meanings and usages of any word in English, even if it is part of a proper name. The site covers pronunciation, function, and etymology, and links words within the definition to similar or related meanings.

For example, entering *bitter* yields nine entries—as an adjective, adverb, and noun; and as part of compound words (bitter almond) or proper names (Bitter Lakes). In the adjective definition, the word *galling* is hyperlinked, as are the related words sour, salt, and sweet. You also can choose the thesaurus section to find synonyms and antonyms. WWWebster includes a word of the day, complete with definition, pronunciation, and use in a sample sentence, and a Merriam-Webster Bookstore. You can also check out the word games and lighter side pages if you're in a less scholarly mood.

Casey's Snow Day Reverse Dictionary And Guru

www.c3.lanl.gov:8064/

This is one of the funkiest of the reference sites (see Figure 16.2). The idea for the site is that when you can't remember just the right word for the concluding sentence in your literary masterpiece, you type in the definition of the word you want and the Reverse Dictionary gives you a list of 48 possible

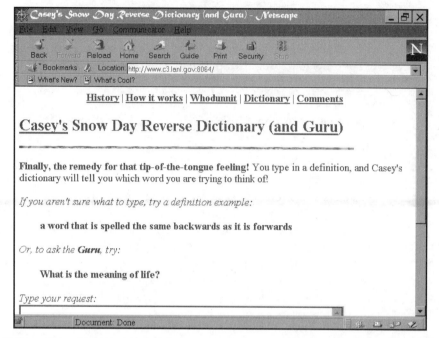

Figure 16.2 *Casey's Snow Day Reverse Dictionary might leave you with more questions than answers.*

choices. You then click on the words in the list for definitions and thesaurus entries. Of course, since words are selected based on statistical relationships between letters and letter combinations *(fuzzy matches)*, sometimes the output is more comical than practical. For example, type in *a feeling of emptiness and sorrow*; you get not only *dreary* but also *seductive* and *cattleman*. Similarly, *burst of light and hope* gives you the understandable *flashlight* and *luminous* and also the more perplexing *cheesecloth* and *landowner*.

Atlases

Dazed and confused? These sites should help you find yourself, wherever you may be.

Map-Related Web Sites

www.lib.utexas.edu/Libs/PCL/Map_collection/map_sites/map_sites.html

This is an index of cartographic references (gazetteers, distance calculators, and tide tables), city maps (global and some real-time traffic maps for major metropolitan areas), and country maps (Belarus to Wales). This site also lists historical maps by region, weather maps (current and interactive), and university, commercial, and media information sources (see Figure 16.3).

Landform Atlas Of The United States

fermi.jhuapl.edu/states/states.html

This has topographical maps of the continental United States and each state individually. States are listed in alphabetical order by postal code (so Iowa precedes Indiana). Just click on a state, then select Topographic Map (which includes latitude and longitude marks along with major physical features), County Map, Yahoo! (which will pull up the Yahoo! page for that state), City.Net, or Virtual Tourist (which marks major cities and interstates as well as relevant archives, data, and indices). There are an elevation key, color palette, and links to other map sites as well.

DecisionWeb

decisionweb.com/dw/atlas/atlas.html

Choose your atlas by clicking on a graphical image of the relevant continent. In addition to basic geographical information, get times around the world, countdowns to various global holidays, and how much time is left till the year

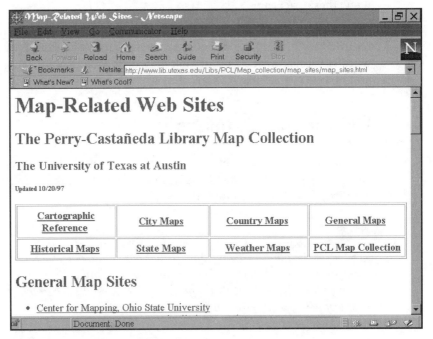

Figure 16.3   Map-Related Web Sites.

2000. In addition, click on a country on the continent map for access to the City.Net directory for that nation.

Thesauri

No, no, that's not the word I'm looking for...

WordNet: A Lexical Database For English

www.cogsci.princeton.edu/~wn/

WordNet is available both on the Web and as an anonymous File Transfer Protocol (FTP) site. The site is somewhat confusing at first—it isn't readily clear how to get access to the database engines—but is worth sorting out. After you read through the introduction, select one of the interfaces listed in the middle of the main page. For example, select the One Touch Web interface or the WordNet 1.5 Vocabulary Helper. Then enter a word or short phrase in English, perhaps *ennui* or *poetic license*. WordNet gives you synonyms, definitions, and senses of use, along with coordinate terms.

Roget's Internet Thesaurus

www.thesaurus.com

Simply place a term in the engine box and select Now. Click on any word returned for a complete definition. There is also a section with the six main word classes, allowing you to look up words according to categories such as matter, space, abstract relations, and so forth.

Library Card Catalogs

So many documents, too little time to thumb through them all? Or maybe you aren't even sure what's available in a collection. Be sure to look at the following virtual card catalogs to find out.

> **TIP**
>
> *Some of the library catalogs you'll find online are not exactly the hope and the future of the great information superhighway. Many of them are still accessible to use only by Telnet, which, as you remember, doesn't have graphics. Don't expect lots of pretty pictures when you're looking up that text on West African agricultural production.*

The Library Of Congress

www.loc.gov

You must access the information service (LOCIS) via Telnet. The process is quite simple: Click on the LOCIS option once you've reached the Library of Congress home page, and your Telnet application automatically connects to the Library of Congress.

LOCIS options are numbered clearly; choose one and press Enter to navigate through the catalog. For example, at the first screen select #1 to get into the Library of Congress main catalog, then select #2 to go through books cataloged between 1950 and 1974. LOCIS gives complete instructions on content, browsing, and searching by phrase or record number. As you can imagine, the library's resources are vast: books, microforms, serials, cartographic items, music, computer files, and so forth. Most are available 24 hours a day during the business week and the majority of hours on weekends (check the site for specifics). You also can find references dealing with federal legislation and copyrights, and Braille citations.

Book Wire Index

www.bookwire.com/index/libraries.html

This has library information by region—including Asia/Pacific, Canada, Europe, Latin America, and the United States (alphabetically and by state)—and special libraries. The U.S. resources vary from AcqWeb (lists of publishers, vendors, and resources for acquisitions librarians), the As-You-Like-It Metaphysical Lending Library (fee-based, it includes everything from astrology to Zen), the Stonewall Library and Archives, and the Yale University Library. Special libraries include the BIBSYS Norwegian book database, the Ronald Reagan Library, and the Labyrinth Medieval Studies bibliographies.

Libweb Library Servers Via WWW

sunsite.Berkeley.edu/Libweb/

Here you can do a keyword search for libraries or look for library resources via world region in a database comprising 1,700 pages from libraries in 70 countries. The United States is broken into six subcategories—academic libraries, public libraries, national libraries and library organizations, state libraries, regional consortia, and special and school libraries. Other categories include regions (Africa, Asia, Australia and New Zealand, Canada, Europe, Mexico, the Caribbean, Central America, and South America), library-related companies, and related sites. The site managers stress that Libweb is not a reference database, but rather a directory of library home pages—searches on specific topics like hanta viruses or stag beetles won't work.

School Libraries On The Web: A Directory

www.voicenet.com/~bertland/libs.html

If you're interested in library resources for K-12 levels, here are links to school libraries in the United States and 10 other countries. There are sections dedicated to school district departments of library/media services, individual states' and provinces' departments of education pages (for the United States, Canada, and Australia), and special resources for librarians. Some of these special resources include reference centers, acceptable usage policy examples, copyright issues, and the future of the Internet and the school library.

webCATS

library.usask.ca/hywebcat/

Want a book from the Seth Wilson Library at Ozark Christian College in Missouri and have no idea where to begin? Looking for a library in Malta? Try webCATS, which has multiple indexes and resources across several categories (see Figure 16.4). In addition to geographical indices, webCATS includes a vendor index (e.g., ALEPH, Gaylord, SIRSI Corporation), indices of libraries by type (from the armed forces to religious collections), and resources related to libraries. The links to Zweb and CARL Web databases contain extensive commentary and evaluations.

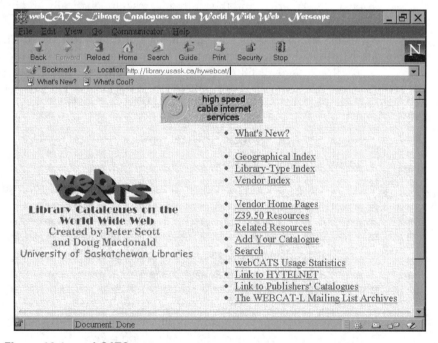

Figure 16.4   webCATS.

WWW Library Directory

www.llv.com/~msauers/libs/libs.html

This gives you access to library resources by country or through an onsite search directory. The search directory includes an explanation of query language, and you need only enter a term to pull up a list of documents to view—then choose a document, click, and read. The countries covered are quite comprehensive; you'll find Croatia and Estonia along with South Africa and Wales. WWW Library Directory also lists 60 companies, 41 nonprofit organizations online, and resources and services relevant to library collections and access.

Ask An Expert

Okay, so you've just got to know how to deal with your stubborn tailor or what the first ionization energy of iron is. Miss Manners is out of town, and you lost your chem book in that little Bunsen burner accident. Fear not! Expert information is a URL and a mouse click away.

New Jersey Networking Infrastructure In Education Project

njnie.dl.stevens-tech.edu/curriculum/aska.html

The Ask an Expert page on this site has nine categories including science, economy and marketing, and literature. Each topic has a form for your name, address, and question, and a few have restrictions or limitations (such as only allowing questions from the K-12 set). They've included a section they call Just Out of Curiosity with subjects from Ask the Amish to the Movie Expert.

Pitsco's Launch To Asking An Expert

www.askanexpert.com/p/askanexpert

This site has links to and information on more than 200 Web sites and e-mail addresses, including information on how to use Web sites and information in the classroom. Click Ready to Ask the Experts to talk to the Broadband Telephony Expert or to a men's executive dress expert. And you never know when you'll need an expert's advice on karate, Java, international trade, or Hilton Head Island.

Mad Scientist Network

www.madsci.com

Mad Scientist Network gives you access to the "collective crania of scientists" in areas from physics to horticulture (see Figure 16.5). The site includes the names, e-mail addresses, and institutional affiliations of the resident scientists and is

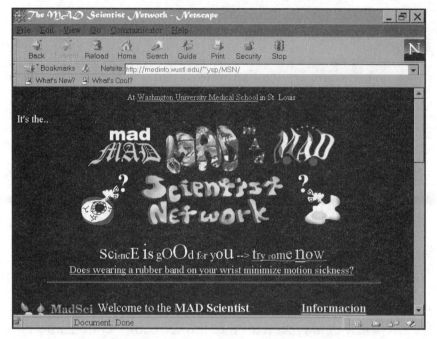

Figure 16.5 Dally with the mad scientists.

searchable by query term and topic. Searches include both the current questions list and the site's archives. You can limit the search by grade level, area, or identification number of a specific message. The site also includes a Mad Scientist Library (organized by science subject) and a list of relevant Usenet newsgroups.

Historical Documents

While your days of flipping through texts and inhaling library dust are by no means over, you often can narrow your search or lighten your load at the archives by searching historical collections and indices available on the Internet. The following are just a few of the Net's resources, but they should get your research going at a smart pace.

Historical Text Archive

www.msstate.edu/Archives/History/index.html

This site has three main sections—regional or national history, topical history, and resources. The regional or national history section has the usual geographical categories (Africa, Asia, etc.) as well as the unusual (Arctic Circle). Topical history comprises subjects from the genealogy of African ancestors to women's historical documents. Resources has addresses, directories, bibliographies, and information on archives as diverse as the Churchill Archives and the Archives of Religion, Death, and Culture in Central Appalachia.

Archiving Early America

earlyamerica.com

You probably can find all the primary source material you ever wanted from the eighteenth-century United States at the Archiving Early America site. In addition to original newspapers, maps, and writings, you'll find the Keigwin and Mathews Collection of Rare and Historical Documents, milestone historical documents (Articles of Confederation, Jays Treaty, etc.), and America's Freedom Documents. They've also attached a useful piece on how to read a 200-year-old document, which should get you around long "s's" and strange syntax.

EuroDocs

library.byu.edu/~rdh/eurodocs/

For documents with a continental flavor, try EuroDocs: Primary Historical Documents From Western Europe (see Figure 16.6). Documents on the site are transcribed and translated along with facsimile images. Most are organized according to country, then listed in chronological order, with document collections at the end of the list. You can find Danish publications forbidden

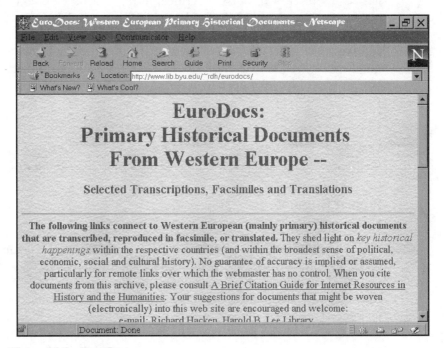

Figure 16.6 EuroDocs.

during the Nazi occupation and Andorra's constitutional agreements and decrees in Spanish translation, along with Medieval and Renaissance European documents, and papers related to Europe as a supranational region.

Texts And Documents

history.hanover.edu/texts.html

Looking for Luther Burbank's "Why I am an infidel"? More historical resources are on the Texts and Documents site of Hanover College. The overall site is broken down into region (including a section on Native Americans). Most sites are then divided into time periods and then subjects. So, to find Burbank's paper, go to the United States, choose nineteenth century, then click Theology. Click on the paper you'd like to view. While some pages are still under construction, the site is already a useful resource for these documents, and links to electronic text collections and Web sites of interest to historians.

Inaugural Addresses Of The Presidents Of The United States

www.columbia.edu/acis/bartleby/inaugural

Still wondering about Rutherford B. Hayes? Go to the Inaugural Addresses of the Presidents of the United States. In addition to full texts of the addresses of presidents George Washington (1789) through George Bush (1989), each entry has a brief discussion of issues critical in that election. So you can find out quickly that there were 20 electoral votes in dispute and that the electoral commission decided in favor of Hayes over opponent Samuel Tilden by a vote of eight to seven. You'll also find a list of all the presidents who never gave inaugural addresses and the reasons they didn't. (You will not, however, find out how President Hayes's mom ever decided on the name Rutherford.)

Literature

If you need to find a literary reference, the Web puts it at your fingertips.

Project Gutenberg

promo.net/pg/

This is one of the oldest and most impressive efforts to make the Internet useful to a broad segment of the public (see Figure 16.7). All files are in plain vanilla ASCII—in other words, so simple that 99 percent of software and hardware can read its files. As the creators stress, the texts available here are meant for general readers and not as authoritative scholarly texts, and their goal is to have 10,000 books in the Project Gutenberg public library by the year 2001.

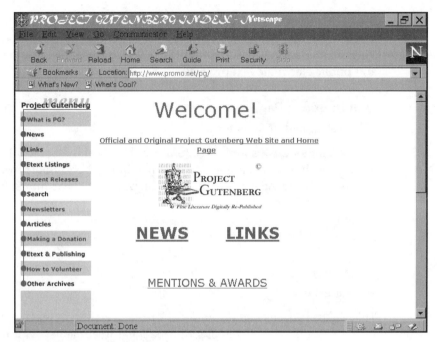

Figure 16.7 Project Gutenberg.

Writings cover authors from Cicero and Descartes to Douglass, Muir, and Zitkala-Sa. There also is a list of other electronic text archives.

Complete Works Of William Shakespeare

the-tech.mit.edu/Shakespeare/works.html

Whether you're a fan of the Bard or just an overworked high school senior, you'll appreciate this site. Shakespeare's works are divided into four categories—comedy, history, tragedy, and poetry. You can get an entire play loaded as one page for easy printing or specify a particular scene in a play and request a list of the dramatis personae. Click on some of the archaic words to find their definitions (a *curtal-axe* is a cutlass, and a *customer* was a common woman). There are several links to Shakespearean resources, a discussion area, and Bartlett's familiar Shakespeare quotations.

University Of Virginia Hypertext Collection

xroads.virginia.edu/~HYPER/Hypertex.html

This is a strong guide to journals and e-magazines related to American studies. Resources include the works of James Fenimore Cooper, Charles Dickens, Dubose Heyward, Charlotte Lennox, and many, many more. Each text has an image of the author and details about its content (language, illustrations, etc.), and whether it is available in full text to the general public or to University of Virginia students and faculty only. You'll also find links to other university and public electronic text projects.

Online Books Page

www.cs.cmu.edu/books.html

This is another great source for literature. The local index includes more than 5,000 English works, and the site is searchable and browsable by author, title, new book listing, or subject. The site also posts special exhibits, from banned books on the Internet to a celebration of women authors. The online books section has links to U.S. general repositories, specialty and foreign repositories, and book catalogs and retailers.

Etext Archives

www.etext.org

This site has dozens and dozens of electronic versions of texts from the sacred to the profane—zines, e-books, sports, legal documents—you name it. The religion section includes Bahai, Rosicrucian, and the Quran. Classical works from Project Libellus (Horace and Virgil, for example) are left untranslated, and they've taken over the old Rutgers Quartz Archives (which has Disney, travel, humor, and other topics).

B&R Samizdat Express

www.samizdat.com

This exhaustive, text-only collection has every imaginable type of document on the Net and off. Users write in to share information about text sources, so the information is not limited by the time or knowledge of the site manager. The index includes information about the National Braille Press, Future Comix, Business on the Net URLs, and the full texts of the play the *Lizard of Oz* (yes, lizard!) and other stories. You'll even find electronic books for sale, and virtual chess and modeling guides.

Bibliomania: The Network Library

www.bibliomania.com

This site includes fiction, nonfiction, poetry, and reference resources. The fiction section has more than 40 classic novels (from Jane Austen to Joseph Conrad), and the nonfiction section has biographies, academic works, and ancient texts. Bibliomania is searchable by page, neighborhood, or for the entire archive at once.

Other Subject Sites

Still haven't found what you need to finish that term paper? Here are some sites dealing with other subjects.

Math Forum

forum.swarthmore.edu

Math resources on this site are organized by subject and grade level. The K-12 section includes arithmetic, algebra, and calculus; the college one has probability/statistics, algebra, and differential equations; and the advanced category has topics such as game theory and programming. In addition to educational material, the Math Forum addresses issues for mathematicians on the job market, equity issues in math and science, the role of math in public policy, and links to organizations, journals, and Web sites covering new directions in pedagogy.

Chemicool Periodic Table

beta-tech.mit.edu/Chemicool

Make your chemistry assignments easier and more fun. Search an element by name or symbol; get a ton of information(see Figure 16.8). For example, enter

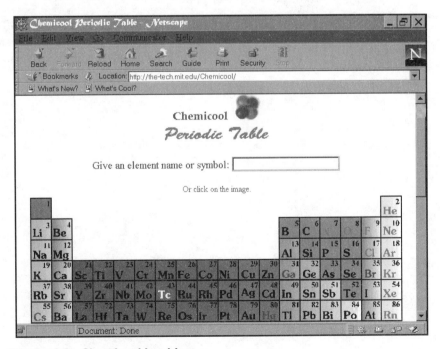

Figure 16.8   Chemicool is a blast.

iron, and you'll get general information (symbol, atomic number, etc.), states (melting point, heat of fusion), energies, oxidation and electrons, appearance and characteristics, reactions, and much more. There are also two onsite chemical calculators (unit conversions and ideal gas law).

Science Matters

www.treasure-net.com/smatters/smatters.htm

This science information site addresses questions ranging from fundamentals (What are quasars? What is the difference between fusion and fission?) to elementary particles and quantum mechanics. Science Matters also has links to other science sites and to newsgroups.

Moving On

As you can see, the Internet has more resources than you'll ever need and probably even know about. While all of this information can be overwhelming—even intimidating—knowing where to start your research can make your task much easier and, who knows, maybe even fun. Most of the resources you've looked at in this chapter will give you solid information about historical, literary, and scientific documents and should help you construct a strong background for your essay or paper.

But unless you're doing a book report or straight literature review, you'll often need up-to-the-moment news to make your work vivid. The next chapter will give you the tools you need to keep current through news sources online.

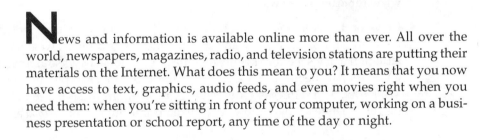

CHAPTER 17

Up-To-The-Minute News And Information

News and information is available online more than ever. All over the world, newspapers, magazines, radio, and television stations are putting their materials on the Internet. What does this mean to you? It means that you now have access to text, graphics, audio feeds, and even movies right when you need them: when you're sitting in front of your computer, working on a business presentation or school report, any time of the day or night.

General News Sources

There are dozens of sites that carry general news and information from the United States and abroad. They cover topics as diverse as religion, sports, and technology.

Newslink
www.newslink.org

We've mentioned Newslink before, but it is well worth looking at again. In addition to its great coverage of political stories in the U.S. and abroad, Newslink connects you to over 7,000 worldwide newspapers, magazines, broadcasters, and news services. You can also tour their Hot Sites, readers' picks, and special online Internet/media columns. Articles are archived and searchable. Newspapers in the U.S. are organized by state, major metropolitan center, type (daily, nondaily), and level of service (limited, promotional). A relatively unique feature is Newslink's collection of links to campus papers from across the U.S. and overseas. Newslink has similarly broad coverage of magazines, radio/TV networks, and resources of general interest to journalists, media buffs, and news junkies.

Kidon Media Link

www.dds.nl/~kidon/uspapers.html

An excellent source from the Netherlands is Kidon Media Link. Organized by region, all newspapers are divided into dailies, weeklies, and electronic deliveries. Media Link is just that—straight links, with no stories carried on the site itself. While the magazine, TV, and radio links are not as strong as other sites, Media Link has unique sections on Teletext feeds, film studios in the U.S. and U.K., and news agencies from Peru to Lebanon. There is also a special Nederlandse Media section devoted to Dutch media.

News On The Net

www.reporter.org/news

News on the Net features an index of major sections in alphabetical order; these are: news, technology and media industry headlines, weather, and international news. Be sure to note that the international news sources may have international themes but are based in the U.S. For example, the newsletter *Main Street South Africa* is about South African affairs but is based in Washington, D.C. There are also a few specialized publications, like *Tripod* and *Tweak*.

Small Hours/News

www.aa.net/~rclark/news.html

Small Hours/News sorts news sources into regions or general news services in English. You can also view the entire list of news sources at once. The site allows you to search the AP news from the past two weeks, check out the AP's top 10 stories, or hook up to the Environmental News Network. In addition to several standard search engines, you can also use finders for Usenet, FTP sites, mailing lists, and Whois (for finding information about a domain name). Small Hours has links to humanitarian organizations and other general news archives as well.

Select ware, inc. presents: alpha complete news index

www.select-ware.com/news/

Select ware, inc.'s alpha complete news index (see Figure 17.1) lists only those publications that are available without charge. Organization is by geographical region, and Select ware describes each link, gives a brief evaluation, and indicates the language(s) of the site, and tells if audio feeds are available. This

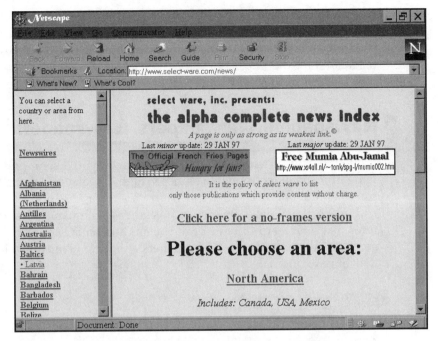

Figure 17.1 *Select ware, inc's alpha complete news index.*

site is an excellent source for European newspapers, particularly if you want them in their respective languages. Select ware also notes if you need special software to read a paper (for example, a Cyrillic viewer for Russian papers).

Ecola Newsstand

www.ecola.com/news/

The Ecola Newsstand carries newspapers, magazines, and computer publications. Newspapers are organized by region, then country or type. They even include Antarctica's *New South Pole Times*. You can go directly to the U.S. News-papers directory and search for a publication by name or state, or specify a type (e.g., daily) and time zone (e.g., mountain states). There are over 5,000 listings, which include U.S. colleges and bookstores. Ecola's links to South American and European news sources are not as strong as Selectware or Newslink. There is also a searchable newspaper archive and a TV remote link to local TV stations.

Enews, The Electronic Newsstand

www.enews.com

If you're looking for yet another general source, check out Enews, the Electronic Newsstand. Divided into two "What's Hot" sections (Heaven and Hell), the Enews newsstand has a showcase area and an "Off the Rack" review section of recent trends and publications. There are over 2,500 titles divided into channels such as business, recreation, and technology. Enews lists the top-10 best-selling magazines for the week. You can even select a username and password and then create a custom newsstand that will carry only your favorite magazines.

Newspapers, Newspapers, Newspapers

While the days of newsprint are far from over, you'll soon find that everything from major metropolitan dailies to high school weeklies are taking their places on the Internet. While most carry a similar core of content—national and international news, sports, and weather—each paper offers unique features that set it apart from its print cousins and online counterparts. Following is an overview of some major papers online, to give you an idea of what they have to offer.

TIP

You don't have to pay a fortune to get your daily newspaper. Most online daily news sites offer a substantial amount of access at no charge.

Metropolitan Newspapers

Here are some excellent regional online newspapers to check out.

The Charlotte Observer
www.charlotte.com/observer/

The Charlotte Observer's Web site is arranged to look like an actual paper, with headlines, columns, and sections that make it a virtual twin to the paper that lands in your gladiolas instead of on your front porch every morning. Major stories have front page summaries with links to the full text, and the *Observer* uses color photos liberally throughout the paper. Many stories have a local flavor (an article on North Carolina college presidents or information about property development in the Charlotte area) as do the area dining, movie, and weather guides. Some stories require a fee-based subscription, although all briefs are free.

The Kansas City Star
www.kcstar.com

The Kansas City Star site features color photos, national news, and events calendars, but it adds opinion forums, live-chat conversations, and the *Star* library—

an archive searchable by keyword and phrase. Story topics vary from baton-twirling competitions to Libertarian party actions against the IRS tax codes, and the business section includes an analysis of the region's top 50 performing companies. Another unique aspect targets the up-and-coming Net generation—"Teen Star" is a segment that is updated weekly and focuses on music (including RealAudio segments), stories, and links of interest to teenagers.

The Sacramento Bee

www.sacbee.com

The Sacramento Bee Web site covers news, sports, leisure, and money. Special features include The Movie Club—a great source of information about what's playing, current reviews, articles about films and the movie industry, and opportunities to win free tickets to advance movie screenings. The paper also has online classifieds; suggestions for travel from California to Europe; and reports "by women, for women" from conferences dealing with business, career, and financial advice targeted toward women.

TIP

*Looking for news that's a little older than yesterday's headlines? Check out Newsworks at **www.newsworks.com**. A single text box will let you search the archives of over 100 newspapers. While the archives don't appear to be more than a couple of years old, the sheer breadth of what you can search means there's a lot of meaningful materials to be found on this site. Best of all, access is free!*

College Newspapers

Regular newspapers aren't the only ones striking out into cyberspace; college newspapers are establishing a strong presence, too. Are you looking for a unique perspective in a very small area of a particular state or country? Try checking out a college paper.

Following are some indexes to college papers, along with an overview of a few "typical" papers.

Kentucky Kernel

www.kykernel.com

The University of Kentucky's online version of *Kentucky Kernel* highlights Current Issues, which are the hottest stories on campus that day. You can also get onsite registration for the Kernel's listserv, and the Sports Smorgasbord serves up the latest news on Kentucky sports if you've got Netscape Navigator 3.0 (frames-supported). The *Kernel* also has searchable archives.

The Arizona Daily Wildcat

info-center.ccit.arizona.edu/~wildcat

The Arizona Daily Wildcat is a campus newspaper that could give the metropolitans a run for their money. Online, you can select sections from a pulldown menu that include news, opinions, sports, police beat, and comics. In addition to letters and classifieds, the *Daily Wildcat* has an archive that is searchable by description or keywords.

The Louisiana Tech Journalism Server

eb.journ.latech.edu

The Louisiana Tech Journalism Server is an asset to online media buffs particularly for its links to publications research. The server has job listings in journalism, college, and high school newspapers and magazines, and FAQs about putting a college paper online. Some of the publication's research links topics include censorship and education, interaction between high school and professional journalists, and a national study of high school and college newspapers.

The College Press Network

www.cpnet.com/college/newspapers.htm

The College Press Network (see Figure 17.2) organizes U.S. publications by state (in alphabetical order) and others by country. CPNet conducts reviews of the Top 25 college publications based on ease of use, daring, up-to-dateness, and good application of new technology. There are also several international college papers listed here, particularly from Canada, but also Denmark, the Netherlands, and Germany. You can also find links to alternative publications such as *Word*, *Hip*, and *Buzznet*, metro dailies, and other news indexes.

Online TV Stations And Networks

Print and audio media aren't the only ones getting online and interactive—so are TV stations and networks. Like newspapers, each television presence has unique features, so it may be worth taking a spin through several sites to see what's out there for yourself.

For example, CNN online (**www.cnn.com**) has the usual U.S., world, and sports coverage, but now lets you get news through a cute little pager on the screen. And ABC online (**www.abc.com**) has Real Audio headlines and video news summaries, links to Disney programming, and trivia games in their CyberCity. NBC online at, you guessed it—**www.nbc.com**—has information on its sitcom stars, job listings, and the Hyperchannels online entertainment network.

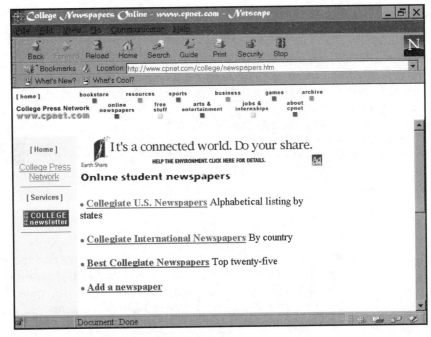

Figure 17.2   The College Press Network.

Magazines And Journals

Chances are that your favorite magazine or journal has an online counterpart, whether it's a political journal, a sports magazine, or an entertainment newsletter. There are hundreds of magazines and journals out there. We've listed several below, but it is impossible to give you even the range of topics in one chapter, so we're including a few indexes where you can find what you're looking for.

University Of Houston Libraries' Scholarly Journals List

info.lib.uh.edu/wj/webjour.html

If you're interested in exploring the more academic-oriented areas, try the University of Houston Libraries' Scholarly Journals list. All journals listed on the UH site are available in English and require no registration fees. The journals are listed alphabetically by title, and there is an ASCII file listing all of the journals on the site as well. You'll find journals from Anthropoetics to Neuroscience-Net and a mailing list archive link, NewJour, which gives you information on forthcoming e-journals.

The MoJo Wire: *Mother Jones* Interactive
www.mojones.com

Mother Jones uses Internet technology to the fullest to get across its political positions and to get you to take action. Hell Raiser Central puts you into the heart of candidates' political speeches and gives you stories about people using the Web to confront political issues and figures online. Steamed about the latest money-raising scandal in D.C.? Plug into the Coin-Op Congress and get the facts to back up your ranting. And if you want to take your ire public, walk into an "Interact and Investigate" chat room of your choice.

BYTE
www.byte.com

You can also find *BYTE* online, with articles that include the print version's cover story of the month. You can search *BYTE* articles and the Virtual Press Room (product announcement section), and find out the latest on telephony and other trends. Files mentioned in *BYTE* articles are downloadable from the site or by FTP, and you can register to have *BYTE* send you e-mail notices about upcoming conferences.

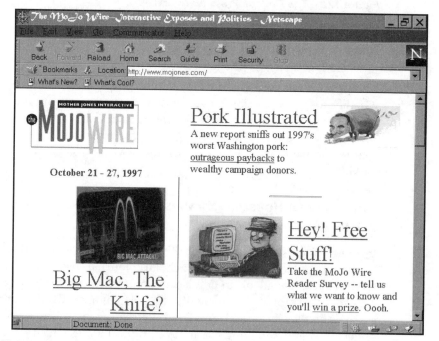

Figure 17.3   Mother Jones *Interactive*.

Elle

www.ellemag.com/

Find fashion fascinating? Visit the *Elle* site. You'll find the expected trend reports, event postings, and articles on this season's fashions. But *Elle* also takes advantage of the Net and gives online users exclusive access to fashion stories not in their print counterpart, as well as the online Model Gallery (photos, photos, photos) and *Elle* Talk message boards.

Aviation Week And Space Technologies

www.awgnet.com/aviation/index.htm

This site isn't fancy, but it provides a lot of solid information on—you guessed it—aviation and space technology. Ever wonder about the level of international support for the Cassini spacecraft launch? Find out here. There's also plenty of space-tech information, as well. A highlight for researchers is the "Intelligence" section, which covers market and industry trends.

Moon Miners' Manifesto

www.asi.org/mmm/

A magazine about the Moon and near-Earth space technology, MMM has seventeen issues online as of this writing. Do you need to find a thoughtful, informed article on the physical and mental traits needed by pioneers to Mars? How about a discussion of "Redhousing," growing plants in the Martian atmosphere? You'll find it here. This magazine is a terrific, intelligent, and slightly offbeat collection of information.

NonProfit Times

www.nptimes.com

NonProfit Times is aimed at executive managers of nonprofits. However, the articles are interesting even to a more casual reader, including the ones on donor research in cyberspace and the need to protect organizations that work with children. Other highlights of this online magazine include a directory of resources for nonprofits on the Web, and a directory of products and services helpful to nonprofits, including legal services, fundraising services, accounting services, and computer software.

Zines

Weird, wonderful, wild, and occasionally offensive, there is nothing like a zine to make you appreciate the anarchic nature of the Net. Zines are small, independently produced publications and cover every topic you can imagine (as well as a few you'll wish you hadn't). Zines are generally done without commercial help or financial gain in mind, and may be the products of passionately committed politicos or simply the rantings of foamy-mouthed narcissists—the two of which are not mutually exclusive.

If you're willing to brace yourself, free your mind, and occasionally hold your breath, the journey through zine-dom will net you news and views you'll find nowhere else. Here are a couple to get you started, plus some sites that list or review many others you can check out.

TIP

Zine editors as a whole tend to express themselves however they see fit, with little more than a cursory regard for mainstream standards of language. With many editors this is okay, since they don't tend to use blue language. A few editors, on the other hand, could make a horse blush. If you're the type that doesn't care for vulgar words or distasteful ideas, tread in these areas only with great care.

Suck

www.suck.com

Suck is a beautifully crafted, self-derisive, and—in its words—self-indulgent cyberrag that doesn't shy away from any topic—God, crack babies, or the Web-as-Giant-Squid thesis. One of the best aspects of *Suck* is that as acerbic as it is toward all creatures great and small, it is also more than willing to turn the acid-splash on itself. Provoking? Yes. A tirade? Often. Journalism? You be the judge—take a look!

Britcomedy Digest

www.prairienet.org/britcom/BD

In the kinder, gentler lane of the zine-side is the *Britcomedy Digest*. From the Black Adder to Monty Python, this monthly zine has gotcha' covered. You can find current and back issues online, as well as articles and snippets on the British comedy scene, the BBC closure of Web sites, or biographies of comedic figures such as Hugh Laurie.

Directory Of E-Zines

www.meer.net/~johnl/e-zine-list

The Directory of E-Zines has a list of over 1,800 zines (and counting!) from around the world. Each entry has a brief description, which you can click on for a full description including format, frequency, keywords, access, and contact information. The site is browsable by keyword and will give you the 80 most popular (travel, TV) or most obscure (bladder, 8-track) keywords, or the whole keyword list, by pressing the appropriate link. Zines are available by Usenet, FTP, Web, Gopher, or e-mail as noted. The Directory also has a list of zine-related sources (events, reviews, guides, and how-to's).

Todd Kuipers E-mail-zines List

www.propagandist.com/tkemzl/

Todd Kuipers E-mail-zines List covers only zines available to your account by e-mail. The List has a full list of topics as well as new additions and is searchable by subject keywords. Each entry has a description of content, frequency of publication, subscription instructions, contact information, other access points (e.g., via FTP or Web), and special notes and descriptive keywords. You'll find zines from Wrestling Voice to the Computer Law Observer.

FACTSHEET5.COM

www.factsheet5.com

Finally, we wouldn't be worth our stripes if we didn't mention the online version of *Factsheet Five*. *Factsheet Five* is a twice-yearly print magazine that reviews zines, both online and offline. The online version runs behind the offline version, but in addition to the reviews there's a bevy of information on the zine world in general and publishing in particular.

What if you don't want to just read a zine? What if you want to be there now? What if you wanna be hip and on the edge?

You take in a live event, of course.

Live Events Online

One way of jazzing up your access to up-to-the-moment news is by "attending" live online events. Many different kinds of events are covered live and online, from sporting events to political coverage to news conferences. By following Usenet, mailing lists, and "what's new" resources you can keep up with what's going on all over the Internet.

Each live broadcast site requires different software to run properly, and we've listed the most important requirements, but be sure to read over all of the instructions and parameters to find out exactly what your system's needs are.

RealAudio

www.realaudio.com

RealAudio lets you download software that plays streaming audio—audio that plays as it downloads (no more having to wait while downloading an audio file). RealAudio has also expanded into video and animation, creating "RealSystem" to complement RealAudio. The site describes all of the features and gives you a demo and the sites using RealAudio—everything from Radio Prague to the NCSU Women's Basketball Team. There is a pull-down menu that lets you select the product you want, along with your OS platform, processor type, and connection speed, and tells you what to do next.

If you have Windows 3.x, you'll need to download the 16-bit version; Windows 95 or NT can use the 32-bit RealAudio versions. The Mac OS version is 32-bit only. As of this writing RealAudio has just released a new 5.0 beta of its RealSystem software, which provides excellent quality stereo sound and video streaming over a 28.8 dial-up connection.

ITV.net

www.itv.net

ITV.net has Real Time Video and a 24-hours-a-day "Netcast" station. Features include celebrity interviews, coverage of events like the Atlanta Olympics, and CU-SeeMee real-time talk and videoconferencing—go around the world without long distance charges since it's all done over the Web. To get ITV's Video On Demand you'll need a PC with a 486/66 or better processor, at least 8MB of RAM and a 14.4 or better modem.

Apple Computer Webcasts

live.apple.com

Apple Computer Webcasts gives you sound, video, and even virtual reality events, including news, concerts, chats, and discussions. The site lists upcoming events and tells you if an event requires a reservation for a spot at the Webcast.

Mediacast

www.mediacast.com

Mediacast gives you access to a variety of Real Time chats, the Digital photo gallery, and QuickTime video clips. First, plug in your connection speed and computer type, and Mediacast will give you recommended configurations. You'll need RealAudio and QuickTime. If you have them, you can listen to concerts and other events from the preshow chat stage all the way through the actual broadcast. Just go to either the Corpcast (business) or Entertainment mediacasts to get the information you want.

Personalized News Services

You probably don't have the time to read the entire paper every morning, and not all of us can afford a personal clipping service. But how can you tell if you've gotten all of the latest information on those hearings in D.C.? Did you ever find out what happened between the biotech companies who had sued each other? Many online news services offer a virtual clipping service that allows you to customize your own paper. This way you'll at least get to the news that is the most important to you. There are also some stand-alone services, such as the following ones.

My Yahoo!

my.yahoo.com

My Yahoo! is a free customized newspaper that includes business news, stock quotes, headline news, weather, and so forth. Just pick a login name and password, and tell My Yahoo! your interests. It will give you suggestions for inclusion in your paper, but the final selections are yours. You can even get city maps and address finders based on your interests.

> **TIP**
>
> *Other search engines and subject index listings offer this same kind of personalization. Try My Excite at **my.excite.com/**, Lycos Personal Web Guide at **personal.lycos.com/**, and Snap! Online's Personal Snap feature at **home.snap.com**.*

CReAte Your Own Newspaper (CRAYON)

crayon.net

CRAYON (see Figure 17.4) also lets you create a personal newspaper online. After you enter your e-mail address and password, you can select your newspaper's name and motto, and then choose whether the newspaper needs a password only for changes, for reading, or for both. You can create your CRAYON paper in two formats: sections (recommended), which is quick loading but slower to scroll through or print, or "Big Form," which is all on one page—much slower to load (over 100K) but easier to print. You can also select subjects that interest you or add URLs that aren't listed on the site (CRAYON gives you a list of all of the news sources it has available and allows you to choose from them). Any time you want an update, just get on the Web and login to your paper.

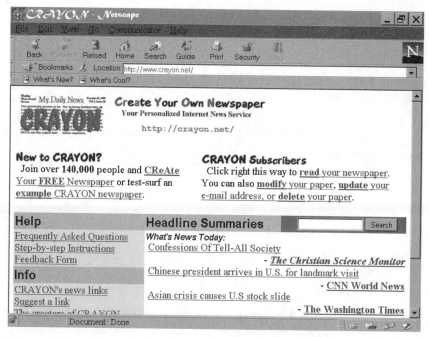

Figure 17.4   CReAte Your Own Newspaper (CRAYON).

Infobeat

www.infobeat.com

Infobeat sends your custom requests to your e-mail box. There are several custom services available, including updates on finances, sports, news, and weather. Infobeat also has a date reminder service. Select one or several dates you need help to remember, then enter the date, what it is (anniversary, birthday), and who it's for (mom, dad, sister), and the reminder service will send you a reminder a week and then a day before the event. The weather service gives you personalized weather forecasts for one or several U.S. cities (enter ZIP code or airport code). The financial section gives you the closing prices and news for your own portfolio of market indices, mutual funds, and securities from three U.S. exchanges.

Moving On

By now you've become something of an expert at finding what you need online—or at least knowing where to begin. Whether you want custom newspapers, live access to a political debate, or a chance to read a zine about tomato caterpillars, you know you can find it through an index or archive online.

But as much as the Internet is an excellent way to find breaking stories, communicate with other activists, or just kick back and relax, it is also susceptible to abuse. All of the features of the Net that make it even better than traditional media can make it even more deceptive if you aren't careful with the information you find. The next chapter will show you how to spot and avoid frauds and falsehoods in Internet resources.

Part IV

Internet Research Issues

CHAPTER 18

Getting The Truth: Legends, Facts, And Frauds

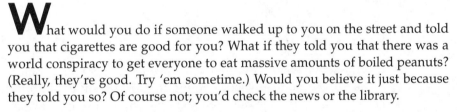

What would you do if someone walked up to you on the street and told you that cigarettes are good for you? What if they told you that there was a world conspiracy to get everyone to eat massive amounts of boiled peanuts? (Really, they're good. Try 'em sometime.) Would you believe it just because they told you so? Of course not; you'd check the news or the library.

On the Internet, you run into this kind of situation all the time. You're reading Usenet postings and e-mail by people you don't know, who have no credibility or history with you. How can you decide what information to consider and what to discard? How do you know you're not being hoaxed or defrauded?

In this chapter, we're going to talk about Internet urban legends, which are usually well-intentioned stories or action alerts, as well as frauds, and Internet time wasters. But before we get into the nitty-gritty of particular things of which you need to be aware, let's talk about analyzing data you find online that doesn't fall into one of these categories. How do you know what's real and what's not?

Verifying Data Found Online

The Internet has a rapidly growing population that corresponds with the mainstream of general culture. However, there are also several not-so-mainstream factions. On your travels throughout cyberspace, you may encounter alternative healing proponents, conspiracy theorists, or psychics. There is nothing inherently wrong with a nonmainstream viewpoint, but the fact remains that nonmainstream viewpoints aren't often covered by the news media. Therefore, it's not as easy to verify claims and information distributed by these factions.

The following hints are designed to help you get the most correct information possible. Use them when you've got the goods, but you're not sure how good the goods are.

Consider Your Source

Currently the assumed credibility of most online information sources is low among many people; only time will develop the reputations necessary for researchers to accept information at face value from certain sources. If you grab a story off an AP wire service, or straight from a company's online database of press releases, it's probably okay. But if you get the information second- or third-hand, double-check it and triple-check it against other resources. (This is especially true of quickly changing data like phone numbers and addresses. If you get an address from one online phone book, try to check it against another before you use it.)

Follow It Back

If you find data that is questionable to you, run it down! If someone tells you that a Survey Company study found that 75 percent of all tortoiseshell cats have tried America Online, then go to the Survey Company Web site and try to find the study. And if you can't find the study, then ask the owners of the Web site about it.

Ask For Attribution

When someone on Usenet or in e-mail gives you facts and figures in the course of a conversation and you'd like to use them, but you're not sure of their validity, ask for attribution. And when they give you the attribution, check it! We cannot emphasize this enough. There have been cases where a Usenet poster has supplemented an argument with dozens of cited sources, and when someone bothered to check the sources, it was discovered they didn't exist.

Consider The Slant

If you ask a Libertarian and a Republican what impact drug legalization would have on the United States, you're going to get two wildly different answers. Each side will present a very convincing argument—one for legalization, one against. Each side will also be backed up by a raft of studies, quotes, facts, figures, and attributions—yet they manage to draw totally different conclusions.

Don't automatically assume that one side is giving you false information. They just know what they believe and have picked the best information to support their position.

These black-and-white perspectives can be a headache. On the other hand, they're great for doing balanced research. The Bureau of Indian Affairs and the Cherokee tribe have completely different perspectives on relations between Native Americans and the U. S. government. If you get both sides of the story, you'll do a better research job.

Don't Use Stale Information

Unless your research covers a specific date range, use the most recent information available. Don't go to a company's site and grab a 1992 copy of the announcement that says they're "phasing into Internet usage." Grab the release from last week that discusses their free HTML classes. Of course, some data—such as literary criticism—is timeless, but before you recirculate information, check the date on it.

Assume You're Going To Have To Check Offline

Humans have been gathering data on paper for thousands of years. We know it hurts to tear yourself away from the computer screen, but sometimes you're going to have to break down and check a source at your local library or get on the phone and call someone. Maybe in a few hundred years everything will be online and everyone will be available by voice chat.

This covers possible misinformation or simply data you're not sure about. But then you've got incorrect data that people will spread to as many people as possible, and swear up and down is true—all with the best of intentions. Take urban legends, for example.

Urban Legends

Have you heard about the lady who tried to dry her poodle in a microwave? How about the guy who found a dead mouse in his soda bottle? You probably have. And did you ever see the stories on the news? Probably not. You didn't because most stories of this type are urban legends, stories that usually have a basis in fact but have been exaggerated or changed.

Urban legends, as part of our culture's oral tradition, are silly and mostly harm-less. They make good funny anecdotes or gross-out stories around the dinner table. You tell 'em, you forget 'em, you hear 'em again later.

On the Internet, however, urban legends are much more powerful and much more insidious. Instead of idly repeating a legend to a couple of people, you can repeat it to dozens or even hundreds of people. Some legends scare people, and others arouse feelings of sympathy and the urge to retell a good story, so the legend gets repeated. Worse, as the legend gets recirculated over and over, it gains an air of authenticity. Soon, it's everywhere. Net citizens spend millions of hours downloading, reading, and responding to the legends. What a mess!

There have been a number of these kinds of legends, but to bring you up to speed, we're going to give you the skinny on the two most popular urban legends on the Internet. If either of these legends makes their way to your computer screen—and they probably will—don't recirculate it. Delete it, and if someone else hasn't set the record straight, do it yourself (nicely—most people redistribute this stuff with only the best of intentions).

Craig Shergold

In 1989, nine-year-old Craig Shergold (also known as Craig Sherwood or Greg Shirgold, etc.) was diagnosed with a terminal brain tumor. He decided he wanted to be remembered in the *Guinness Book of World Records* for receiving the most get well cards. In 1990 he had received 16 million—yup, million—cards and held the world record. In 1991, Craig's tumor was removed and his health improved, but his request for cards wouldn't fade away. Cards and letters poured into the hospital where he'd stayed. Even worse, other organizations were dragged into it.

The following is excerpted from a news release by the Make-A-Wish Foundation (see Figure 18.1). You can read the whole release at **www.wish.org/wish/craig.html**.

```
Shergold's tumor was successfully removed in March 1991. However, the
cards and letters continue. Several versions of the letter exist, most
of which wrongly claim that the young boy remains terminally ill and
now wants to receive the largest number of business cards. The
addressee is encouraged to gather business cards, forward them to an
incorrect address in Georgia, and then forward the chain letter to 10
friends.

"The chain letter claims that Make-A-Wish is involved," stated James E.
Gordon, Chairman of the Board of the Make-A-Wish Foundation of America.
"That is not true. Our organization is not, and has never been
```

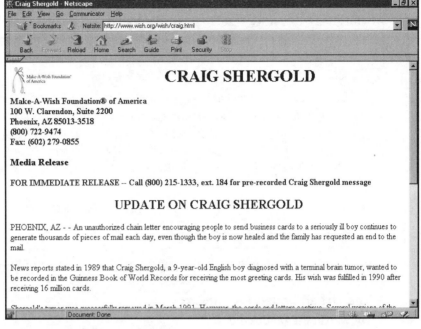

Figure 18.1   The Make-A-Wish home page.

associated with the letter. Yet our office continues to receive numerous phone calls each month about the letter, diverting our staff time and resources from our mission. The Make-A-Wish Foundation requests that people please stop sending business cards or greeting cards to Craig Shergold."

From a dying boy's wish to a major headache for a large children's charity. Poor Craig! Poor Make-A-Wish!

Good Times

Good Times is probably the urban hoax that has damaged the Internet the most—and it's less than five years old.

The first confirmed sighting of this bogus virus warning, according to the Good Times FAQ (check it out at **www-mcb.ucdavis.edu/info/virus.html**), was in mid-November 1994, but the content hasn't changed much over time.

Generally, the message says that a virus called Good Times is being carried by e-mail. It warns that reading a message with Good Times in the title could mess up your computer or destroy your hard drive.

The legend plays on the good intentions of the Internet community; when faced with such a threat we want to warn our friends, so we unwittingly circulate a completely false piece of information. There is no Good Times virus. Relax.

TIP

Just for the record, it would be nearly impossible for a plain-text e-mail message to carry a virus. A virus hides in an executable program and is activated when the user runs the program. There's no place in a plain-text e-mail message for a virus to hide! On the other hand, an attachment received by e-mail could easily carry a virus. That's one of the reasons why it's considered bad manners to send attachments without asking permission first.

Urban Legend Resources

For more information on urban legends, try the following online resources.

The Urban Legend Archives

www.urbanlegends.com

This site covers online and offline urban legends—a lot of them. If you think something is too funny or unusual to be true, check and see if it's mentioned here.

Cyberlore

www.pass.wayne.edu/~twk/cc.html

Cyberlore covers computer folklore, in addition to urban legends. If you're interested in computer culture and anthropology, check this site out.

The Eff Hoaxes Archives

www.eff.org/pub/Net_culture/Folklore/Hoaxes/

This is an archive of online hoaxes and urban legends. Get the straight dope on the modem tax, the man who wrote a friend about spaying his cat and was arrested, and the energy matrix virus.

April Fools On The Net

www.2meta.com/april-fools/

April Fool's Day has traditionally been a time of great humor and creativity online. While April Fool's postings and e-mails are not urban legends, per se, their mischievous information can cause a lot of trouble. When a press release was circulated saying Microsoft had bought the Catholic Church, it caused a furor that took a long while to die down. Check these archives (see Figure 18.2) for pranks pulled over the past several years.

Computer Virus Myths

www.kumite.com/myths

In the dozen or so years that we've been using BBSes and the Internet, how many viruses do you think we've gotten on our computer systems? Two. That's without anything other than basic virus control measures. If you listen to the mainstream media, it can sometimes seem that computer viruses are as common as flu viruses, but that isn't true. This site does a good job of cutting through the hype and giving you hard facts about computer viruses.

What happens when you go from accidental to deliberate misinformation? You encounter fraud.

Online Fraud

You post a message asking about the penny stock market. You receive an e-mail message from someone offering you a book on the subject—all the information

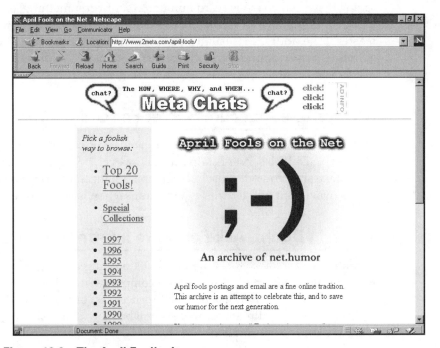

Figure 18.2   The April Fool's site.

you need—for just $9.99. Just send your postal address and your Visa card number, the message says, and they'll mail you the book immediately.

You'd never fall for this, would you? But you'd be amazed how many people do.

In your research, you may encounter folks who are trying to defraud you. While there isn't a lot of this going on now, expect scam attempts to increase as the population of the Internet increases. You can take the following steps to protect yourself:

- Don't disclose personal financial information.
- Always use a secure server for online transactions.
- When in doubt, ask for more information.
- If you're still in doubt, call the Better Business Bureau.

We'll get more into protecting personal privacy in Chapter 21.

Don't Disclose

Don't ever give out your credit card number, checking account number, or any other information that could be used to access your finances through e-mail or on a Usenet newsgroup. Never, never, never! If someone sends you e-mail saying they need your Visa card number to confirm something, or your checking account number as verification to win a free prize, send it to your postmaster. (The address is usually **postmaster@***company.com*. If your e-mail address is **person@mindspring.com**, your postmaster's address is **postmaster@ mindspring.com**.)

Always Use A Secure Server For Online Transactions

The risk of someone intercepting a transmission made between your Web browser and a Web server is fairly low. However, if you really want to play it safe, make sure you only disclose personal financial information on a secure server (Navigator will tell you when a transaction is secure or not secure).

When In Doubt, Ask For More Information

If you're not sure about a company that's offering a product or service, ask them for more information about their company—how long it's been in business, when and where it has received its licenses, or testimonials from satisfied customers. Legitimate companies will be more than happy to supply you with this kind of information.

If You're Still In Doubt, Call The BBB

If you've talked to a company and you still have questions about it, contact the Better Business Bureau (BBB) in the state where the company operates. The BBB can supply you with information about the company and whether or not it has been the subject of investigations or complaints.

A good place to find information about fraud online is the National Fraud Information Center at **www.fraud.org**. The NFIC (see Figure 18.3) has a variety of information, including reports of fraudulent Internet activities, tips for protecting yourself against fraud, and contacts for reporting or prosecuting fraud.

Time Wasters

Spams are not always fraudulent, but we wanted to give that great time waster its own category.

Spam

As we told you before, spam is the posting of a message to a large number of mailing lists, newsgroups, or even private e-mail. The first nationally recognized

Figure 18.3   The National Fraud Information Center.

spam was probably the Green Card spam, put out by a couple of lawyers a few years ago. Since then advertisements, religious admonitions, rantings, and urban legends (like the Shergold story) have been distributed to thousands of places throughout the Internet.

But who cares, right? It's just one message and you press the Delete key and it goes away. What's the big deal?

There's a serious problem with that attitude. There are lots of big deals. Mainly, it costs Internet providers money to shovel text around and store it on their hard drives. And when that cost is significant enough, it's passed on to the customers either in the form of higher prices or more stringent terms of usage (the list of conditions under which your Internet provider agrees to provide service). Furthermore, spam has the potential to choke off rational discussion on newsgroups and mailing lists. What would you do if you got a mailing list that was constantly putting huge amounts of spam into your mailbox? You'd probably unsubscribe. You've lost the benefit of the discourse, and they've lost the benefit of your perspective. Everybody loses except the spammer.

If you're getting hit by spam, check the return address. Forward a copy of the spam to the postmaster and the abuse address of the return address's domain name. For example, if the return address on a spam was **spam@stupidspam.com**, forward the mail to **postmaster@stupidspam.com** and **abuse@stupidspam.com**. If you find the spam harassing or containing content you find offensive (perhaps of an extremely graphic or sexual nature), you should forward it to the postmaster of your domain. There's probably not much they can do about it, but they should know about it.

Do not send abusive or angry messages to the postmaster or abuse addresses. These people take a lot of heat, but the activities of their customers are not their fault. If someone runs over your mailbox and then drives away, do you swear at the police officers who show up to investigate? Of course not. You'd treat them with courtesy and respect. Do the same for postmasters.

You can try replying privately to the spam itself, but we wouldn't advise it. Anything you say can escalate rapidly into a flame war. It's not worth it.

For more information about spam legislation, news, and activities, check out The Coalition Against Unsolicited Commercial Email at **www.cauce.com**. For the sake of disclosure, we should note that this is a very anti-spam site.

Make.Money.Fast

Make.Money.Fast (MMF) is a special hybrid of spam and a chain letter. We don't mean special in a good way; we mean special like it plucks our very last nerves.

The Make.Money.Fast chain letter starts out salivating over the fact that the sender made 80 billion zillion dollars sending out the chain letter and now the sender doesn't work, eats out every day, and flies around the world party-hopping. (Or something like that.)

The letter goes on to explain that you too can participate in this amazing moneymaking process by sending a buck to five people on the list. This will get your name on the list, and as copies of the letter circulate through newsgroups and mailing lists, zillions of people will send you a buck and you too will be rich and sit at home all day eating ham and cream cheese burritos.

Please don't buy into this scam. First of all, it's fraudulent. Second, you will earn the undying enmity of many people on the Internet. Third, those people whom you have irritated have your name and address, because you had to put it on the letter in order to get all that nifty money. This is neither a safe nor comfortable situation to create for yourself. So-called Net vigilantes might do something extra-special to reward you for wasting Net resources, like mailbombing (sending extremely large e-mails designed to flood your provider). Note: This kind of extreme reaction is generally reserved for repeat offenders, though you probably don't want to risk it. Double note: We do not approve of this kind of behavior. Two wrongs don't make a right, and all that.

For more information on the MMF scam, check out the MMF Hall of Humiliation (see Figure 18.4) at **www.clark.net/pub/rolf/mmf**.

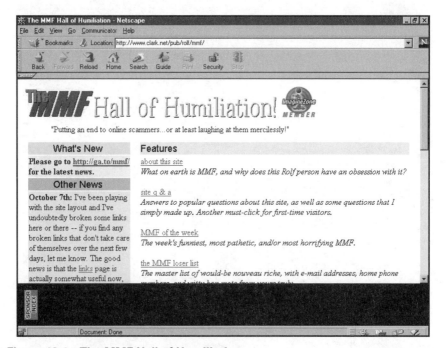

Figure 18.4   The MMF Hall of Humiliation.

Moving On

Although it's unrealistic to expect any large collection of data to be error-free, hopefully this chapter has taught you a little bit about when the red flags should be raised and when you should be suspicious of information.

Some folks would argue that things like spam and hoaxes could be taken care of through judicious government regulation. We are more inclined to argue that an educated Net citizenry, with commonly understood rules, can live in online peace and harmony. Time will tell.

In the meantime, let's talk a little bit about spending money. Sometimes during your Internet research you get what you pay for, which isn't a whole lot. However, with wise investments in online information services, you can get a lot more than what you pay for.

CHAPTER 19

Fee-Based Databases: When Should You Pay?

Not everything in life is free, and neither is everything on the Internet. The Internet is not like America Online, which has premium services that cost over and above the basic fee. However, there are independent companies that set up shop online and charge a fee to browse this information.

As the Internet gets larger, we suspect that you'll see more information collections accessible for a fee. Every database is valuable to someone, but it may not be valuable to enough people to exist on the Internet as an advertiser-supported resource.

At the moment, databases contain general types of information you cannot find on the Internet at large—at least, not in such nicely organized collections. Fee-based databases can be stand-alone pages or a subsection of a Web site, such as the archives of an online newspaper, collected archives of several publications, or collections of compiled information.

Advantages Of Fee-Based Databases

The adage of "you get what you pay for" is occasionally all too true on the Internet. Sometimes the stuff you can get for free just doesn't satisfy your research needs. In this case, a pay-for-play database has several advantages.

Information Is Collected In One Place

With a fee-based database, everything—text and multimedia, if available—is all on one site. In addition, since the information is the primary income generator, the keepers of the site have a strong incentive to keep their information free of strangely formatted text or dead links, things you've probably encountered using general search engines.

Searching Is Faster

With all the materials gathered in one place, the searching process is both faster and easier in a fee-based database. Of course, some online databases have a long learning curve (see "Disadvantages Of Fee-Based Databases" later in this chapter) that take a while to learn.

Credibility Is Less Of An Issue

When you get information from an online fee-based database, you're getting mostly prechecked information from verified services. After all, pay databases won't stay in business long if they're regularly selling erroneous information from unverified sources.

Materials Are High Quality

When you subscribe to a quality online database, you're not getting "he said, she said," you're getting the skinny straight off the press or the wire. There is so much online information that an online service can't get away with selling you the same old stuff. They have to offer you unique, timely material—and most of the time they succeed.

Disadvantages Of Fee-Based Databases

Of course, pay databases are not all beer and Skittles. There are some definite disadvantages to using them, as you'll see in the next few pages.

Pricing Structures Aren't Usually Meant For Individuals

Back in the old days, the only folks who had access to computers for research were hobbyists and professional researchers, or institutions that needed to do research, like corporations or libraries. This led to an expensive pricing model that could be afforded only by professional researchers or institutions. This structure survives today in online databases like LEXIS-NEXIS or DIALOG. (In all fairness, though, these databases are such enormous repositories of information that their prices are more than reasonable.)

Fortunately, as more people have gotten online, some databases have developed fee models more accessible to the casual researcher.

Coverage Of Nonmainstream Data Is Limited

If you're trying to hunt down a timeline of Bill Clinton's activities or grab a couple of candid shots of Socks, a pay database can give you a lot of information. But what if you're trying to get information on 1996 presidential candidates Harry Browne or Monica Moorehead?

Most fee-based databases carry fairly mainstream information, unless they're very technically or industry-oriented. If you're looking for cultural information not often covered by major media—like on small record labels, for example, or little-known political parties—a fee-based information site might have little more than a smattering of information.

Pay Databases Can Have A Long Learning Curve

If you've signed on to a database that charges you by the hour or by the query submitted, you may run up quite a bill just figuring out how to get the information you need. Even with a certain amount of free time each month, you may still end up spending money to learn.

A Few Good Pay Databases

As you can see, there are good and bad points to using online fee-based databases. If you keep an eye out and look for databases that feature flat-rate costs (a weekly, monthly, or yearly fee that allows unlimited access) and easy-to-use material, you can get a lot of benefits out of the access. Our two favorite pay databases are NewsPage and the Electric Library.

NewsPage

www.newspage.com

NewsPage (see Figure 19.1) is a daily news service that provides a dazzling array of information for a low monthly price.

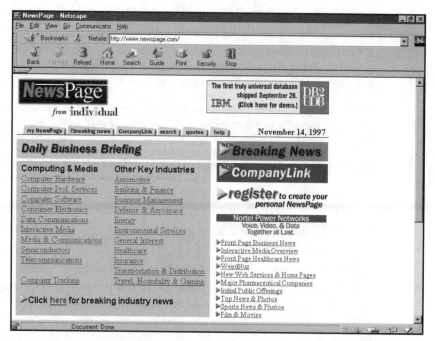

Figure 19.1   NewsPage offers a great way to keep up with the day-to-day news.

Every day, NewsPage receives up to 20,000 news stories from over 600 sources. The sources are many and sundry, with both regular news and industry-specific information about everything from accounting to transportation. The news stories are filtered and put onto NewsPage's Web site by topic. (There are over 2,300 topics; news stories are posted to more than one topic as necessary.)

You are free to explore all the topics and stories as a full service user, with the exception of the pay-per-view stories (but we'll get to those in a moment). However, NewsPage gives you a nice notification every weekday with NewsPage Direct.

When you sign up for NewsPage, you fill out a news profile of topics in which you're interested. You can choose up to 10 topics. Every weekday you'll get an e-mail with information on up to 20 stories covering the topics in which you're interested. The 10-topic, 20-story limitation is a bit frustrating when you're a news junkie. However, you can read as many stories as you like once you're at the Web site, and the daily e-mail is at least a good daily reminder to go check on your pet topics.

NewsPage offers a certain amount of material for free. Story headlines and briefs, for example, are available at no charge. A full subscription costs $6.95 a month; it gives you access to almost all the news stories online except the pay-per-view ones. The pay-per-view stories cost a fixed amount per retrieval; most of the ones we've seen cost between $1 and $3. (It should be noted that the pay-per-view stories on NewsPage constitute a very small percentage of NewsPage's stories.) They have "are-you-sure" screens to make it impossible to choose a pay-per-view story accidentally.

If you need a day-to-day way to keep up with news, especially industry news, NewsPage is an incredible value. The only complaint we have is with the pay-per-view stories. They're not useful often enough, and you only see a limited amount of the story before you've ponied up your money. Still, there's so much available and the price for everything is so good that this is only a minor complaint.

TIP

Online databases have different rules about what you can do with material retrieved from their sites. Be sure to review these rules and abide by them.

The Electric Library

www.elibrary.com

While NewsPage is ideal for day-to-day news, The Electric Library (see Figure 19.2) is ideal for more general reference work. Their selection is also

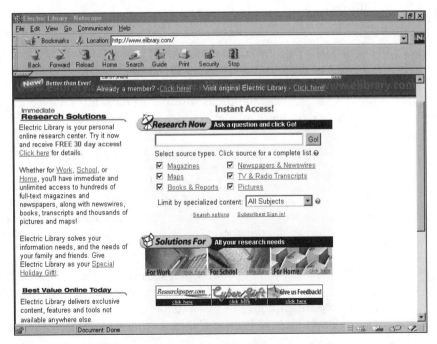

Figure 19.2   The Electric Library is ideal for all types of reference work.

more multimedia than NewsPage. Electric Library offers thousands of photographs and maps in addition to several newswires, hundreds of periodicals, and a variety of reference works, including *Compton's Encyclopedia*.

Searching is simple—enter a few words in the search box and away you go. You can also narrow your search by choosing what document type(s) you're looking for—photograph, newspaper, map, and so on. The Electric Library's photograph collection in particular is excellent.

The Electric Library costs $9.95 a month for an individual, with unlimited use. There are other plans available for multi-user and institutional access. Its extensive references, including the Bible, complete works of Shakespeare, and *Webster's* dictionary, combined into one easily searched location make it a great stop for students, while its extensive photograph and periodical collection make it good for more general research needs.

Other Pay Services

An exhaustive list of pay services on the Web would take an entire book. We'll include more examples here of online services to give you an idea of the kinds of things available.

Inquisit

www.inquisit.com

Inquisit (see Figure 19.3) is a personal agent service. For $12.95 a month you can set up unlimited search agents to review the contents of over 400 publications from around the world and search for the keywords you specify. Inquisit can deliver the information to your e-mail box and can even page you when information becomes available.

The Wall Street Journal Interactive Edition

www.wsj.com

The Wall Street Journal Interactive Edition (see Figure 19.4) is only one of many online newspaper services available. We include it here both as an example of a fee-based newspaper service online and because it's an excellent value for its price ($49 a year).

In addition to the content of the domestic print of *The Wall Street Journal* online, *The Wall Street Journal Interactive* features additional coverage for the Asian and European editions of its newspaper. You also get searching access to the terrific Dow Jones Publications Library, though actually retrieving articles costs

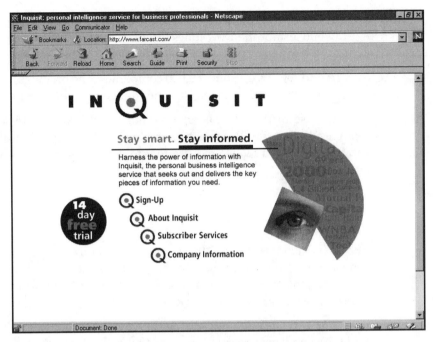

Figure 19.3   Inquisit's agents work for you 24 hours a day.

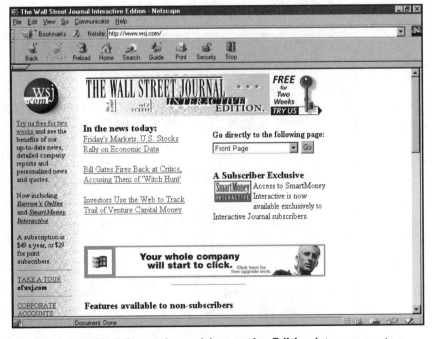

Figure 19.4   The Wall Street Journal Interactive Edition lets you create a customizable profile to give you just the news you want.

extra. If you do a lot of media research, you might find subscribing to the *WSJ* worthwhile just for the Dow Jones Publications Library access.

The Wall Street Journal Interactive Edition also offers Briefing Books, which are background reports on almost 9,000 companies. The briefings are available as hyperlinks whenever a company is mentioned in a news story.

To make use of the site easier, *The Wall Street Journal Interactive* offers a customizable profile. Readers can create a profile consisting of their topics and industries of interest, and use that to display the news in which they're interested.

Hoover's Online

www.hoovers.com

Hoover's Online (see Figure 19.5) has information about more than 11,000 companies around the world, both public and private. One of the great things about the Hoover's site is that it offers extensive free information, such as company search by name or stock symbol.

Once you've ponied up your subscription money (subscriptions start at $12.95 a month), you'll get access to Hoover's Online Library, which has hundreds of archives of business publications. You'll also have access to over 8,000 of Hoover's Historical Financials, which cover sales, net income, and stock price data.

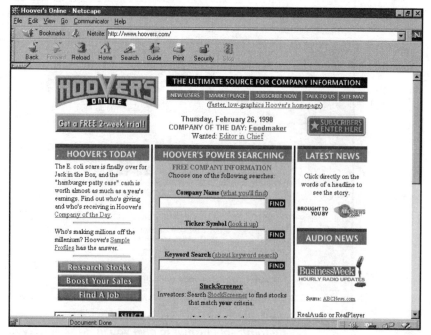

Fig 19.5 Hoover's keeps you up-to-date on a variety of business information.

Moving On

Carefully choosing an online database can augment your research without breaking your budget. Remember to consider your needs carefully—we bet you'll find a winner online.

But even with all this great news and information at your disposal, can you keep up? Can you use the vast resources of the Internet to keep up with the growth and new additions to the Internet itself?

The short answer is no. But turn the page anyway.

CHAPTER 20

Help! How Do I Keep Up?

How do you keep up with all the resources that show up on the Internet as it grows by the second? Sorry; you don't. Even with a dataport straight into your brain and a computer screen in front of your eyes 24 hours a day, you can't keep up. Tara tried, once. She read every Internet magazine available and every announcement service online. Then, one day, her husband asked if she planned to run any errands and she answered that she needed milk@foodlion.com.

That was enough of an alarm that she gave up and concentrated on finding things when she needed them instead of tracking them at all times.

This shouldn't bother anyone, but strangely enough, it does. People seem to assume that just because it's online it should be easy to track. However, the sheer volume of the material makes this impossible. Look at it this way: Do you try to keep up with every new book that gets published? Of course not. Consider the Internet—and especially the Web—the same way.

The best thing to do is to keep in mind a few tips for tracking the materials in which you're most interested. Do we have those tips for you? Of course we do.

Rules Of Thumb For Keeping Up Online

Many Web search engines have a substantial delay before a new resource is added to their database. The next time you want to hunt a new resource, use a newsgroup or mailing list search engine first, such as Deja News (**www. dejanews.com**) or Reference.COM (**www.reference.com**). This is especially important with breaking news.

Take, for example, a pirated site. Sometimes a Web site is *hacked*—broken into—and its images and text are replaced with something else. When this happens, the hacked site may sometimes be made available on *mirror sites*—Web sites that didn't have anything to do with the hacking but have a historical interest in the event. This happens so quickly that often you won't find the mirror sites by using search engines until long after the invasion of the site is old news. However, you will find the mirror sites' URLs with a quick search of Reference.COM or Deja News if people are talking about them (and they usually are).

TIP

What else can you find in newsgroups that you can't find in a timely way by searching Web sites? New game hints, breaking news, opinions about recent events, sports rumors, and so on.

Cultivate A Circle Of Friends

Software agents can make some amazing recommendations, but they're nothing compared to a circle of friends. If you've got regular e-mail correspondents, send them URLs and resource announcements in which you think they'll be interested, and invite them to do the same for you. Sometimes they'll do the job too well. Tara once received 15 notices for the same Web page. But even that can be helpful for letting you know the popularity of a new resource. (Warning: Be polite. If one of your correspondents doesn't want to be included in your resource-fest, don't push it.)

Use Compilation Sites

Small, independently managed specialty index sites (see Figure 20.1) that list links pertaining to a particular subject can add sites much faster than a larger Web search engine. Check with your favorite appropriate specialty indexes when looking for a new Web site. (And remember, **www.clearinghouse.net** will help you find these specialty sites.) Keep in mind that it works the opposite way, too—sometimes small specialty index managers don't have the time to keep the site updated. It might be months before a new link is added. Check the Last Updated On date that's usually at the bottom of a Web page.

Figure 20.1 *Specialty index sites, such as this one about lighthouses, can help you track your favorite topics, sometimes better than general search engines or subject hierarchies can.*

Stalking The Wild Specialty Index

It's a bummer, but sometimes you just can't find a specialty index covering the subject you want. Don't despair, though; a lot of times you can find what you want just by knowing one Web site and going *backward*.

Say you're looking for online information on books and book sales. You have one site to go on: **www.bookzone.com**.

Go to AltaVista or HotBot and do a backward link search on this URL, as we explained in Chapter 11. You'll get some clinkers and some lists of resources relating to books and publishing.

This doesn't work with every last URL, but the more specialized the site for which you're checking, the better it works. (Yahoo! and Netscape, obviously, don't work very well at all.) Try it.

Read

If you have a general interest in Web resources, you might want to subscribe to a couple of magazines that cover the Internet (our favorites are *Internet World, ZD Internet,* and *Fast Company*). The sites they discuss have usually been on the Web for a few months, which is a disadvantage. However, they'll have reviews on them and more detailed information than you'll get from a search engine. This is a handy way to hear about the good sites you might have missed.

Don't Sweat It

When you're searching the Internet for new material, don't constantly worry about the great places you might be missing. The wrong question to ask yourself is, "Have I found everything that relates to this subject?" The right question to ask yourself is, "Am I getting everything I possibly can out of the information I've got right now?"

Resources For New Stuff On The Internet

Giving you a complete list of online resources that covers new stuff on the Internet would fill up an entire book. (We know we say that a lot, but it's true.) We've got six favorites to share with you.

Net-happenings

scout.cs.wisc.edu/scout/net-hap/

Net-happenings (see Figure 20.2) is far and away the most extensive "what's new" list with the highest signal-to-noise ratio available. Everyday, Gleason Sackman, moderator of the Net-happenings resource, distributes announcements for new resources to a mailing list, newsgroup (**comp.internet.net-happenings**), and Web page. The resources run the gamut, from lesson plans to online events to books. This is our favorite way to keep up with new resources—it gives lots of good information with few "clinkers."

A searchable database of the announcements is available at **scout.cs.wisc.edu/ scout/net-hap/**. The database is also available as a list of the day's or month's articles, or as a historical archive, broken down by month, going back to 1994.

If you're prepared to get a lot of e-mail or a large digest file daily, you can subscribe to the Net-happenings list by sending the command **subscribe Net-happenings** *firstname lastname* to **listserv@lists.internic.net**.

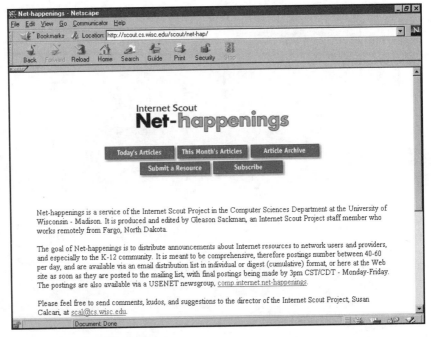

Figure 20.2   Net-happenings.

The Scout Report

scout.cs.wisc.edu/scout/

The Scout Report (see Figure 20.3), a weekly newsletter produced by Susan Calcari, is focused on resources of interest to the education community. How lucky for us that a lot of the resources covered are beneficial to researchers, as well. The report doesn't go for giving you an exhaustive list of new sites; rather, each resource is accompanied by an extensive review of what the resource contains. This is a wonderful newsletter. Subscribe by sending the command **subscribe scout-report** *firstname lastname* to **listserv@lists.internic.net**, or get more information at **rs.internic.net/cgi-bin/lwgate/SCOUT-REPORT**.

What's New Too!

newtoo.manifest.com

What's New Too! (see Figure 20.4) is probably not as well known as Net-happenings, but this does not stop it from listing over 500 new resources a day. What's New Too! makes no visible attempt to monitor the list, so the announcements run the gamut. One recent day's highlights included a Web site for a bed-and-breakfast in Quebec, the home page for a wheelchair manufacturer,

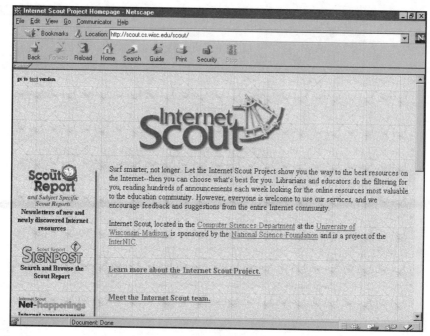

Figure 20.3 *Researchers and educators especially will get a lot out of The Scout Report.*

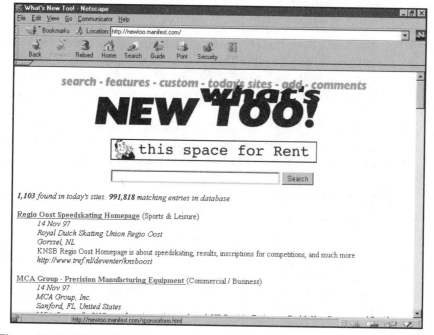

Figure 20.4 *What's New Too!*

and the online gallery of an Oregon artist. You may be getting the impression from all this that you'll have to dig a little to find what you want, and that's true. However, the What's New Too! Web site allows for simple searches that should save you time.

Edupage

Okay, okay. Edupage is not a resource listing, per se; it's a thrice-weekly report on information technology. We include it here because as a repository of technology news; the trends you can read about are rapidly reflected in new resources of interest. For example, if Edupage runs a brief on new concerns about network security, you may see a sudden surge of announced white papers or conferences on network security a few days later. Edupage gives you the whys and wherefores of some of the new site trends that might be confusing you. Subscribe to Edupage by sending the command **subscribe Edupage** *firstname lastname* to **lisproc@educom.unc.edu**. If you really like this resource, you may want to subscribe to the bimonthly print magazine, *Educom Review.*

Net Announce

www.erspros.com/net-announce/

Though smaller in scope than Net-happenings, Net Announce (see Figure 20.5) is a similar kind of service. It's delivered twice a week via e-mail and includes a variety of information, including new site announcements, event listings, and content updates.

Instead of receiving all the information via e-mail, the Net Announce subscriber receives a summary page that lists the titles of all the latest announcements available. Subscribers can either click on the title and go immediately to the Web page containing the announcement, or receive the announcements they want via e-mail.

A subscription form is available at the Web site, or your can send an e-mail to **nalist@erspros.com** with the word "subscribe" in the body of your message.

The Green Eggs Report

www.ar.com/ger

For a completely different take on new URLs, check out The Green Eggs Report (see Figure 20.6). It is a collection of Web site addresses pulled from Usenet postings. They're arranged on the Green Eggs Web site by the Usenet group from which they were taken—scroll down to the newsgroup in which you're interested, click, and there you are. Green Eggs collects over 1,500 URLs a day, and while it may take a little digging to find something really good, it's a completely different source of URLs than the others we've given you in this chapter.

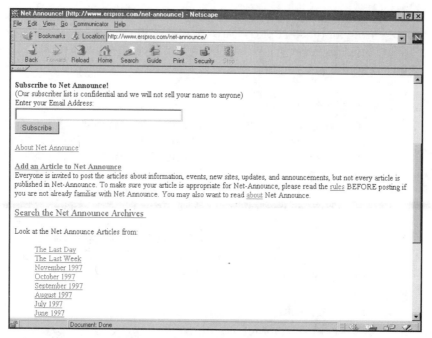

Figure 20.5   Net Announce.

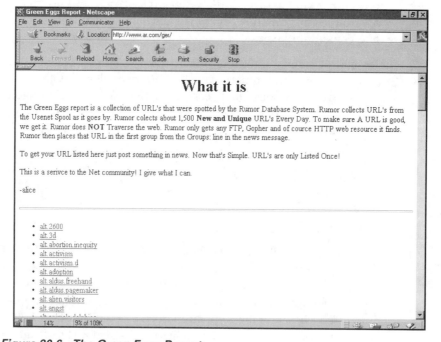

Figure 20.6   The Green Eggs Report.

Moving On

The Web gets bigger every day. These tools should help you stay on top of it as much as you need; remember—you don't have to know everything that's going on.

But by being online so much, you might be concerned about your privacy. Now let's talk about protecting yourself online.

CHAPTER 21

Protecting Yourself: Privacy On The Internet

This is a difficult chapter for us to write. We have spent so much of this book telling you about the possibilities of the Internet, about all the great things you can find, and the research you can do online.

But at the same time we have to be realistic. The Internet has some dangers: Just like a city has wonderful sites to see—but at the same time dangers—the Internet contains good things and bad things. (And the Internet, as you probably realize, is the about the biggest city of any.)

So in this short chapter we're going to be taking a look at the ways you can protect yourself. You don't have to be a computer whiz to take advantage of this information; it's pretty easy to follow.

Let's start out with the first and best tool for protecting your privacy: *your brain* (well, your common sense, actually).

Using Your Brain

Okay, we admit we're horsing around a little bit, but it really is true that basic privacy protection starts with using your brain. That's because the first and most important thing you have to protect is your password. Actually, you've probably got several passwords you want to protect.

Let's talk first about creating passwords. We encourage you to create weird passwords—the weirder the better. Don't settle for a really basic password like your spouse's middle name or the date of your birth. If you have what you consider to be a dull job and you're looking for a creative outlet, apply it to your password. You won't regret it.

Use upper and lowercase letters, like this: ExAM562G. Use numbers and letters at the same time, like this: WH44hoIk7. (These are just examples, of course; make your own.) Don't attach meanings to them. Make them long if you can (some passwords can only be eight or 12 characters). And please, please, please—*do not use the same password for everything you use that requires a password*. If the security on that one password is compromised, you're in real trouble. Use many different passwords.

Now, if you've used the Internet for even a little bit of time, you've probably accumulated plenty of passwords. Some newspapers, for example, give free access but require that you register with a username and password. You might also be using a couple of pay services that require usernames and passwords. And you might be getting mad at us for suggesting that you make up all these passwords and then keep up with them. After all, you already have to remember phone numbers, PINs, identification numbers, and all kinds of other data strings, and here *we* are telling you to cook up a few more and remember *them*. We have some nerve.

One of the things that might make your life a little bit easier is a password manager. These are programs that keep your passwords all together in one safe place, while *encrypting* the information to keep it safe. (More about encryption later in the section, "Encryption: Making a Code.") If you want to see one of these programs in action, check out Password Manager from Celerity Consulting Services. This program stores your passwords and displays them when you enter the master key (so you have to remember only one password instead of a couple dozen). It can also generate passwords for you and set expiration dates for passwords, so you remember to periodically change your passwords. It's shareware and at this writing costs only $14.95 for a single-user license. You can download a 60-day trial version at **www.celcoserv.com/**.

Why oh why are we harping on passwords like this? Because passwords are like the keys to your house. Someone who has the keys to your house can get in and do all kinds of mischief when you're not home. Obviously you would not give away your house keys to someone unless you trusted them completely. Yet sometimes people have a much more cavalier attitude about their passwords. They write them down anywhere, they share them...this is a really bad idea.

People can violate your privacy in other ways, but they can do it very easily if they get your passwords. Start protecting yourself online by protecting your passwords.

In addition to protecting your passwords, you also want to protect personal information. Think two or three times before making your phone number publicly available, or your street address. Don't ever share your social security number. And of course, don't share financial information or any other sensitive data online unless you're participating in a secure transaction.

Okay, enough with the common sense. Let's talk about real nuts-and-bolts privacy. You can look at your privacy online in two basic ways: one is how messages are passing back and forth from your computer to the Internet, and the other is the messages available on the Internet itself. We'll look at the traffic between your computer and the Internet first.

Encryption: Making A Code

When you send out an e-mail, or send a command to a Web page, it can be intercepted. It's not very likely, but it's possible. The analogy that you might have heard is that sending an e-mail is like sending a postcard, which members of the postal service can read if they want to. Of course, they have their own lives and their own things to do, but theoretically they could read your mail.

It is the same way with Web pages. If you send information to an unprotected Web page, it is possible that someone can intercept that information.

The response to that possibility is a technology called *encryption*. What encryption does is scramble your document with a code that can only be unlocked with a particular "key." It puts your communications in an "envelope," so to speak, and makes them more difficult to view.

A variety of different software is available that you can use to encrypt your e-mail and make it safe. The most well-known one in the U.S. is probably PGP, or "Pretty Good Privacy" (see Figure 21.1). You can download a demonstration copy of this program at **www.pgp.com**.

Please note that this software has severe restrictions. As it says on the Web page, "Please remember that all cryptographic software is classified as export-controlled by the U.S. Department of Commerce. If you are a citizen of the U.S. or Canada, or have permanent alien resident status in the U.S., you may legally purchase and download the software."

Figure 21.1   Pretty Good Privacy's Web site.

The procedure for protecting the information that flows between Web pages is a little different, but it's just as important. Say you want to order a book from the Internet. You want to give your credit card number, but you don't want to run the risk of someone intercepting it. Netscape servers and the Communicator browser are equipped with a security measure called the *Security Socket Layer (SSL)* protocol. Basically, a site secured with SSL encrypts the data that's being transmitted, so that even if someone manages to intercept it, it's just so much hash.

TIP

Wondering if the Web page you're looking at is secure? Look at your Navigator screen, in the lower left corner. You'll see an icon that looks like a little padlock. If it looks open, the Web page is not secure; if it looks closed, the Web page is secure. You can also find out the status of a page by choosing Security from the main Navigator menu bar.

But of course, securing the credit card transmissions isn't going to matter at all if you send the credit card number to the wrong place. That's what site certificates are for.

Digital Certificates

Are you sure that the Web page you're looking at is the company or retail site it claims to be? Are you sure?

Web pages can't be issued driver's licenses to confirm their identity, and birth certificates are right out, too. The identity of a page is instead confirmed through the use of what's called a *digital certificate*. The certificates are unique and prove that a Web site is what it says it is (see Figure 21.2).

The certificates are issued by certificate authorities, just like a driver's license is issued by the DMV. One of the better-known CAs is VeriSign, at **www.verisign.com**. You can get information about a site's certificate, if any, by clicking on the security icon in Navigator's menu bar.

At this point you might be thinking, "Gosh, digital certificates sound like a good idea. They should make those for individual people so that people can prove to Web sites that they are who they say they are." You're one step ahead of us (which is good because otherwise we'd be short one segue). They do make personal digital certificates, (*personal certificates* for short). You can use a certificate to sign an e-mail message and assure correspondents that it's really you—things like that. Are you interested in getting a digital certificate? Check

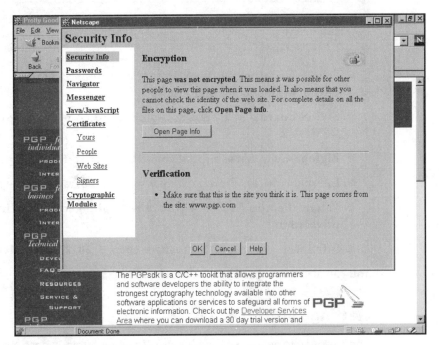

Figure 21.2   The security information of a site, along with certificate information.

out **certs.netscape.com/client.html**. Warning, though: The certificates cost money, and how thorough they are depends on the level of the certificate.

Okay, now you know how you can prove who you are and how a Web site can prove what it is. Now let's take a look at how you can remove yourself from information repositories.

Getting Out Of The Databases

Several places online store information about you, especially if you have a listing in the phone book. Some places build a directory of information starting from phone book listings.

So, obviously the first thing to do if you don't want your contact information available online is to make sure your number is unlisted. However, other types of information are available online as well, like e-mail addresses. You might have a listing without meaning to, simply because you posted a message in a public forum.

Getting Out Of Contact Information Databases

Several Web sites house contact information, as well as removal information, too. Here is a listing of URLs you can use to learn how to remove yourself from various databases:

- **Four11** Go to the main Four11 site at **www.four11.com** and click on Help/ FAQ in the menu bar on the left.
- **Switchboard** Go to **www.switchboard.com/faq_pepl.htm#RES_ REMOVE**.
- **Bigfoot** Go to **www.bigfoot.com/RUN?dyn=&FN=FAQ_EDIT**.
- **Internet Address Finder** Go to **www.iaf.net/frames/delete.htm**.
- **Yahoo! People Search** Go to **www.yahoo.com/docs/info/people_ privacy.html**.
- **InfoSpace** Go to **in-132.infospace.com/_1_60127106__info/faq.htm**.

You can also get out of Deja News, if you like, as we explain next.

Getting Out Of Deja News

The best way to get out of Deja News is to never let your posts appear there in the first place. Putting X-No-Archive in the headers of your messages will assure that your messages aren't archived (this applies both to Deja News and Reference.COM).

However, if you want to get out of Deja News after a posting, you can still do it. Visit **www.dejanews.com/forms/nuke.shtml**. You'll be asked to give the e-mail address for the posts you want to "nuke," and you'll have to go through an e-mail confirmation process for each message that you want to remove from the Deja News archive.

Because each removal has to be confirmed by e-mail , this process will not work for an e-mail address you no longer have.

Now you know how to protect your communications and how to keep personal information out of databases (or get it out after the fact). But if you're a parent, you're going to want to protect one more thing: your kids.

Protecting Your Kids

This doesn't quite fit the heading of protecting your privacy, but it's as good a place as any for discussing protecting your kids from things that you don't want them to see online.

> **TIP**
>
> *We're discussing Web pages in this section, but your kids probably do some online chatting, too. Make sure they know the basic "don't talk to strangers" rap, and make sure they know never to give out personal information like their address or phone number on the Internet.*

You have beliefs and a culture into which you want to raise your child. And that means that you don't want them to have access to certain images and ideas. And you know what? That's your right and responsibility as a parent. We have the right to free expression in this country, but we also have the right to protect our children from what we consider dangerous or inappropriate ideas or resources—whatever they are. In the past this has caused a deep conflict between public information resources, like libraries, and people who wanted material removed from these resources because they disagreed with them.

The technology surrounding the Internet, however, has developed software that allows you to pick and choose from information on an individual level. This kind of software is called *filtering* software. It filters Web site information—sometimes based on actual URLs of resources, and sometimes based on keywords—and helps assure that your kids are not looking at things that you don't want them to look at.

Bear in mind that this doesn't always work perfectly. Keyword blocking software may block your kid's research on "breast cancer." And a URL-blocking program might not cover the subjects that you find offensive if they are beyond what the general cultural standards consider decent. (For some reason, for example, you may consider information about thumbtacks offensive and not want your children to have access to it.)

Bottom line: Filtering software might be a good addition to your use of the Internet. Is it *not* a substitute for your brains, your judgment, and your supervision of your kid. Yet at the same time, the more people who take advantage of individual-level content control, the better we will be able to enjoy our rights of free expression. (It's a thin line, isn't it? Well, nobody said maintaining civil liberty was easy.)

For more information about filtering software, check out Filtering Facts at **www.filteringfacts.org**, which is very pro-filtering. For an anti-filtering perspective, look at Peacefire at **www.peacefire.org**.

Moving On

Hopefully this chapter has given you a few ideas on how you can better protect yourself online. We hope we haven't bummed you out, but rather given you a little practical instruction on making the online experience safer for yourself and your kids.

Next, we're going to get into how you can track your searches once created and how you can make the most of your archived information. Let's talk archiving…without pack-ratting.

Part V.

Internet Research For Scholarly Types

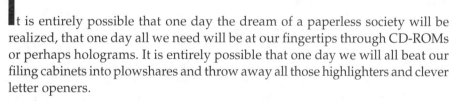

CHAPTER 22

Archiving: Keeping Track Of Research Projects

It is entirely possible that one day the dream of a paperless society will be realized, that one day all we need will be at our fingertips through CD-ROMs or perhaps holograms. It is entirely possible that one day we will all beat our filing cabinets into plowshares and throw away all those highlighters and clever letter openers.

It is also entirely possible, as Dorothy Parker once wrote, that the Statue of Liberty is situated in Lake Ontario.

Let's face it—paper is invaluable simply as the lowest common denominator of data storage. You don't have to worry about paper being incompatible with the particular pen you're using. You don't have to worry about a General Protection Fault with pressed wood pulp. You may spill coffee on it, but even then it's unlikely that you'll have a complete data loss.

When your hard drive crashes, you can lose data forever. Heaven help you if you don't have a backup. Of course, having a backup can set you up for that double-whammy of a research nightmare: the corruption of your backup.

The ideal situation when archiving your research efforts is balancing your electronic archiving with paper supplements. This chapter will discuss just that—archiving, but without pack-ratting.

Analyzing Your Research Needs

The first question is, "Do you need to even archive in the first place?" Let's look at your situation.

How Serious Is It And How Serious Are You?

If you're doing research for academic or commercial reasons, we'd say that you are pretty serious and should probably do a more extensive job of archiving the materials you come across while researching. But what if you're a more casual researcher? Your archiving needs are not as extreme. As you go through this chapter, bear in mind that what should be standard operating procedure for an academic might be overkill for an armchair Sherlock.

How Much Do You Need To CYA?

That's *Cover Your Archives*, regardless of what other words you've assigned to that friendly little acronym. Are you going to have to cite your sources (we'll talk about that in Chapter 24), or are you going to have to "show your work," as they said in calculus class? Is the research you're pursuing more like a "hunt," where you're zigging and zagging and going through several complex steps to get what you want, or are you just "gathering" data? The first might require an extensive log of activity, especially if you're doing a lot of work over a long period of time, while the second might require just a list of URLs.

> **TIP**
>
> *Not all research projects are huge, immensely complicated beasts. At our company, we sometimes get requests from clients or peers to do quick projects—a 30-minute drill, if you will.*
>
> *These are quick answers to a research question or problem. For example, we recently got a call from someone who wanted figures on direct mailings that had more than a 10% return rate.*
>
> *After 30 minutes of research we had a dozen examples, complete with URLs. The 30-minute drill is excellent exercise and something you might want to try the next time you have a research problem. Just set your timer to 30 minutes and go.*
>
> *The question is, what do we do with this information once gathered? If it is nonsensitive information, we have a variety of options, and so do you. Here they are:*
>
> - **Put it on your Web site or in your library.** *This means you'll always have the information at your fingertips, but at the same time you might not*

ever need it again. Unless you really think you'll use the information again, don't try this option.

- **Create a case study.** *In a few paragraphs (see "The Single-Page Case Study"), we'll be discussing creating a case study. Unfortunately, creating one sometimes takes more time than actually doing the 30-minute drill.*

- **Share it.** *When it's possible, pass on the information to a group that could use it. For example, if you're involved in a marketing discussion group, share with them the list of direct mailings that had more than a 10% return rate. They can use it, they may pass it on—and someone might end up archiving it anyway.*

Archiving Strategies

You can probably shuffle paper 50 million ways. We could also say that about organizing an archive. The way that has worked for us is a single-page case study model. It allows you to vary the complexity according to your needs, while allowing you—at any level of complexity—to use the same model.

TIP

This is the way we like to keep track of our important research problems. You may have something different, or you may want to integrate your research into your current archiving. That's fine. The important thing is that you're able to arrange your materials in such a way that you both learn from them and benefit from their use.

The Single-Page Case Study

The core of your archiving effort should be the single-page case study. By starting with this format, you can get either as detailed as you wish, or restrict your record of a research effort to the bare minimum of who, what, when, where, why, how, and 32- or 16-bit. (Okay, we made that last one up.)

Format your case study like this:

- **Date** The date you did the research.

- **Topic/Title** Make this a meaningful line that you can remember.

- **Description of Problem** This should be a description, in a few sentences, of your research need or problem.

■ **Special Circumstances** If special circumstances surround this research effort (for example, if you had access to unusual resources or you were restricted in the resources you could use), put them here.

■ **Solution** Write down your footsteps here—what you went through to find the information for which you were looking. This might be a sentence for an easily solved project or several paragraphs for a more extensive solution.

■ **Action Taken** Whatever action you took, if appropriate.

TIP

If you've already got a filing system for your records, you might want to add a Related Case Studies field to the preceding ones, so you can cross-reference them within your filing system.

Want an example of the case study sheet in action? Take a look at this:

■ **Date** October 10, 1997.

■ **Topic** Push technology.

■ **Description** Find third-party products that help create channels for push technology.

■ **Special Circumstances** None.

■ **Solutions** Went to CMP and ZDNet sites, searched for articles on push software. Went to Yahoo! and skimmed the software section. Finally downloaded several trial versions of software, including Hotdog Professional 4 and FrontPage 98.

■ **Action Taken** Sidebar on channel-creation software for article.

This case study could stand by itself and be referred to later when we're ready to do another article. We could see where we went last time and pick up our tracks where we left off. Or, we could attach a great deal more information on the sites where we had been—printouts of the articles we found, contact numbers of PR people, or product information sheets. Either way, the single-page case study sheet acts as the core of the archived research, gathering and summarizing the information.

How To Create And Organize Your Archive

A one-page case study could be created on your computer in a variety of ways: as a note in InfoSelect, as a document on your favorite word processor, as an entry in a database, or even as an e-mail you send yourself. We tend to prefer either InfoSelect or using a word processor—it's easier to convert the document to plain text and share with other people.

InfoSelect (see Figure 22.1) lends itself well to creating lists of material that can go with your case study. For example, CWR used to do public relations work for a television station's Web site in Raleigh, NC. The site is marvelous but so extensive that we had to publicize it through a number of channels. Every week we created a "PR Report," which detailed who we had approached for coverage consideration, whom we had asked for a link to the Web site, and so on. We made out this report in InfoSelect as a "public version" of the case study document that we could give to a client. These kinds of lists could also be used to supplement a case study, or as a summary of efforts made and sites contacted.

How you should organize your materials is a different matter. We have a few suggestions, like always, but you're free to invent your own styles. Try organizing your materials:

- **By date.** Ideal when your research is corporate or otherwise professional and you can trace a day on your timesheet to a case study.

- **By academic category.** If you're a student, try breaking down research problems by category, and from there break them down by date, class, or individual assignment.

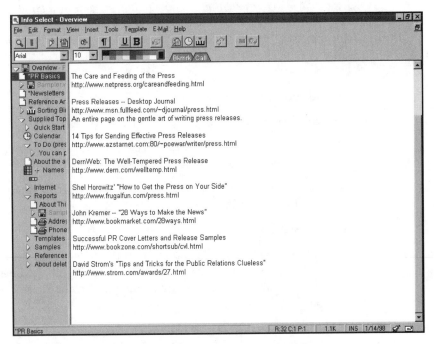

Figure 22.1 InfoSelect is great for making summary lists.

■ **By type of problem.** If you don't plan on archiving many details, you may want to break your materials down into two simple categories: "hunting" for a solution, or "gathering" about a subject or topic.

■ **By client or job.** If you're working on a corporate or institutional level, incorporating your case studies into a current division of archives by clients and jobs could save you time—the filing system is already set up.

Now you know how to archive and have some ideas about how you could organize your materials. But what should you archive?

What To Archive

When we say *attach* materials to your case study sheet, we don't mean print out every last little Web page and Internet resource you come across—good grief, no. You'd quickly run out of room in your filing area and start having bad dreams about old-growth forests.

Instead, we've got a list for you of things you probably do want to archive, in addition to things you might want to think twice about.

TIP

> *Don't compare your potential archives to this list and then blindly archive everything we recommend, okay? We don't want you to feel like this is the be-all, end-all, must list. Make sure it's relevant to your research, and worth keeping, before you include it in your case study.*

You should probably archive these:

■ **E-mail correspondence.** If you don't archive this, who will?

■ **News stories.** Don't assume they'll get picked up in an archive. If it's not a major story, it may just drop off the wire.

■ **Nonarchived mailing lists.** This is another type of information you might not be able to find later.

Think about archiving these:

■ **Temporary Web sites.** Sites that are put up for a special reason, like to promote a movie or album, are sites that aren't going to be around long. If they add value to your research, you might want to print them out and keep them.

- **Usenet posts.** Some users use a header option called *x-no-archive* to avoid having their posts archived on Usenet. If you're not sure if a Usenet post is going to be archived or not, you may want to keep it.

- **Search-generated material for a Web site.** If you've just run a search for a set of addresses or a certain amount of text, you might want to print out the search results and keep them, especially if the search took a while.

TIP

You might have noticed that we don't say anything here about stable Web sites, like those of large corporations or organizations. That's because there's no reason to archive them—they should be around as long as you need 'em.

Maintaining Your Archives

We've already covered how to arrange your archives, in what order to put them, and what to actually include. Now let's talk about how to maintain those archives so you can actually use them:

- **Save postings and e-mails in their entirety.** That means including the headers that tell where it came from, when, and the e-mail address of the person who sent it. Don't rely on your memory to retain this information.

- **Put additional notes directly on the material being archived.** If you've got a bit of information you need to add, don't use another sheet—just write it on the post, e-mail, or resource to which it pertains. Be sure to use a vivid ink or other marking device that sets the notation apart from the other information.

- **Keep an updated paper and electronic record.** Keep your archives in both electronic and paper format. Make sure both types are kept up-to-date. Keep case study records in individual folders on your hard drive, and don't forget to do a periodic backup.

- **Spring clean.** Periodically go through your files and toss the case studies you no longer need or use. If you're a student, you may want to clean your files once a semester. If you're a professional, perhaps once a quarter. And if you're a slacker, every time your filing cabinet is about to explode should do the trick.

Moving On

It may seem a little disloyal for computer geeks to have such a fondness for paper. But paper's a lot less complex and therefore subject to fewer complex problems. Perhaps one day a simple, foolproof way will exist to electronically store and retrieve data without ever having to worry about disk corruption or drive crashes.

Unfortunately, no matter how carefully you gather your information or do your archiving, you sometimes don't get the information you need in the format you want. Sometimes you need to change the format a little; sometimes you need to convert it completely. Chapter 23 discusses making those kinds of changes and the tools you'll need.

CHAPTER 23

Moving Information Around

You're doing a research paper comparing the poetry of Ted Hughes and Ogden Nash. You're surfing around the Net checking out poetry references. Suddenly, you find it, the great resting place for your madness—the official Ted Hughes/Ogden Nash Web site, including a rare photo of when the two were at Vo Tech together. (Perhaps for the sake of clarity and because this is a humorous example, we should explain that we are making all of this up; as far as we know, these two fine poets never participated in vocational education, much less together.) Anyway, the photograph and a couple of quotes from the site would make a great addition to your paper. So how do you grab the information?

Whoa. Hang on a minute there. Before we get into how to grab information, let's talk about copyright.

Copyright Resources On The Internet

The Internet is a great place to learn about copyright and other intellectual property issues. You'll find online official government sites, nonprofit clearinghouses, and commercial legal centers, all of which offer different perspectives and information. Here are some places to start your research when you're not sure if your use of material is "fair use" or fairly illegal.

The United States Copyright Office

lcweb.loc.gov/copyright/

This is the official U.S. copyright presence and is carried by the Library of Congress site (see Figure 23.1). You can find out everything you ever wanted to know about copyrights, much of which you probably didn't even know to ask. The About the Copyright Office section posts hours of service, location, and phone numbers, but it also has a detailed history of the U.S. Copyright Office. You'll find the original idea for intellectual property protection outlined in Article I, Section 8 of the U.S. Constitution, and the origins of the Office itself, its role, mission, and administrative structure. The Office lists each division and a brief description of its responsibilities, and gives you notable dates, a list of all Registers for the Office, and a guide on how to get more information.

This historical information is only the beginning of the site, however. The Copyright Office also posts information on current issues such as legal protection for databases and the waiver of moral rights in visual artwork. You'll also find the latest scoop on the ongoing, multiyear project known as CORDS (Copyright Office Electronic Registration, Recordation and Deposit System), which is projected to allow applicants to apply for copyrights via digitized applications over the Internet. You can even learn how to conduct online searches for copyrights via Telnet.

Figure 23.1   The United States Copyright Office.

Copyright Clearance Center Inc. Online (CCC)

www.copyright.com

This is a nonprofit company organized at the request of the U.S. Congress to help companies and organizations comply with U.S. copyright law. The Copyright Clearance Center Inc. Online (CCC Online) runs collective licensing programs that allow authorized users to make photocopies from their collection of over 1.75 million titles and still be within the law. The site is searchable by company type (academic, medical organization, information broker, etc.) or service type (FEDLINK, international, all services, etc.).

CCC Online (see Figure 23.2) also has a catalog of titles that you can browse to see if the works you need are registered. The service catalogs include a range from FEDLINK, which gives blanket licenses to federal library members, to Annual Authorization Service (AAS), which gives blanket licenses to corporations and organizations with 500 or more employees. CCC Online's Some New/Some Newer Stuff section gives you a "question of the week" (largely trivia), access to the Electronic Rights Management Service (which will help you with getting the right clearance electronically), and a list of speakers dealing with intellectual property. CCC Online also maintains a body of press releases and articles dealing with copyrights and intellectual property.

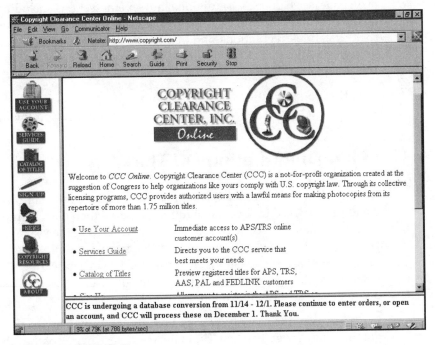

Figure 23.2   CCC Online.

EINet's Intellectual Property Page

www.einet.net/galaxy/Law/Intellectual-Property.html

This site deals with the broader issues of intellectual property, but it also has information dealing with copyrights and new media. In addition to its two major sections on international and networked communication issues, EINet maintains a New Items section, which releases information that is less than seven days old. It also posts announcements on stories such as "Intellectual Property and the National Information Infrastructure," and has a good list of collections and directories on copyright issues. You'll also find a few periodicals, such as the *Richmond Journal of Law and Technology* and the *Texas Intellectual Property Law Journal*, with Internet presence. Last, but certainly not least, is EINet's collection of organizations on the Web that link you to general, academic, commercial, nonprofit, and other organizations specifically dealing with copyrights or intellectual property rights.

Copyright & Fair Use—Stanford University Libraries

fairuse.stanford.edu

Plain rather than fancy, the Stanford site nonetheless has amazing amounts of information for you to learn about the issues of copyright and fair use. Its main page (see Figure 23.3) is divided into several sections, including Resources on the Internet; Current Legislation, Cases, and Issues; and Primary Materials such as statutes, regulations, and treaties. Its Resources on the Internet section is especially good, including a huge list of government agencies, Web sites, and mailing lists.

Now that you're a little more savvy about copyright, fair use, and not getting sued to high heaven, let's talk about pulling information off the Internet.

Pulling Information Off The Web

Getting information from a Usenet post or e-mail is pretty simple—highlight it and press Ctrl+C to save the highlighted parts, then paste it into a new text document, database, or wherever you want to keep it, then save it. No biggie. However, when you do this with a Web document, you might get more or less than you bargained for—strangely formatted text, disappearing words, or sections of text that require a lot of reworking before they're even readable. That doesn't even say anything about the graphics.

There are a couple of ways to save text files and one very easy way to save graphics files. If you're using Clipmate, InfoSelect, or any of the other tools we told you about in Chapter 4, you're a leg up on keeping your information in a usable format.

Figure 23.3   The Copyright & Fair Use site isn't fancy, but it contains a huge number of resources.

Saving Text Files

Go under the View item on Navigator's menu bar, and choose Page Source. A screen will pop up with the text version of the Web page on it—it'll have a bunch of strange letters and characters. That is HTML coding—we'll talk about that in a minute. In the meantime, you can use the screen in which the text version popped up to save the material as a text file (see Figure 23.4).

TIP

> *If you didn't get a screen that popped up with the text version of the Web page in it, but instead got an error message, you probably haven't set your text viewer properly in your preferences. Go to Edit\Preferences\Applications. You should have something designated as your "Text Document" application. If you don't, and you don't have a favorite text editor, click on the Edit button to the right of this screen, then click on the Applications radio button and type* **c:\windows\notepad.exe** *in the white space. That should do the trick.*

Another trick you can use, is mailing the document to yourself. Choose File\Send Page. A mail screen pops up with the Web page you're on listed as

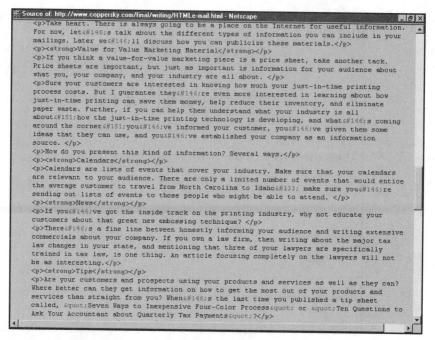

Figure 23.4 A text version of an HTML document.

an attachment (see Figure 23.5). You may also choose to click on the Quote button at the top of the screen. This will paste the Web page, sans HTML code, into the body of the e-mail message. (Be sure when you do this that you delete the attachment, or you'll get the same Web page twice—once as an attached document, and once as part of an e-mail message.)

Saving Graphics

Saving graphics is simplicity itself: Find a graphic you like and right-click (not left-click) on it (see Figure 23.6). You'll get a variety of options, but the two that should interest you at the moment are View Image and Save Image As. View Image shows you a copy of the picture all by itself on a page, without loud background images or surrounding text. The Save Image As option allows you to save the picture onto your hard drive. (Navigator will automatically put the proper file extension on the graphic, so you don't have to worry about figuring out if the picture is a .jpg, .gif, etc.)

So now that you've got the documents, what do you do with them? Many times, nothing. You're able to use them as-is, or print them as-is. But sometimes you need to remove the coding from an HTML document or save a picture in a different format. What do you do then?

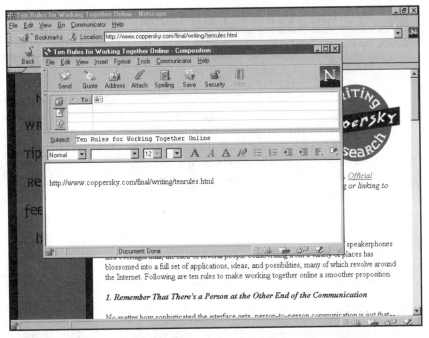

Figure 23.5   You can mail documents to yourself as well as clip them.

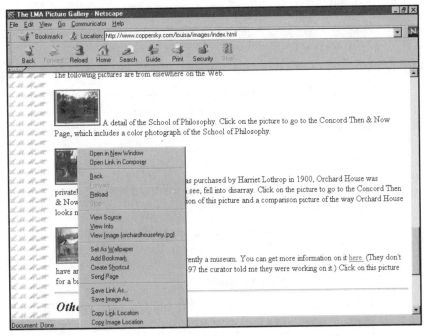

Figure 23.6   You can do a number of things with a simple right-click on a graphic.

Working With HTML Documents

Most text files on the Web are in HTML format. Let's talk about HTML a little bit.

HTML stands for HyperText Markup Language. (You can pronounce it as an acronym, or if you want to be funky you can refer to it as "Hot Metal.") A basic HTML document starts life as a text file. Markup codes are inserted into the text file to change the attributes of the text, such as style and size. However, you will not see the effects of the markup codes until you load the HTML document into a Web browser (or unless you have an HTML editor that shows you what the markup codes do as you add them to the text file). The Web browser really does all the work of presentation, showing you the HTML file with its own interpretation of the markup codes.

For example, say this is your initial text file:

```
My niece, Sam, doesn't like oranges.
```

That's a nice sentence, but when you put it on your Web page you want to emphasize the word "doesn't." You would put an italic markup code in and put tags at the top and the bottom to let Navigator know that this is an HTML document:

```
<HTML>
My niece, Sam, <I>doesn't</I> like oranges.
</HTML>
```

You can still read that with your text file reader, though it looks kind of funny. If you load this file into your Navigator browser, however, suddenly it takes on a different look:

```
My niece, Sam, doesn't like oranges.
```

Now you can tell that Samantha really doesn't like oranges, thanks to the markup code.

HTML can do all kinds of things to a Web page and the text in it. And while HTML can't actually alter an image file, it can refer to graphics and include them in a Web page. It's an incredibly flexible, easy-to-learn language, and it's being added to all of the time.

The example of Samantha and the oranges was very simple. Imagine those kind of codes—<I> and </I> are just one example—scattered on every single line, sometimes two and three at a time. If you want to use the information as a text file, it can get very annoying and time-consuming to load the page into Navigator every time you want to make sense out of it.

You can quote the file into an e-mail message to yourself and go from there. You can also take advantage of programs that remove HTML codes and leave ordinary text files behind. These programs are called—you got it—HTML strippers. Two examples of HTML strippers—there are several available on the Internet—are Opposite Software's HTML to Text Converter and Bamboo Soft's DE-HTML.

HTML To Text Converter

HTML to Text Converter is a little more sophisticated than a software application that merely takes away the HTML tags and leaves the text. This converter removes the markup but leaves some of the formatting from the original document, making it easier to read. HTML to Text Converter maintains headers like headings, titles, lists, and paragraph breaks. This program is now part of Opposite Software's HTML Power Tools for Windows, which you may want to investigate if you're on the way to becoming a sincere HTML-head.

DE-HTML

DE-HTML is an MS-DOS converter that creates ASCII text files from HTML files. It's quick and simple; if you're comfortable with DOS and just want to get your files converted without any fuss, it's a good choice. You can download it from Bamboo Software's Web site at **www.halcyon.com/frog/bamboo.htm**.

Handling Images

Sometimes text just won't do it. You need to handle an image—either change its format to use in your research or just look at it outside of Navigator.

You may have a favorite graphics application to use already. If you don't, consider LView Pro. LView Pro can view a variety of image types, including GIF, JPEG, PCX, TIFF, BMP—in short, almost every image type you'll find on the Internet. It's an excellent application for viewing graphics without opening Navigator. You can find out more about it and download a trial copy by going to **www.lview.com**.

But say you need to edit an image because it's in the wrong format or you want to crop it. An excellent program to consider is Paint Shop Pro. Paint Shop Pro is a much less expensive alternative to full-scale graphics programs such as Adobe Photoshop. However, that is not to say it's a lightweight; it supports over 30 file formats and has a variety of drawing and painting tools. Load a file you pulled off the Internet, edit it as you wish, and then save it in another file format—very simple. If you're not an artist, but just need a graphics application that isn't weighed down with a lot of curlicues, Paint Shop Pro is for you. Check it out at **www.jasc.com**.

Moving On

You've done the research. You've checked your copyright. You've gathered the materials and put together a case study sheet. You've altered the graphics into the proper format for your programs. But before you turn in your project...

Have you cited your resources?

Aha! We knew it. Unfortunately, putting together a bibliography using Internet resources isn't exactly a cake walk. However, there is hope. Cite right with the next chapter.

CHAPTER 24

Citing
Electronic
Information

Ah, to be a pioneer in Internet research. And here you thought it was going to be sunny skies and roses, something to tell your grandchildren about when they're turning in their term papers and research reports on bio-organic chips instead of floppy disks.

Not quite. There are still a lot of questions that need to be answered and paths that need to be blazed. Nowhere is this more apparent than in the field of electronic information citation.

There's no widely accepted style of citation yet, though there are several ideas floating around. In this chapter, we will discuss the most prevalent of those ideas and give you several sources to look into for deciding how to cite your Internet information resources.

> **TIP**
>
> *This chapter covers only the Modern Language Association style of electronic citation, though many of the resources covered in this chapter also touch on the American Psychological Association style. For a nice work on citing document styles in relation to the Internet, check out Xia Li and Nancy Crane's book,* Electronic Styles: A Handbook for Citing Electronic Information, Revised Edition, Information Today. *You can get more information on this book at **www.uvm.edu/~xli/reference/mla.html**.*

General Tips For Citing Your Sources

Regardless of what style you end up using, there are some things you need to keep in mind as you put together your works-cited page.

Check Formatting Requirements

Before you put together any kind of works cited list, discuss the format of the list with your professor, boss, client, or whoever is going to see it next. Ask them what style they want the list in and what sources they'll find acceptable. (For example, since it is not publicly available, they may not want you to cite personal e-mail correspondence.)

Don't Assume Print And Online Versions Match

You may be tempted to cite an online magazine as a print magazine to save time and trouble—on the assumption that the print and online version will match.

Don't give in to this temptation. Sometimes the print version of a magazine will match the online version, but a lot of the time it won't. Look at it this way: The online version of a magazine has more space to print stories, less lead time to add stories, and a much larger potential audience than the print version. For a magazine to make sure that its online and print versions match would be a huge waste of time and resources on its part.

If you have both the printed and online resources available, by all means check both! But if you've only got one, then only list it in your works-cited list.

Make Sure You've Got The Right Source

If someone sends you a Web page by e-mail, you don't want to cite the information in the Web page as coming from their e-mail. You want to check the page they sent you, and cite that.

This is a special hazard of the Internet. We learned in the last chapter how easy it is to extract materials from the Web and Usenet and forward them to people. Sometimes these alterations of sources are pretty obvious—if someone forwards you an AP news story, for example. But what if someone extracts materials from a Web page, then sends you the extraction of the page along with their commentary? Be sure to look carefully at where the original material came from, and give proper citation.

Check The Date And Version Number

Obviously your mother-in-law's e-mail to you about the new season of *Suddenly Susan* is not going to have a version number. But many Internet resources do—most notably, FAQs.

Part of the reason that you even have a works-cited page is so that some other person can come along behind you, read your work, and then follow your references. If they can't follow your references, the page isn't doing what it's supposed to be doing. Two things that will help them follow your references are dates on everything and version numbers if they are available.

For example, say you're writing a dissertation on the use of religious symbolism in the works of Louisa May Alcott, from *Hospital Sketches* to *Jo's Boys*. You use the FAQ from rec.arts.books.alcott for part of your material. The version you cite is 2.1, and the date on it is December 1997. The paper is a tremendous success and is archived in the university library.

Two years later, an Alcott researcher stumbles across your paper while researching his own masterpiece. He eagerly hunts down the resources you've included in your works-cited page. He's stunned when he looks up the **rec.arts.books.alcott** FAQ and discovers that it doesn't include the information that you've put in your dissertation!

But wait; there's a quick answer to the mystery. Somehow, the Alcott researcher has managed to get hold of a very old version of the Alcott FAQ—from April 1995, actually. He looks a little more, finds the FAQ you actually cited, and continues with his research.

So you see, when you write a paper and include a works-cited page, you're not doing it just for yourself, but for the people who come after you who might want to build on your work. Keep that in mind.

Do The Cite Thing

The Modern Language Association (MLA), in the fourth edition of *MLA Handbook for Writers of Research Papers* (written by Joseph Gibaldi, published by the Modern Language Association of America) covers the citation of Internet resources. There have been expansions of this citation style as Internet researchers provide their own ideas on how sources should be cited.

Citing With The MLA

All of the following formats are taken from the *MLA Handbook for Writers of Research Papers, Fourth Edition*. It covers a huge number of citations both online and off; if you write research papers regularly, pick up a copy.

Citing From Electronic Journals, Electronic Newsletters, And Electronic Conferences

These citations require the following items:

- Name of the author, if given

- Title of the article or document, in quotation marks

- Title of the journal, newsletter, or conference, underlined

- Volume number, issue number, or other identifying number

- Year or date of publication, in parentheses

- Number of pages or paragraphs, if given, or n. pag. (which means "no pagination")

- Publication medium (online, not Internet)

- Name of the computer network (Internet)

- Date of access

The MLA also makes optional supplementary information at the end of the document giving the address used to access the document. If you choose to or are required to give this information, precede it with the word "Available" and the kind of information it is.

Example:
Powers, Stacy. "Pigs In a Blanket." <u>Stuck in Traffic</u> 13 (October 1996) 2 pp. Online. Internet. 2 Nov. 1996.

Citing Electronic Texts Or Books

Sometimes you'll find a text online that is also available offline, like classical literary works or historical documents. You need to treat these like online documents and cite them appropriately. These citations call for the following items:

- Name of the author, if available

- Title of the text, underlined

- Publication information for the printed source

- Publication medium (online, not Internet)

- Name of the online area where you accessed the electronic text

- Name of the computer network (Internet)

- Date of access

Also in this citation style, the MLA makes optional supplementary information at the end of the document giving the address used to access the document. If you choose to or are required to give this information, precede it with the word "Available."

Example:
Bricktoss, Prunella. <u>Betty and the Book Example</u>. Whatever, 1881. Online. The Gutenberg Project. Internet. 13 Nov. 1996.

Citing E-mail And Usenet Documents

E-mail documents are simple: include the name of the e-mail writer, a description of the document that includes the recipient, and the date of the document. The e-mail's title (subject) should be enclosed in quotes and put right after the document writer's name in the citation. (Be sure to ask permission to cite a personal e-mail before you do it!)

Example:
Nystrom, Jill. "Screenshots for Chapter 14." E-mail to Tara Calishain. 12 Oct. 1997.

Usenet posts require the following:

- The author's name

- Title of document (This is usually the subject line, unless they post a formal title in the body of the message.)

- Date of posting

- A description, "Online posting." followed by the name of where you found the post (alt.pez-tossing, for example) and the name of the network (Usenet).

- The date of the access

Examples:
Jordan, R. "Cell Biology and Ribosome Structure." 11 August 1996. Online posting. sci.biology.cell. Usenet. 2 Sept. 1996.

Dupree, B.F. "Sawmills in Harnett County, NC." 15 September 1996. Online posting. triangle.sawmills. Usenet. 3 October 1996.

Expansions To The MLA Style

You may think, when looking over these styles, that they're a little thin; they don't completely encompass the wealth of document types that the Internet offers.

You're not the only one. There have been several discussions and proposed evolution of the MLA citation style, with particular emphasis on each of the different types of Internet information, be it from Gopher, Usenet, or Web.

Janice Walker, of the Department of English at the University of South Florida, has compiled her own standards in a paper called "MLA-Style Citations of Electronic Sources." (The paper is available at **www.cas.usf.edu/english/walker/mla.html**.) While her proposed style makes use of the MLA format whenever possible, she also takes into account the punctuation used on the Internet and tries to avoid confusion by changing the presentation of information at some points.

Andrew Harnack and Gene Kleppinger, of Eastern Kentucky University, have expanded on Janice Walker's ideas with "Beyond the MLA Handbook: Documenting Electronic Sources on the Internet." The paper is available at **falcon.eku.edu/honors/beyond-mla**.

TIP

While the proposed changes to the MLA delineation style are interesting, they are not "official." Be sure to ask your publisher, teacher, or boss what style they prefer, and if they mind your using "evolved" styles to cite your information.

Other Sites For Information On Citation

The citation formats for Internet-based information will change, of course. Even if the formats themselves never change, the types of information available online will change.

Our favorite site for keeping up with how to cite electronic sources is the Purdue University Writing Lab's page on the subject, which can be reached at **owl.english.purdue.edu/files/33.html**. It's an excellent overview of both MLA and APA style guides, and it offers a number of links to other sites that discuss the issue of electronic document citation (see Figure 24.1).

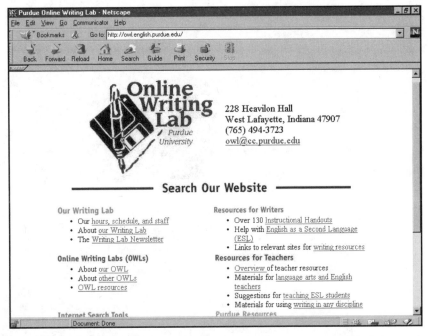

Figure 24.1   The Purdue University Writing Lab provides valuable information on how to cite electronic sources.

Moving On

The fundamentals of electronic citation have been established, but the details have a long way to go. Be sure to keep up with the latest happenings online and get guidance from your teacher or boss concerning the type of citation they prefer.

Well, you're almost done. You've found the information you're looking for, you've archived the results—you've even cited your sources. What the heck do you do now?

You give it back, of course!

CHAPTER 25

Giving Your Research Back To The Internet

Just imagine—several hundred pages and many hours ago you were a different person. But that was BIR (Before Internet Research). Now, after a whirlwind tour of all the corners of cyberspace that we could fit into this book, you re-emerge, pumped up on information, crackling with data. You've learned how to gather data online, how to archive it, and how to cite it.

So what do you do now? You've done the research, created the archives, cited the works. What happens next? Do you log off, kick back, and go downtown to catch the Jackie Chan film festival? Do you pop open a Snapple and put on a Mickey Hart album?

No way. Remember, this is the Internet. This is the place that was built by folks who were willing to contribute their ideas, research, perspectives, and time to add to the storehouse of information online. You can do the same thing; give it back with your personal touch.

Of course, you can't just wave your hand and have the information appear online. You also don't have free rein to distribute it wherever you think it needs to go. No, you need to think about several things before you add your masterwork to the Internet. This chapter discusses those ideas and hopefully puts you on the right track to giving as good as you got. We'll start with examining your research.

Evaluating Your Research Piece

When we say *evaluate*, we don't mean evaluate as in *grade*. What we do mean is that you're going to have to ask yourself some questions about your material. The answers to those questions will determine where your material is best suited for distribution. You have several options—e-mail, the Web, Usenet, and so on. What's best for you and your research depends on several factors.

Of course, you also have the option of publishing offline on paper. We'll be talking about that in this chapter, too, but first, let's talk about online publishing and your options.

What Kind Of Information Is It?

What kind of information do you have? Is it plain text? If it's just text, then you can distribute it anywhere—via e-mail, Usenet, or the Web. But what if it's partially or mostly graphics or some other form of multimedia? If the graphics are only a small part of the research and leaving them out doesn't make a large impact on the data, perhaps you could distribute two different copies of the research—one on the Web and one via e-mail. Of course, if the bulk of the research material is graphics or another type of multimedia, you are not going to be able to distribute it anywhere but on the Web.

How Timely Is It?

Is this research you've done time-sensitive, or is it something that'll be relevant ten years from now? If you've written an analysis of Ibsen's *The Doll House*, you probably have no need to get it circulated to Ibsen fans quickly. You can easily put it on the Web to be found by playwrights and actors one, two, and ten years from now.

On the other hand, perhaps you're writing about the current elections or the efforts of special interest political parties during a certain time frame. That, too, will have its historical significance, but it also has an urgency about it; students of political science could make good use of your materials now. In this case, you might want to consider e-mail or Usenet distribution instead of Web-page distribution, as it will get to the interested parties faster.

Is The Information Going To Change?

How is the information you're presenting going to change over time? Is it a one-shot deal, like an essay on contemporary economics, or is it something that will require frequent updating, like an ongoing study of a certain stock or industry? If it's something that's going to be updated, maybe you want to create a regular mailing list for updates of the research, or perhaps you just want to keep updating a Web page periodically.

How Long Is It?

If you've got a one- or two-page report or perspective, it would probably be okay to distribute that to a newsgroup or mailing list, as long as you were sure that the topic was appropriate where you wanted to post it. But if you've got a long paper—say, over 7 or 8K—you'd want to ask before posting it anywhere. Though they might be low on graphics content, these papers can also make for good Web pages, as you see in Figure 25.1.

How Committed Are You To Maintaining A Web Site?

Are you committed enough to put your materials on a Web site, and then do the updating and other maintenance that a Web site requires? If you're not, perhaps you should consider approaching a Web site that covers the topic of your research and allowing it to maintain the archives of your research.

For example, say you do a newsletter on Norwegian genealogy, but you don't have the time or resources to put together a Web site for back issues of your newsletter. So instead of just putting the back issues away, you approach a

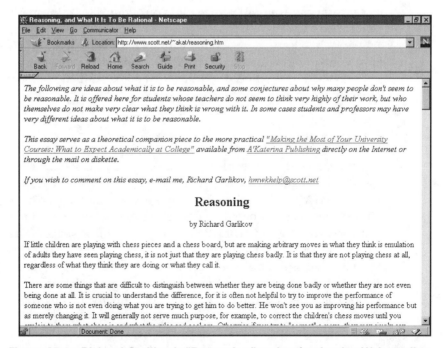

Figure 25.1   Richard Garlikov's "Reasoning" makes fascinating Web reading.

Web site devoted to Norwegian genealogy and offer to let them put your newsletter online.

You both benefit. The Web site gets to put up original content from your newsletters. You benefit by having the back issues of your newsletters online and available to anyone who's interested.

But say you do have the time to keep up with your Web pages. Do you have time to learn how to make them? Learning to make Web pages with HTML is pretty easy, but it can require a substantial amount of time and effort in the long run. If you're not sure you want to make that commitment, but you still want to put your materials on the Web, consider an arrangement like we just explained for the Norwegian genealogy newsletter.

So what is it going to be? Do you have a long-term, stable project that you don't mind putting up on a Web page? Do you have a one-shot deal that you want to distribute through e-mail? Do you have something extremely topical that you think would look good on Usenet? Let's discuss the pros and cons of each method, starting with the Web.

The Web

We've told you about the Web and how it uses hyperlinks to establish a non-linear form of media. We've also told you about HTML, the markup language that's used to create Web pages. Now we're going to tell you where you can go on the Web to learn more about creating Web pages, because if we wanted to give you a thorough tutorial on HTML, it would take—you guessed it—an entire book. First you need to learn the language, then you need to find the tools, and then you need to get the space.

Language

Are you one of those people who breaks out in a cold sweat when you hear the word "language?" Did you flunk Pig Latin in third grade? If so, don't sweat it. HTML is sort of like chess—it's easy to learn how to play, but you can gain additional skills based on how enthusiastic you are about it. You can be someone who can make a functional Web page, you can be someone who makes a neat-looking Web page, or you can devote a lot of time and energy to becoming a Markup Master. The level you want to reach is up to you, but it doesn't take a lot to get started. As you can see in Figure 25.2, an HTML document viewed outside a Web browser doesn't look much different from a regular text document. (By the way, if you want to see more examples of plain HTML documents, choose View | Document Source while in Navigator. This is a good way to learn more about HTML once you've got the basics down.)

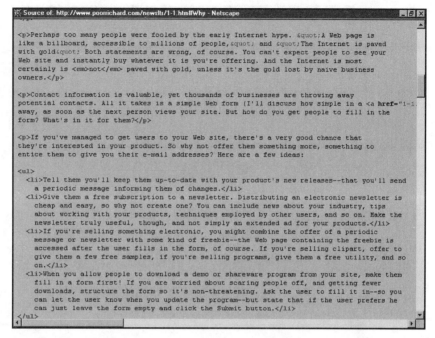

Figure 25.2 **A plain HTML document looks a lot like a plain text document.**

WebMonkey

www.webmonkey.com/teachingtool/

Are you the type who has to try something as soon as you learn it? This site, which is extremely thorough, includes a really neat feature called "Monkey See, Monkey Do." Once you've learned a tiny bit of HTML—how to create italics and bolds, for example—you can try out your knowledge. You're presented with a split screen and told to input HTML text in the box on the right, with the goal of mimicking what appears on the left side of the screen.

Once you've filled in the box, you can click on the Go button and your formatted text is shown on the screen. If it doesn't look like the left side of the screen, you can click on the View button on the left side of the screen and compare your code to the WebMonkey's code. This is a great site for you if you don't want to slog through lots of lessons but want to start playing right away.

UserActive

www.useractive.com

Similar to WebMonkey, UserActive (see Figure 25.3) offers a text box into which you can type HTML and then press a preview button to see how the HTML is going to turn out. The HTML is divided into several different lessons (HTML structure, links, graphics, etc.). You can also find lessons available in JavaScript.

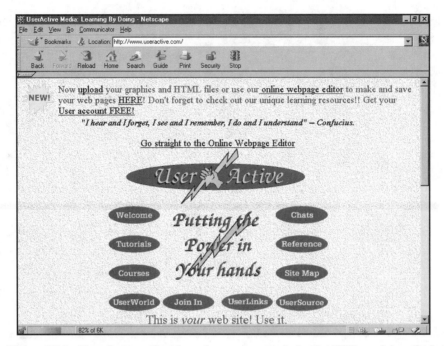

Figure 25.3   UserActive offers learning resources in both HTML and JavaScript.

This site also offers an extensive HTML reference as well as college credit courses in HTML and JavaScript.

TIP

If you want a book instead of a Web page (being able to thumb through a book is sometimes comforting), try HTML 4 for the World Wide Web: Visual QuickStart Guide *by Elizabeth Castro, published by Peachpit Press.*

Once you've got the know-how, you'll need some tools. You can create HTML files with an ordinary text editor like Windows Notepad, but unless you're a serious HTML head, it's like eating peas with a knife. Communicator includes Composer, a WYSIWYG (What You See Is What You Get) editor, which you can use if you like. (For more information on using Composer, pick up *Official Netscape Composer Book: Windows 95 & Windows NT*, by Alan Simpson. If you want to try something different, however, or you're looking for some jazzy graphics and icons, keep reading.

Tools

You don't have to have an HTML editor to make Web pages, but it's a lot easier for a beginner. HTML editors include easy ways to include the HTML markup codes. Sometimes they include extras, like "wizards" that walk you through the process of making a Web page.

If it were just software you needed to make a Web page, you could go to a software archive like CNET's Download.Com (**www.download.com**) or Tucows (**www.tucows.com**) and pick up whatever HTML editor you wanted. (So many of them exist, built for so many different levels of expertise, that we don't feel comfortable making a recommendation. Fortunately, most editors offer demonstration copies that you can try before you buy. You can even find free editors out there.)

However, you need other things for a Web page. Graphics, for example. Even if you don't want to use large pictures, small "bullet" and "button" graphics go a long way towards breaking up the text on a page and making it more interesting to view. And then there's the HTML reference pages, and recommended styles, and examples, and…

Fortunately, several pages are available to bring all of these resources together.

The WWW Home Page Starter Kit

www.geocities.com/SiliconValley/Lakes/3933/kitrex3.html

This site has a variety of materials available for you to build your HTML page. The WWW Home Page Starter Kit (see Figure 25.4) also has a lot of great attitude,

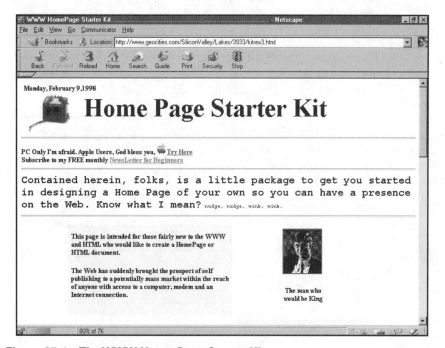

Figure 25.4   The WWW Home Page Starter Kit.

as well as plenty of guidance to make your page full of great information, and not just pretty to look at.

The HTML Assistance Page

www.ipr.nl/developr/roland/assist.htm

This site is both pretty to look at and full of great information. It has lots of links to tools, graphics, references, and guides to writing good pages. The English is a little spotty in some places, but it isn't a hindrance to taking advantage of this resource.

Space

Even the most beautiful Web page in the world is not going to make much of an impact unless you've put it online. For that you need Web space. If you're going to be putting up pages that are mostly text, you don't need a lot of space—1MB should do you just fine.

Before you get into this section, check with your Internet service provider and find out if your Internet account makes Web space available to you. A lot of providers include a certain amount of Web space for noncommercial activities. Go ahead, check. We'll wait.

Back? All right. Unfortunately, you might be one of those people who doesn't get free Web space. That is indeed a bummer. But don't despair; you can still have a page.

How? Many places offer free pages, based on different requirements; some sites have pages for non-profits, some for students, even some for those organizations involved in animal rescue.

For indices of free Web space, check out **www.freehomepage.com**, or Sites that Offer Free Web Pages at **members.tripod.com/~jpsp1/sites.html**. These indices offer you a wide variety of options for hunting down Web space.

Wait, we can hear you now: "WHAT? You've got 500 pages to noodle around in and you can't even tell me where to get free Web space?" Fear not. If you need a personal home page that isn't going to be used for commercial applications, and you don't mind conforming to content and usage guidelines, a free home page can be yours. Let's take, for example, GeoCities and Tripod.

> **TIP**
>
> *Free Web page services tend to have a variety of restrictions on them. Please follow these terms to assure that the services will continue to be offered.*

GeoCities

www.geocities.com

GeoCities (see Figure 25.5) is one of the largest, if not the largest, free Web service on the Internet. Its users' pages are divided up into 27 different "communities," each of which has a different theme, ranging from Area51 for science fiction and fantasy buffs to Yosemite for the outdoorsy type, you can move into the neighborhood that's best for you.

You're allowed 3MB of disk space with which to create your page, and GeoCities has various programs to expand that amount; 3 MB is a lot of space for just text, though—this should be plenty for you to work with unless you want to create a site heavy in graphics or a very extensive site.

GeoCities has a number of terms of service of which you should be aware. First of all, it requires that you have a reference back to GeoCities in your pages—either a reference to the "community" in which your page is placed, or the GeoCities home page. It also prohibits materials that are grossly offensive, promotion or instruction of illegal activities or bodily harm, pornography, posted materials that violate copyright, and pages that consist mostly of hyperlinks to forbidden materials.

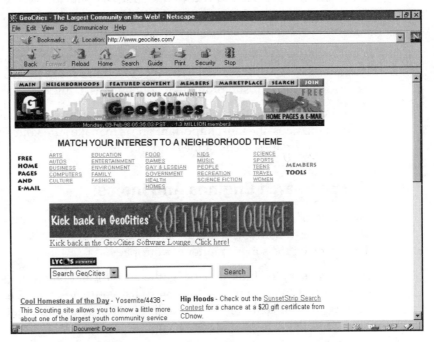

Figure 25.5   GeoCities offers free Web pages in a community-type setting.

A few more rules exist, but these are a good overview. Because GeoCities is giving you a page for free, treat your Web page as a guest on its computer, and be sure that your guest is following all the "House Rules."

Tripod

www.tripod.com

Tripod (Figure 25.6) also offers Web pages, with many of the same types of restrictions as given by GeoCities. You may notice that these standards are pretty much the ones condoned by "mainstream culture." That's as it should be; Tripod and GeoCities are offering their free pages to a potentially huge audience, and it's reasonable for them to want all their members to feel as comfortable as possible. It's not easy for many people to feel comfortable with large amounts of pornography, illegal activity, and violence.

Both Tripod and GeoCities are good choices if your provider doesn't offer Web space with your account.

Promoting Your Web Site

You've learned HTML, and you've put your Web site up. You are not finished. You've got to let people know your Web site is there, right? How much fun is it going to be if no one comes to visit your home page?

A zillion years ago, Tara worked in PR. She developed a plan for promoting Web sites called a "PR Sweep." The PR Sweep has four steps to cover all the bases of getting your site promoted. Following is a quick look at the sweep.

The process of promoting your site is very time-consuming. If you don't want to do all the steps, the most important one is to make sure your site is listed in all the appropriate search engines and indices.

Utilize Search Engines And Indices

Take the time to make sure you're in all the major search engines and indices. More of these than you think are around—it could be dozens and dozens, depending on the subject matter of your page.

Some places on the Internet have gathered information on these listing sites into one area to make it easy for you to list your sites. Some, like Submit-It! (**www.submit-it.com**) allow you to fill out a form and automatically submit your information to several search engines.

If you want to do a more thorough job of listing your sites, you should check out two places.

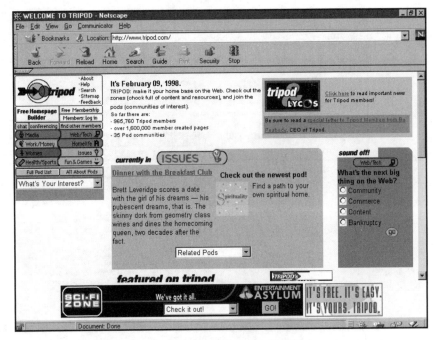

Figure 25.6   Tripod is another good option for free Web space.

WebStep Top 100

www.mmgco.com/top100.html

This is a frequently updated list of the 100 most popular places on the Web to list your resource. They're not all going to be appropriate for your page (some are for commercial sites only, some are for certain regions), but it's a good place to start.

VirtualPROMOTE

www.virtualpromote.com/

Everything you wanted to know about promoting your Internet site—and more. VirtualPROMOTE (see Figure 25.7) has engines in which to register your site, places to nominate your site for awards, links to other site promotion resources, and more, just like we said. (You'll also find information on Meta tags, reading your site logs, banner advertising, etc.)

Nominate Your Site For Awards

Literally hundreds of awards are out there for Web pages: best of, worst of, funniest, most pointless, and so on. If you think your site has what it takes,

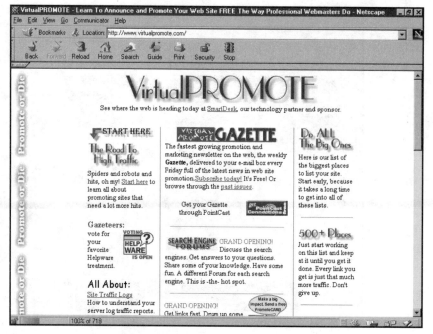

Figure 25.7   VirtualPROMOTE.

then nominate your site for an award. Yahoo! has a comprehensive listing of awards—do a search for "Web awards" and you'll see what we mean.

Of course, if you've spent a grand total of five minutes putting up your site, don't nominate it for any awards—you may find yourself on a "worst site of the day" list.

Send Out A Press Release

If you're feeling really loud and proud about your new site, write up a press release and send it out to the editors of computer magazines.

Use your good sense when you do this, though. Don't send a press release to announce your Windows research site to a Macintosh magazine. Don't send a release announcing your Web site, "An exhaustive study of socialsexual relationships," to *Family PC*.

And, above all, don't bulk mail a bunch of editors. Send each one an individual note, with their name at the top, before you get into the boilerplate (the press release and all the standard information that you want to send to everyone). It's so easy to be rude on the Internet and so easy to be courteous as well. Stay on the side of good manners.

Research Reciprocal Links

Finally, a good thing to do is research other sites that have content and interests similar to yours and request a reciprocal link from them—if they link to you, you link to them. This is a good way to attract visitors who are already interested in the topics that you're covering.

Of course, this is applicable only for materials on the Web. What are you going to do if you want to put your materials on Usenet or mailing lists?

Putting Your Materials On Usenet Or Mailing Lists

If you've got material that's mostly text, and you don't want to keep up with a Web page, you may find it best to post your materials to Usenet or a mailing list. If you do want to do that, though, keep the following things in mind.

Ask First

If you're not sure if the charter of the mailing list or newsgroup you're interested in accepts articles, ask. E-mail the owner of the list or post a message that says something like, "I have an article on thus-and-such I'd like to post. May I?"

Many times it'll be okay. But if it isn't okay, or if these materials aren't appropriate, offer to e-mail the material to those who ask for it off-list (by sending e-mail directly to you).

Don't Crosspost

You may be understandably very proud of your materials, but don't give in to the temptation to post your article in thirty places at once. Limit your distribution. It's too easy to go from posting a well-researched article to the places where it will be most appreciated to a downright spamming of Usenet. When in doubt, err on the side of conserving Internet resources.

Present Readable Materials

The more readable your materials are, the more people will read them. (Blindingly obvious, isn't it?) Don't present your material as one huge chunk of text. Put lines between the paragraphs, and don't make your lines 80 characters long—make them about 60 so that everyone will be able to view them comfortably with their e-mail application. Also, if you've written the paper in a word processor, make sure that all the special formatting characters are removed before you post it. The special characters don't translate well into plain text, and can mess up some news readers and mail applications.

Don't Overdo It

Even the most tolerant mailing list or newsgroup might get sick of you after a while. Be careful about how often you post materials. Once every couple of months is probably okay; once every week may not be. Be sure to ask, and if someone asks you to stop, don't redouble your efforts out of a misguided sense of revenge. It's not worth it and could escalate into a huge "flame war."

Now you know about mailing lists and Usenet, but what happens when you want to take your research efforts offline? Where should you go? Don't turn off your computer just yet—the Internet can still help you out.

Taking It Offline: Resources For Writers And Publishers

Sometimes the Internet is not the publishing option you want to consider. Sometimes you want to see your thoughts and ideas on pressed wood pulp. Take heart: Whether you are an experienced writer looking for your next story idea or a neophyte trying to get through a major block, the Internet is a good bet for surviving the chaos of writing and publishing. You can cut back on a lot of legwork and headaches by taking advantage of the research already done by these site owners, and use all of that extra time for being creative and getting work published.

General Writers' Resources On The Web

These sites cover topics of general interest to all writers, regardless of skill level. Most of them cover a broad range of genres and several have interactive features such as cafes, puzzles, and newsgroups.

Inkspot
www.inkspot.com/

Inkspot (see Figure 25.8) covers writing topics ranging from how to begin your first novel to marketing your fabulous book on travel tips in Tibet. The Beginning Writer's FAQ section includes links to resources for young writers, an index of questions about preparing and submitting manuscripts, getting an agent, and the pros and cons of self-publishing. You'll also find several unmoderated Writers' Forums. Remember your Netiquette, though: Writers' Resources requests that you not post your writing samples or inquiries about agents on these forums, as they provide a separate place for these features.

The genre links on this site are diverse enough to cover almost every aspect of a subject that you can think of. For example, the Children's category has a link to The Children's Literature Web Guide, which lists movies and TV shows based on children's books, best book lists, bestsellers for kids, and links to resources. The main Writers' Resources site is also packed with notes on writing as a craft: where to find writers' associations, the latest on conferences and multimedia resources, a reference desk, and a range of grammar and style guides.

Online Writing Lab

owl.english.purdue.edu

Online Writing Lab includes several writers' standards such as style guides and dictionaries, but it also has strong sections on business and technical writing, ESL-related sites, and links to professional organizations. But don't think that standard means boring. The style guides include a link to the Editorial Esoterica quiz and a directory of grammar hotlines throughout the United States. The business and technical writing links include chapters from NASA's own handbook.

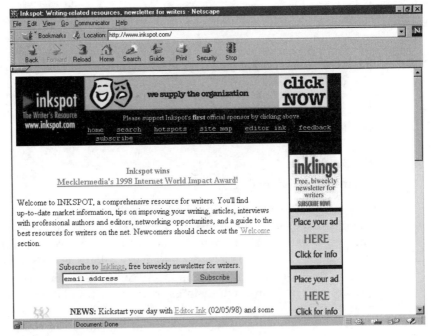

Figure 25.8   Inkspot is a great spot for writers.

Readers' And Writers' Resource Page

www.diane.com/readers/

Readers' And Writers' Resource Page compiles daily newspapers, writing tools, quotation sources, and other links of use to writers, publishers, and illustrators. Some of the writing tools include the Copyright Clearance Center Online, Advice on Novel Writing, and Semiotics for Beginners. They also have connections to online bookstores, ranging from **amazon.com**'s million titles to other, less-known shops. You can also submit your own list of favorite books or search the Web with its online search engine.

WritersNet

www.writers.net

WritersNet is a searchable directory of published writers. You can browse by author or category or search by keyword. To do a search, set the output level to "terse" (displays a list of names only) or "verbose" (displays full information). For example, if you enter "Jordan" you'll get several names, including "Jordan Elgraby," the screenwriter and producer of the film "Aberration." The terse output level gives you just the names, though you can click on the hyperlinked name to get a verbose output. Verbose gives you the author's name, biographical information, e-mail, and physical addresses, publications, and interests.

WritersNet also sponsors several discussion groups, including Editors and Editing, Publishers and Publishing, and Writing Assignments.

Publishers' Indices And Resources

These sites tackle the basics of book trade issues, finding the right publisher for you or getting information about print brokering, bookmaking, and self-publishing.

Books AtoZ

www.booksatoz.com

Books AtoZ (see Figure 25.9) covers professional and creative services, bookmaking shops, and self-publishing guides. It also features an exhaustive alphabetical listing of dozens of links and resources on several topics. For example, the Creative Freelancer's Registry allows you to list yourself in a profiles database that potential employees can access to find designers, writers, and filmmakers. Some of the listings are fee-based, and they typically list your name, education, work history, and online samples of your work if you have them available. Listings are broken into broad categories (for example, artistic/graphics) and subcategories (caricaturists, medical illustrators, muralists).

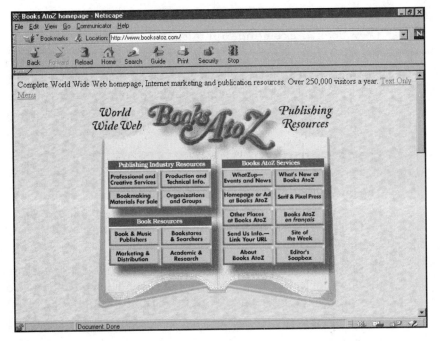

Figure 25.9   Books AtoZ.

The rest of the Books AtoZ site covers practical issues and has a Bookmarks section, with links to pages from outside of the United States or that offer book-related services (print brokering, book consulting, and the like) and journals. The site is also available in French.

Book Stacks Unlimited

www.books.com

Book Stacks Unlimited is another searchable site that lists over 400,000 titles and provides access to book forums, interactive cafes, and audio feeds from literary-oriented interviews and reports. It has two main search functions: a "help" engine (by word, located on every main page) and a "search shelves" engine (by title, author, keyword, or ISBN).

The Author's Pen has over 550 authors listed alphabetically. You can search this section by author's name (last name, first name). Each author's page has a brief biography, a selected bibliography, and links to home pages both official and unofficial.

Book Stacks' Book Forums cover everything from "lateral thinking" to out-of-print books. If you just can't find that perfect venue, you're welcome to suggest a forum that you'd like to moderate.

The BookWire Index Of Publishers

www.bookwire.com/index/publishers.html

This site has eighteen categories listed alphabetically that include associations, computer books, multimedia resources, and specialty shops. In turn, each category has an alphabetical listing of links to publishers, plus a brief description of services and business approaches (nonprofit, co-op, etc.) where available.

Conclusion

The Internet is here to stay and here to change our lives forever. It's great, if you think about it—you personally have access to a larger store of information than anyone in history, right at your fingertips, available at any hour of the day or night.

This information has the potential to give you a tremendous amount of power: the power to learn, grow, create new ideas, and defend or detract old ones; the power to better understand everything from a neighboring country to a new exercise program.

We hope that what we've tried to teach you in this book leads to you using these powers wisely and responsibly, for the betterment of yourself. But above all, we hope you have fun and find what you're looking for. That's what it's all about.

Onward!

The Reverse-Gutenberg Revolution: The Need For A New Expertise

By Tara Calishain

Johannes Gutenberg didn't have a clue. When he set the last lines of type for his 1454 printing of the Bible, he couldn't have known about everything that would come later; AA Milne and Pablo Neruda, The Communist Manifesto and Danielle Steele. The values, needs, and dissentions of hundreds of cultures, distilled down into a few handfuls of type and a sprinkling of punctuation marks.

Gutenberg was the first to liberate information. He made owning collections of information affordable. He brought movable type to the Western world and at the same time created a revolution of the mind throughout all Europe, widening horizons and initiating literacy among the non-aristocratic public.

His invention also created the need for writers; people to feed the pipeline that he made, people to package information into the format that he publicized. Unfortunately, writing became, and still is to some, an "elite" activity that requires inbred talent or a bolt of divine lightning. It takes several steps to get a book published, and sometimes a large sum of money. Gutenberg created an inexpensive method of compiling information, but not for creating or distributing it.

Now we have the Internet. It is a pipeline much like Gutenberg's, only on a much more massive scale. With the creation of the WWW, the Internet has gained the easy-to-use interface it needs to become widely used by all kinds of people at all education levels. The critical difference is that it's as easy to *create content* as it is to *access content*.

In a way, the Internet is reverse-Gutenberg. Instead of movable type, we have "type movable"—one copy of a newsletter, book, or magazine can be circulated literally millions of times. Better yet, it can be archived for later retrieval.

What does it mean, when everyone can create sets of information that can be reproduced an infinite number of times all over the world? First of all, it means that the amount of information available to everyone is going to increase by a scale unimaginable. And what happens when the supply of a commodity increases? Right; the value of the commodity drops. And so it is with writing.

Sort of. Writing is a subjective commodity, the value of which varies wildly from person to person. Still, there will be a measurable increase in the amount of information available, and it will be such a large increase that it will impossible to avoid an increase in the amount of valuable information available to any one person (unless one has absolutely no interest in anything.)

In the face of this tide of information, the current generation and surviving generations before it find themselves ill-equipped to make sense of it. They have the wrong skill.

Our educational system prides itself on teaching children to write, to express themselves articulately in print. This is admirable, and quite understandable when the commodity of written information was forced to go through a very expensive and narrow pipeline; many, many students are taught to write, and relatively few grow up to feed the pipeline and bring the commodity of printed material to those who enjoy reading. Now the pipeline is huge. Almost anyone can put materials on the Internet to be read. Writing enables one to add to the flow of information, but not to harness the stream of materials constantly moving on the Internet.

Now is the time to deliberately advance the evolution of a skill that is usually taught only in higher-level courses, a skill that will enable future students to evaluate the materials circulating in the pipeline and make the most out of what they see. In its simplest form, the skill is called reading.

Now, theoretically, we are all taught to read in elementary school. We sound out words, get together in groups and follow the adventures of Dick and Jane, and gradually move up to Hemingway and Parker. However, the reading taught at this level is merely the interpretation of symbols. It is STOP and GO and THE CAT SAT ON THE MAT, but it is not understanding the material, it is not any kind of criticism, it is not a knowledge of how different pieces of writing go together.

The understanding of how different things link together is the lynchpin of the new reading skill. Fragments of information will be available everywhere. It will be up to the reader to catalogue this information, evaluate it for relevance, and, most important of all, connect it to other fragments of information to create new information that has a very high subjective value to him or her (and hopefully some concrete usefulness.)

I am not calling for the abolishment of writing courses. What I am calling for is the understanding that writing should now be the secondary skill. It used to be that reading was the secondary skill; one learned to read in grade school and from then on through college, the emphasis was on writing, perfecting spelling and grammar skills, learning proper form, and so on. I feel that a more proper education would be reading in grade school, a couple of years of writing to learn to communicate clearly, and then nothing but reading. Reading for thorough comprehension, not just to spit back a temporary understanding. Reading to remember later and link to a new piece of information. Reading to understand and empathize with a different culture, a different experience, a different need, a different perspective (all things readily available on the worldwide Internet.)

In short, reading as an experience of depth, designed to change one subtly with every paragraph, every new word, every discovered fact. Readers will be needed at all levels of the Internet to comb through information and organize it before passing it on to the next level of readers, until it finally gets to the "general public;" those who have specific and narrow needs and rely on the readers to correctly evaluate and filter information before delivering it to them. They are the "end users," they want only the gold. They are not the readers who pan the information stream, who find the gold but also find dirt, diamonds, and dynamite.

The pipeline of words has been unleashed; *time* is now the rare commodity. It is only through a new set of skills and understanding that humans will be able to harness and tame the tide that we add to second by second.

Index

C

D

G

J

K

O

Q

R

S

X

Y

Z